COVER PHOTO:

Mar. 18, 1945 – During the attack on Kyushu, Japan,
a twin-engine Betty kamikaze, attempts a suicide dive on the
Intrepid crashing close off the starboard bow, spewing flaming
gasoline and shrapnel onto the hangar deck.

G.P. Books, P.O. Box 788, South Salem. NY 10590
ISBN 0-9746916-0-7

Printed in the United States of America
Mount Kisco Printing

A WW II Memoir by Raymond T. Stone

"My Ship!"
THE U.S.S. INTREPID

in.trep.id\ *adj* [L *intrepidus,* }: characterized by resolute fearlessness, boldness, courageousness; indomitable, gutsy, nervy, ballsy, spirited, dashing, daring, adventurous, brave, valiant, audacious, heroic, gallant, resolute, and quite invincible.

★ ★ ★ ★ ★ ★ ★

U.S.S. INTREPID ★ CV-11

"My Ship!"

THIS BOOK IS DEDICATED TO:

★ **The Plankowners.** The 3,000 officers and
enlisted men in the original crew who gave this
Fighting Lady her life, soul, invincible spirit–and
a pair of brass balls for good measure.

★ **The pilots and their crewmen** who flew from
Intrepid's flight deck attacking and destroying more
planes and sinking more ships than the Japanese did
in their sneak attack on Pearl Harbor.

★ **Especially dedicated to those valiant heroes**
who lost their lives while fighting under Intrepid's
battle flag.

★   ★   ★

I'm proud to be one of the Plankowners
who earned the right and honor of calling
the U.S.S. Intrepid, "My Ship!"

– Ray Stone

During WWII, the U.S.S. Intrepid was "the most hit carrier," surviving first a torpedo hit at Truk, then kamikaze hits off the Philippines, Okinawa and the coast of Japan. Battle-scarred but never bested!

INTRODUCTION

Looking back, some details about people and events are as vivid as yesterday. Others, filed away in a corner of my mind, had to be tugged out of hiding.

The view is from my then–teenage perspective, expressed in the everyday language of the time (a Japanese was a Jap). It's how I saw it. How I felt about people and events when they happened.

My story is buttressed by accounts of my radar buddies: Jack *Botts* Alexander, George *Polack* Vogrin, Leon *Smitty* Smith, Jack Norton, Enos *Leaky* Evans, Jake Fegley, and other shipmates: Winston Goodloe, Tony Zollo, Lou Valenti, Ed Coyne, Felix Novelli and Gerry Goguen. Each telling it the way he saw it, as it happened.

The story, people and events are real; one or two names have been changed to avoid embarrassing shipmates or their families.

CONTENTS

On Dec. 7,1941, 16-year-old Ray Stone was finishing this poster, for a contest, as news of the Japanese attack on Pearl Harbor was being broadcast over the radio.

"–a date which will live in infamy"

Sunday, Dec. 7, 1941, began quietly. Church in the morning, family together. The dining-room table cleared after a typical early Sunday midday meal of roast chicken, mashed potatoes and apple pie. Mom in the kitchen doing dishes; Dad reading the Sunday newspaper while a large Philco radio filled the room with music by the New York Philharmonic. A usual Sunday scene, as set in Cedarhurst, Long Island, and across much of America.

The dining-room table now covered with tempera paints, ruling pens, brushes, t-square and triangles as I put final finishing touches on an *Army Air Corps* recruitment poster. Mr. Page, my high school art teacher and friend, urged me to enter the poster contest; he was stopping by to check some unfinished lettering: *LET'S GO! U.S.A. KEEP 'EM FLYING!*

Mr. Page arrived as the last stroke of paint was applied.

"Finally finished! I couldn't believe it."

"Never thought you'd get it done on time, Ray, especially without some of your usual smeared paint. Way to go, guy. Good job!"

I let go a couple of resounding yippies when Dad advised,

"Quiet! Something has happened!"

The music stopped. The silence broken by a somber-voiced announcer tersely reporting:

11

We interrupt the program to bring a special news bulletin. The Japanese have attacked Pearl Harbor, Hawaii, by air, President Roosevelt has just announced. The attack was also made on naval and military activities on the principal island of Oahu.

Mom came into the living room, drying her hands in a dish towel. My older brother Lou sat staring at the radio; younger sister Dolly began to cry, not really knowing why. Tears started flowing down Mom's cheeks, too. Dad withdrew, silently thinking about what war, as he experienced it, meant. Something he never discussed. We had read about some of dad's WWI experiences from an old framed newspaper interview that we found tucked away in a drawer. For a minute or more, all were too stunned to speak.

Finally, Mr. Page broke the spell, excusing himself to call Mary Ace, his fiancee. "I have to talk to Mary...get back later."

I exploded: "Why those little, slanty-eyed bums. We'll kick their butts soundly! How dare they attack us? They're only good at making cheap little metal toys out of used Campbell's soup cans. We'll show them. Won't we, Dad? Where in the heck is Pearl Harbor, anyhow? I'll get the geography book, find it on the map." (As the war went on, the map of the Pacific and its remote places became all too familiar: Wake, Midway, Guadalcanal, Iwo Jima, Rabul, Leyte, Formosa, Eniwetok, Ulithi, Peleliu, Saipan, Guam, Okinawa.)

Like many Americans, I knew of the ongoing meetings in Washington, D.C., between two Jap diplomats and Secretary of State Cordell Hull, but didn't really know, or care much, about why the meetings were being held. My teenage focus was zeroed in on our high school football team, cheerleaders, ice-cream sodas and getting an old jalopy to drive to school.

As history shows, these two bowing, formally-attired diplomats were stalling, well aware of the impending sneak attack on Pearl Harbor by the Imperial Japanese Navy. They were waiting for final word from Tokyo on the exact timing of the attack, planning to then present a declaration of war, sanctioned by Emperor Hirohito, to Cordell Hull when the assault began.

However, a decoding snafu and an ancient typewriter delayed delivery of the document to the Secretary of State until nearly an hour after the sneak attack on Pearl Harbor had begun.

The first of 3 Extra editions of the Honolulu Star-Bulletin reported:

The Japanese attacked Pearl Harbor from the air and all naval and military activities on the island of Oahu, principal American base in the Hawaiian Islands.

Oahu was attacked at 7:55 this morning by Japanese planes.

The Rising Sun, emblem of Japan, was seen on plane wing tips.

Wave after wave of bombers streamed through the clouded morning sky from the southwest and flung their missiles on the city resting peaceful in Sabbath calm.

The Honolulu Star-Bulletin published two additional Extra editions that Sunday, amplifying reports on damage and casualties suffered on Oahu. For me, the rest of Sunday was a blur of raging angry thoughts, wary anticipation and additional nighttime prayers.

The following day, President Franklin Delano Roosevelt delivered his famous "date in infamy," address to Congress.

"Yesterday, December 7, 1941 – a date which will live in infamy – the United States of America was suddenly and deliberately attacked by naval and air forces of the Empire of Japan.

The United States was at peace with that nation, and at the solicitation of Japan, was still in conversation with its government and its Emperor looking toward the maintenance of peace in the Pacific.

Indeed, one hour after Japanese air squadrons had commenced bombing in the American island of Oahu, the Japanese Ambassador to the United States and his colleague delivered to our Secretary of State a formal reply to a recent American message. And while this reply stated that it seemed useless to continue the existing diplomatic negotiations, it contained no threat or hint of war or armed attack.

It will be recorded that the distance of Hawaii from Japan makes it obvious that the attack was deliberately planned many days or even weeks ago. During the intervening time the Japanese Government has deliberately sought to deceive the United States by false statements and expressions of hope for continued peace.

The attack yesterday on the Hawaiian Islands has caused severe damage to American naval and military forces. I regret to tell you that very many American lives have been lost. In addition, American ships have been reported torpedoed on the high seas between San Francisco and Honolulu.

Yesterday the Japanese government also launched an attack against Malaya.

Last night Japanese forces attacked Hong Kong.

Last night Japanese forces attacked Guam.

Last night Japanese forces attacked the Philippine Islands.

Last night Japanese forces attacked Wake Island.

And this morning the Japanese attacked Midway Island.

Japan has, therefore, undertaken a surprise offensive extending throughout the Pacific area. The facts of yesterday and today speak for themselves. The people of the United States have already formed their opinions and well understand the implications to the very life and safety of our nation.

As Commander in Chief of the Army and Navy I have directed that all measures be taken for our defense.

But always will our whole nation remember the character of the onslaught against us. No matter how long it may take us to overcome this premeditated invasion, the American people in their righteous might will win through to absolute victory.

I believe that I interpret the will of the Congress and of the people when I assert that we will not only defend ourselves to the utmost but will make it very certain that this form of treachery shall never again endanger us.

Hostilities exist. There is no blinking at the fact that our people, our territory and our interests are in grave danger. With confidence in our armed forces – with the unbounding determination of our people – so help us God, I ask that the Congress declare that since the unprovoked attack by Japan on Sunday, December 7, 1941, a state of war has existed between the United States and the Japanese Empire."

My Air Cadet Recruitment Poster was due Monday, Dec. 8. I skipped school, borrowed Mr. Page's car and drove to the Post Office in Jamaica with my good pal Bob Lavery. The woman who received the poster gave us a big hug, a "God Bless" and off we went. On the way out, we passed a Navy recruitment room. In we popped, trying to enlist: "We want to be Navy pilots!"

The Petty Officer listened patiently, then gently advised, "Come back when you're 17. Be sure to bring written permission from your parents. You'll need it to enlist."

"The war will be over before I'm 17! It will only last a couple more months, at the most, won't it?"

"Don't worry. I'll save a couple of Japs just for you two."

Bob and I left, vowing to return. During the drive home, we were full of patriotic rhetoric aimed at the Japs:

"Those little runts are going to find out they picked on a giant! What treacherous, devious, dishonest little shits; you and I could kick the crap out of a dozen of them with one hand tied behind our backs."

No doubts on our part. Americans were strong; all Japs wore thick glasses and had buck teeth.

Bob and I couldn't wait to get our hands on them. We were going to kick ass. (Bob became a paratrooper in the 11th Airborne, seeing action in New Guinea and the Philippines. He kicked ass.)

Robert J. Lavery
11th Airborne

Later in the day, news of the number of ships, men and airplanes lost at Pearl Harbor hit home like a giant shock wave. Fortunately, our aircraft carriers were safe. The *Yorktown* had been detached in April for Atlantic duty. The *Saratoga* was stateside for repairs. The *Lexington* and *Enterprise* were at sea near Wake and Midway Islands. Other very important survivors of the attack were the repair ships and huge oil tank farms–all were left intact.

Pictures of the horrors from bombings began appearing in newspapers. In this pre-TV era, movie houses showed film by Fox Movietone News which provided dramatic coverage of the devastation, as a sobering window introduction to war's horrors, with pictures of the sordid destruction.

It took some time to sink in before we understood that America was facing a well-prepared Japanese war machine: ruthless and dedicated to conquest throughout Asia. "Ruthless" is a carefully chosen word; the atrocities committed by Japanese soldiers throughout Asia were as horrible or even surpassed those of their Nazi allies in Europe.

With America reeling from Pearl Harbor losses, the Japanese wave of conquest and control spread quickly from one end of the Pacific to the other. Gen. Douglas MacArthur had escaped to Australia 10 weeks before Corregidor was surrendered by Lt Gen. Jonathan Wainright. Wainright and X,000 of 15,000 American and Filipino troops survived the horrible Bataan death march.

Prior to Pearl Harbor, much of America shared an isolationist creed: *It's Europe's war, not ours.* Attitudes changed immediately. The sneak attack got America's dander up, uniting the people in a common cause: victory over the Axis trio of Hirohito, Hitler and Mussolini.

Air Cadet, Louis J. Stone

The manufacturing muscle of the United States did a quick switch to wartime production. No more civilian cars. Jeeps, tanks and airplanes began rolling off assembly lines. A work force known as defense workers emerged almost overnight. More and more women left homemaking to become welders, riveters and assemblers on production lines.

My brother Lou worked for Liberty Aircraft before going into Cadet Training in Texas for the U. S. Army Air Corps. (Score one for my high-school recruitment poster!) Lou was a radio gunner on a B-26 bomber with the 9th Air Force. He flew on a total of 65 low-level bombing missions during the invasion of France.

Prior to the war, Japan flooded the United States with cheap tin toys and goods, marked *MADE IN JAPAN*. To counter American's growing resentment, it started stamping goods *MADE IN USA*. "USA" was a city the Japs renamed to deceive us about the country of origin.

Significant Early WWII Dates

Sept. 1, 1939: War in Europe starts when the Germans invade Poland without a declaration of war. By Dec. 7, 1941, German armies have blitzkrieged Europe and are overextended, fighting a fierce Russian counteroffensive all along the 500-mile Moscow front.

Dec. 8, 1941: The United States and Britain along with Australia, the Netherlands, the Free French, Yugoslavia and several South American countries, declare war on Japan. China declares war on Germany, Italy and Japan.

Dec. 11, 1941: Germany and Italy declare war on the United States. Congress replies with a declaration of war and notes U. S. forces can be dispatched to any part of the world.

Dec. 17, 1941: Adm. Chester Nimitz is appointed to command the U.S. Pacific Fleet, relieving Adm. Husband Kimmel.

Feb. 22, 1942: Gen. Douglas MacArthur is ordered to leave the Philippines and establish his headquarters in Australia.

April 1, 1942: Japanese continue attacks on Bataan. Some 24,000 American and Filipino troops are weak and exhausted from existing on quarter rations and suffering from tropical diseases.

April 9, 1942: Gen. Ernest King surrenders 75,000 troops (12,000 American) to Gen. Masaharu Homma on Luzon. Prisoners are marched to San Fernando, 100 miles away, with many thousands dying due to mistreatment by the Japs. Gen. Jonathan Wainwright still holding out at Corregidor.

April 18, 1942: Gen. James Doolittle's 16 B-25 Mitchell bombers are launched from the U.S.S. Hornet for the first air raid on Tokyo.

May 6, 1942: Gen. Wainwright surrenders Corregidor with 15,000 American and Filipino troops.

Slinging Hash Instead of Ammo

Two months after my 17th birthday, I graduated from Lawrence High School with as much determination as ever to enlist in the Navy, but I had to put it on hold for a while.

Dad had purchased a new diner just before the war started and was putting all his resources and energy into holding on and making a go of it. I was a resource, having helped out as a dishwasher on Saturdays since age 13 and by now was a reasonably good short-order cook. Help was scarce; men and women were drawn to higher paying jobs in nearby defense plants, like Grumman in Farmingdale, where they turned out fighter planes.

The diner was open around the clock, 24 hours a day, 7 days a week. After graduation, my good pal Bob Lavery and I started working the night shift, 6 in the evening to 6 in the morning, and on occasion, when someone didn't show up for the day shift, I worked right through the lunch rush until 2 in the afternoon.

It was hard work, but Bob and I took it in stride, kidding with customers, making fun, increasing the night business and making good money from our base pay plus tips. Twenty-five cents was average; some people tipped only a nickel or a dime. The town's bookie left a dollar tip when he had a good day or a few too many good drinks.

A lawyer and his wife were among the regulars who came in for dinner two or three nights a week. One night, while the jukebox was blasting out "Rosie The Riveter," one of the biggest WW II hit songs, he told me he wrote "Rosie". It was catchy and had a great beat and lyrics that put a smile on your face when you heard them.

The song celebrated women who left their traditional homemaker role, rolling up their sleeves and working in defense plants to help build our country's mighty arsenal.

"ROSIE THE RIVETER"
While oth-er girls at-tend their favorite
cock-tail bar,
Sip-ping dry mar-tinis, munch-ing cav-i-ar,
There's a girl who's real-ly put-ting them
to shame-
Ros-ie is her name. Etc.

1999- Rosie Stamp

Other diner regulars included the town's
night owls, who regularly closed bars at 3 a.m: bartenders, bar-flies, bookies and assorted patrons, mostly male, either finishing the night or starting the morning with bacon and eggs, omelettes, steaks and hamburgers. The generous tipping bookie insisted we conjure up a different omelette every night. We did, throwing in leftovers, anything in sight. His favorite was sardines and meatballs. It became known as the Sweep Up the Kitchen for a Sucker Omelette.

Strangers in the night stood out like sore thumbs in this small town. Two, who started having late suppers, looked and acted as if they were right from central casting – Hollywood type G-Men, tall, clean-cut, white shirts, dark ties and navy blue suits.

One night, after showing me F.B.I. identification, they asked if I had a ladder they could borrow? I wanted to ask why, but didn't and said, "Sure." They remained out of sight in the kitchen until a big black Packard limo pulled into the parking lot. They drove off with the ladder on top and returned about 45 minutes later, placed the ladder against the wall and, without a word, drove off.

I could see two more people, a man and a woman, in the back seat of the limo. I heard later that a couple of German spies with a short-wave radio had been caught on Washington Avenue, a couple of blocks away.

As the war continued, there were more tales of locally-captured spies, but you soon learned to treat most rumors with a grain of salt.

During the war, women working in a Washington State shipyard worked hard and long for their pay. A typical unskilled worker, after putting in six eight-hour days, took home $23.20 from her $29.00 salary. (Twenty percent was deducted for taxes.) Some male shipyard workers made more than that in one day.

Slinging Hash Instead of Ammo

However, Long Island beaches were considered ideal spots for German submarines to put saboteurs ashore, especially out toward the less populated eastern end. One group of German agents who landed from a submarine encountered a Coast Guard man on beach patrol and offered him a bribe that he pretended to accept, although he immediately reported them to his commanding officer. The Germans were kept under constant surveillance as they moved about the country, until they and their contacts were all eventually rounded up and arrested in Chicago.

WW II Rationing in the United States began four days after the attack on Pearl Harbor under the Office of Price Administration with the goal of equal distribution of commodities and price control.

Dec. 11, 1941: Sale of new cars and passenger tires banned.

February 1942: The last civilian cars produced.

March 1942: Gasoline rationing at the discretion of the service station owners. Dubbed "Mother Hubbard" by *Business Week* Magazine.

Ration books for food, sugar, coffee and shoes, were distributed directly to consumers for rationed items. Surrender of coupon books was required within 10 days after death of the holder.

May 2, 1942: Sugar Rationing Book 1 initiated.

May 15, 1942: Eastern States gasoline rationing announced with three gallons per week allotted for nonessential vehicles.

May 1942: Mandatory 35 m.p.h. speed limit implemented.

Nov. 29, 1942: Coffee rationing begins.

Dec. 1, 1942: National gas rationing takes effect.

Jan. 7, 1943: "Pleasure driving" banned on the East Coast.

February 1943: Shoe rationing begins.

Mar. 29, 1943: Meat rationing begins. (Once, while home on leave, I used many of Mom's ration coupons for a leg of lamb. It was the toughest meat I ever tried to carve.)

Aug. 15, 1945/VJ Day: Ration restrictions lifted on processed food, gasoline, fuel oil and oil stoves. By the end of the year, restrictions on everything, from men's rubber-soled work shoes to tires, was lifted.

Time to Level

Since Lavery went off to the Army, I was running the diner alone at night, stalling and putting off talking to Dad about enlisting in the Navy. Time was running out, my 18th birthday was a couple of months away. I would be drafted and probably end up in the Army. Finally, over a cup of coffee, I leveled with my father.

"Dad, I'll be 18 soon. I'll be drafted. I want to go in the Navy, not the Army."

"Son, you've been a big help here, I appreciate it. Been doing some thinking about things myself. I know how strong you feel about enlisting in the Navy. I'm with you there. When you go, we'll close the diner at night and will only have to handle getting through the days."

"Dad, I feel bad, I..."

"Raymond, don't worry. Mom and I will work it out. Something will turn up."

We hugged; both were teary-eyed. I felt relieved; the bittersweet mixture of joy, sadness and guilt.

Dad said: "Can you give me a hand in the morning? Another batch of draftees are leaving on the 8:04; you'll be able to serve some of your buddies coffee and doughnuts...say goodbye."

"Sure Dad, I think Fitzgibbons and Doran are leaving then. Dad, wait and see how many girls come to say goodbye to Fitz. He'll have one at either end of the station platform and another in the middle."

People were issued ration books with stamps for food and gasoline. A family of four was allotted enough food stamps to have meat every other day, etc. A civilian gas allotment was 3 gallons of gas per week. A small businessman who needed his car, as my father did, got a "B" Ration Book which allowed extra gallons of gas per week.

21

Time to Level

My father served free coffee and doughnuts to all draftees departing from the Cedarhurst Rail Station. The scene was, as you might expect, very emotional. Young men trying to act and look brave. Parents sad, tearful, also trying to be brave. Young girls unabashedly kissing their high-school sweeties in public, in front of parents, no less. Young married couples, some with infants, speaking softly, staring deeply into one another's eyes at the past, at the future.

Seeing loved ones off to war was heart-rendering and painful, for those going and for those staying. What would happen? Would you ever see one another again? Unspoken fears swelled forth as the train edged out of the station

Some people not on the train should have been, but they were cowardly and cunningly avoided serving their country. Draft dodgers, *manufactured 4-F's,* with faked illnesses documented by paid-off doctors; greedy, selfish cowards who would do anything to avoid being drafted, to avoid putting their ass on the line, students, aided by bribes supplied by wealthy parents. War was bringing out the best in most, the worst in a few.

It was especially delightful when one of those bastards was caught, exposed, tried and sent to jail. The phony 4-F's and black marketers dealing in food and gasoline, the enemy within, were loathed almost as much as the Japs and Germans.

A couple of days after seeing my pals off, I caught the 8:04 to New York's Penn Station, took a subway downtown to the Wall Street area, found the Navy Recruiting Station, showed my baptismal certificate (for age proof), my parental permission letter and the process started.

"Fill out these papers, print if you know how. Stop calling me *sir*, I'm not an officer. Put the filled-out papers in the box on my desk then get in line over there to see the doc. He's an officer, call him *sir*."

"Ever had any serious diseases?"

"No, sir."

"Breathe in, deeply. Hold it. Exhale. Do it again."

"Alright, drop your pants, bend over, spread your cheeks, smile."

"Do what?"

"The same as that guy is doing over there."

"Move along."

"Cover your left eye, read this line"

"E F P T O Z"

"Your right eye."

"L P E D F E C D".

"O.K., now take one of those jars, pee in it, and give it to the yeoman who has your papers. Next!"

I grabbed a jar, and headed for the head thinking, so far, so good. Got it made in the shade. There must have been 20 guys lined up peeing or trying to pee in jars. The guy next to me was a *trying to*. He said, "I've been here for 15 minutes, can't pee. They won't let me in the Navy if I can't pee!"

"Go over to the sink, turn on the faucet, listen to the running water; that's the way I was trained to pee before going to bed when I was a little kid. It might work."

I filled my jar halfway and walked over to the yeoman's desk. He labeled it and I was about to move on when "TT" rushed up with a full jar shouting: "I did it! I did it!" As he tried to pass the jar to the surprised yeoman, it slipped from his hand, spilling all over the desk.

"You dumb son of a bitch, look what you've done!"

"I'll dry 'em. I'll dry 'em, I'm sorry...sorry"

"Get out of my sight before I kill you. Out! Out! Out!"

"Do you need another sample?"

"Out, out, I said, out!"

The place was rocked by laughter; everyone except the yeoman and poor TT were splitting their sides.

I left in high spirits. Everything seemed to be going well, and it was.

A couple of weeks later, my orders came: Report to Grand Central Palace at 480 Lexington Ave., Room 1400, N.Y.C. at 1800 hours. I couldn't believe it, I was finally on my way to be sworn into the U.S. Navy on April 13. It was a tough day, saying goodbye to Mom, Dad and my sister. It was so hard on all of us. Somehow we managed to keep up a false front in this fragile, emotion-packed situation. Each of us tried to make it easier on the other when really, there was no way to make it easy. As we hugged and kissed, I wondered if and when I would see them again. Maybe Mom and Dolly, but Dad was quite ill. He looked frail, not his usual robust self; his eyes were languid, weary. For the first time ever, I felt my father was vulnerable, not invincible...that he was fighting a losing battle and that I was leaving him to fight his battle alone.

Time to Level

My cousin Frank Moore, a New York City detective, drove me into the city. He was my idol. A superstar athlete in three or four sports, while on scholarship at Riverdale Country Day School. Frank could have had an academic or athletic scholarship to any college in the land.

He graduated during the height of the Depression, skipped college, married young, worked in Florida for a while and eventually became a policeman and then a detective.

Frank was about 28. I wondered why he wasn't in the service, but didn't ask. When he let me out on Lexington Avenue, he joked, "Now that you're going into the Navy, Ray, this war will be over soon. God bless!" and off he drove.

Off I went to find room 1400. There were about 100 enlistees milling around there, waiting to be sworn in. No overture played before the dramatic moment. An ensign entered the room and a yeoman bellowed:

"Raise your right hand...repeat after the officer."

"I (Raymond Stone) do solemnly swear that I will bear true faith and allegiance to the United States of America, and that I will serve them honestly and faithfully against all their enemies whomsoever, and I will obey the orders of the President of the United States and the orders of the officers appointed over me, according to the rules and articles for the government of the Navy.

And I do so further swear that all statements made by me as now given are correct."

An unscheduled hooray followed the oath!

We shook hands in celebration, now sailors in the U.S. Navy (though in reality, lowly apprentice seamen).

A star flag was proudly displayed by families proclaiming the number of sons and daughters serving in the armed forces. Each blue star represented a family member, while a gold star indicated a son or daughter had given his or her life for their country.

Fortunately, the flag proudly displayed in my parents' window had two blue stars.

24

Feelings of joy, pride and patriotism crested in my mind, finally certain that I was heading on the course I wanted. I was ready to embrace duty to country the same as I did religion–with faith, dedication and trust, not as a martyr about to face the lions but more as a warrior about to do battle and win.

All the new "boots" seemed to be feeling older, taller and stronger, filled with heightened self-esteem since taking the oath.

We formed-up on 46th Street and Lexington Avenue to march–first crosstown and then downtown to Penn Station–behind a fat, swaggering boatswain's mate. As we marched through the Times Square area, sidewalk crowds stopped to cheer us on.

"Go get 'em!"

"We're proud of you guys!"

"Kick their butts!"

"God Bless America!."

The cheers made us stand straight as we tried even harder to march in step while waving back to the people like victorious, not fledgling, warriors.

We marched into Penn Station about 8:30, just after the evening commuter rush.

The salty boatswain's mate, with a couple of hash marks on his sleeve signifying at least eight years in the Navy, bellowed:"We managed to arrive at Penn Station without suffering casualties en route. So I'm going to release you until midnight. You are not to leave the station. I will personally kick the ass of any f*** who doesn't f***** return to this exact spot by f***** midnight. Understand?

This was my first encounter with use of the "f" word in all its glory; noun, verb, adjective, punctuation! I didn't realize it would soon become my common denominator when expressing joy, sorrow and pain. (I had been instructed by my father to throw out any man in the diner who used lesser profanity whenever ladies were within ear-shot ... which I did on several occasions).

A crisp $20 bill, my birthday present from Mom and Dad, was burning a hole in my pocket. I picked out a guy about my age, Ed Hadley, from a town in Connecticut, and said: "How about joining me in the Savarin Bar? At midnight I'll be 18, old enough to legally drink in New York".

Time to Level

Ed bellied up to the bar and we started. After downing six, seven or more *Three Feathers* rye and ginger ales, I gave the barman a $2 tip, floated out the door and joined the group boarding the train for an overnight, long, long, meandering trip to the Sampson Naval Base in Geneva, New York.

Sampson Boot Camp

It was an unforgettable train trip, which I spent sprawled on the floor, with my head in a toilet bowl, upchucking my brains, getting hit in the head every time someone swung the door in. I was totally *non compos mentis* as the train wove through Pennsylvania and back to New York State, picking up batches of "boots" at stops along the way. Fortunately, upon arrival late the next morning, we were loaded onto open-air trucks for the drive to Sampson. Rushing fresh air helped to clear out the fog in my head a little – just a little.

The truck finally came to a stop at a large building, a drill hall. We went in, lined up on marked squares, stripped off our civilian clothes and placed them in a box to be sent home.

To start, each man was issued a ditty bag containing a tooth brush, comb, razor, etc. Next, we were attacked by corpsmen armed with needles, injecting us from both sides. I was still so numb that I didn't feel or notice a needle still sticking in my arm as I shuffled down the line for the next hit.

After the shots came lunch, consisting of a cheese sandwich on dry white bread, an apple and a container of warm milk. Standing around naked while eating lunch was a bizarre introduction to Navy chow.

(The ID Card photo, taken later that morning, is

Sampson Boot Camp

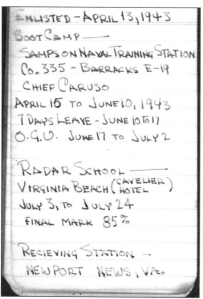

```
ENLISTED - APRIL 13, 1943
Boot Camp —
Sampson Naval Training Station
Co. 335 - Barracks E-19
    Chief Caruso
April 15 to June 10, 1943
7 Days Leave - June 10 to 17
O.G.U. June 17 to July 2

Radar School —
Virginia Beach (Cavelier Hotel)
July 3, to July 24
Final Mark 85%

Recieving Station —
Newport News, Va.
```

First page from the unauthorized diary I carried throughout the war. Other diary pages follow in chronological order, detailing the action and significant events. Then, as now, my spelling was flawed.

a constant reminder of how badly I felt, and looked, while nursing the worst hangover of my young life).

"Now, dump yer plates in the barrel and follow me."

"Sound off yer size at each station! Keep moving!"

We were then issued skivvies, socks, shoes, undress blues, dungarees, shirts and "boots," those ever-loving leggings you would lace up and wear, day after day, until boot camp was finished.

"Alright now, everyone listen up when I call your name. Stone?"

"Yo!"

"Over here with this group going to E-19. Get dressed, put your extra clothes in the sea bag. Move it."

"Yes sir."

E-Unit had 10, brand-new, identical two-story wood-frame barracks, plus a chow hall, indoor drill hall/gym and administration building, all surrounding a four-acre drill field. We were quartered on the lower deck, which we still called the ground floor. About 80 of us packed in one huge bunk room with a small open space and a table at one end, near the head with its sinks, toilets and showers. At home, the room shared with my brother had twin beds. This was sort of an extension, with 40 double-deck bunks. We were settling in when the bugle sounded what was to become a favorite–chow call. Da-da-da-da-da-da: "Come and get your beans boys–come and get your beans."

Our leader, Chief Caruso, lined us up on the drill field, said he wanted us to look smart and proceeded to march us to and up the broad steps of the mess hall. It was immense, with rows and rows of tables.

Cigarette smoking and cursing became habitual. Cigarettes sold for 50 cents a carton; at 5 cents a pack; you couldn't resist. Some popular brands were: Lucky Strikes, Camels, Old Golds and Chesterfields.

28

Food was plopped on the tray as we filed past the steam table, served by other boots who had K.P. duty that week. The meal was a palatable meat loaf. Things were looking up. Most of us were nestled in our "fart-sacks," as we soon were calling them, before taps sounded. Tired as I was, my thoughts were home. How were Mom, Dad and Sis? What will happen tomorrow? I drifted off to sleep with a smile and a deaf ear to a cacophony of snoring, farts and muffled sobs.

A bugle blared: "Ya got ta get up. Ya got ta get up. Ya got ta get up in the morning." Getting up at dawn wasn't all that bad; getting up, dressing in zero time, lining up on the drill field and doing morning exercises was pure agony. Chief Caruso's jumping jacks, toe touching, deep knee bends and push-ups were not my idea of how to start the day, especially without a cup of coffee. After a couple of days, I found that by laying flat in the middle of my sagging mattress, pulling the covers over my head and placing the pillow on top, I could avoid both detection and early morning torture while getting an extra half- hour's sack time. It was my maiden voyage into the realm of artful goofing off.

The only nautical training remembered during our eight weeks at Sampson was one day of tying knots, another day of rowing a long boat on Lake Geneva, and passing the swimming test that required you

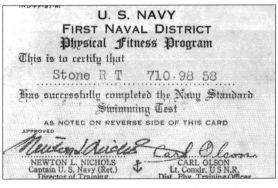

to jump off the high platform, swim to the other end of the pool, back, and then swim across the pool underwater.

Everything else was marching and drilling and as far as I was concerned, prep for infantry duty. Hikes, long hikes, double-time hikes. Daytime hikes, nighttime hikes, all carrying a heavy rifle that we didn't know how to load or fire. It was totally ludicrous to me; the rifle, an ancient bolt-action model, was a prop, used solely for drilling, discipline and as I soon found, for punishment.

One day, Chief Caruso caught me shouting right, instead of left, during our cadence marching chant. "You hadda good job and you left, (right), first they hired you, then they fired you, then by golly you left (right)," and so on. Caruso lost his cool and laced me out and as punishment, while the rest continued marching, I had to stand spread-eagle, holding the rifle over my head. It was a hot, muggy day and I was soaked with sweat, my muscles cramping and aching. After about a half-hour doing penance, Caruso allowed me to bring the rifle down to my shoulder for the next half-hour. Lesson No. 1: *Don't be a wise ass* – was learned and remembered.

We drilled, drilled, drilled until we were better at marching than any of the other two left-footed boot companies in E-Unit and ended winning the coveted Red Rooster Flag (we called it the Bloody Red Rooster), which earned us one day of liberty in Geneva.

As a liberty town, Geneva was pretty dull, but any place away from the base, away from the daily routine, was appealing. Boots were not usually entitled to liberty until after finishing training. It was ironic, earning a day without marching, by marching.

Dress blues had not been issued, so we dressed in our work blues and the obligatory leggings that branded us as boots on the loose. Spirits were soaring as we boarded buses: here comes the Navy; get ready Geneva! "Hey there mister, ya had better hide your sister, 'cause the fleets' in, the fleets' in!"

Bounding from the buses with smiles of expectation, this liberty party quickly learned liberty was restricted for boots. Boots were not allowed in bars and couldn't buy booze in liquor stores. We could go to the movies and could get an ice-cream soda. So much for the fantasy of being a salty sailor enjoying the fruits of a wild liberty. After downing a coffee ice-cream soda, I wandered around aimlessly until I heard loud voices coming from a parking lot.

Some boots had managed to con a civilian into buying them a bottle of whiskey. A few of my buddies were passing around the bottle, already three sheets to the wind when I joined the gathering behind some cars.

My barracks buddy, Kelly, greeted me. "C'mere Stoney, c'mere and have a swig!"

After a swig I advised, "Hold it down guys, the Shore Patrol's 'round the corner."

Kelly's response: "F*** them! I'm on my first liberty."

"Which just ended," one burly S.P. said, as he the took bottle from

Kelly, pouring whiskey on the ground. The S.P.'s herded us into a basement brig in the cellar of the town's courthouse, to be held until our bus departed for the base.

The sloppy drunks were put behind bars; the rest of us sat on benches or squatted on the floor. Most of us were very scared about what was going to happen when we got back to Sampson. Not Kelly, though. He was shouting, rambling and raging on, in ossified Bronxese, about his sea duty, ships served on, battles fought...

"How can you treat a war hero this way? I've been..."

"Pipe down, you asshole. You never even been on board the Staten Island ferry. Shut up!"

Nothing quieted Kelly's drunken fury and fortunately nothing happened to us. We could have been charged and convicted of something, putting an indelible blotch on our thus-far pristine service records: "Drunk and disorderly on first liberty." A stigma that would surely raise eyebrows on future duty assignments.

Thankfully, we were turned over to Chief Caruso and bused back to base. Within minutes of hitting our sacks, the entire barracks was ordered to fall out, with rifles, for a 10 mile nighttime hike. Everyone had to pay for the transgressions of the few who screwed up.

The question asked was: "Why everyone? Why not just those jerks who got caught?" Our no-marching day, earned by precision marching, ended in punishment marching. Tails were dragging when we got back to the barracks, and if there was a lesson to be learned, it was something like: that which doesn't quite kill you makes you strong.

Jim Roche, my boyhood pal from home, had finished his boot training at Sampson a month earlier and was awaiting shipping orders in G-Unit. On a visit, he told me that beer was served in his PX. The chapel was located between his unit and mine. I became a regular nightly chapel visitor. Entering by a side door, kneeling in a rear pew, I'd remove the boots, stuff them under my jumper and nonchalantly walk past the guardhouse as if I were returning to G-Unit from chapel. It worked, without a challenge.

James J. Roche 1943

31

Jim would be waiting in the PX bar. You had to be 21 to legally get a beer. So Jim and I had to wait until a fight broke out, usually after about 15 minutes. We'd slip under the velvet ropes that separated the drinking area, grab a vacated empty beer glass and wait for the S.P.s to restore order. The empty glasses were presented at the bar and refilled with no questions asked. We usually drank our fill, departing before lights out

Back at the barracks, they couldn't figure out how I went to chapel most nights and came back smelling like a brewery. I kept mum, knowing it would blow my cover if too many others got my religion.

The mixture of farm boys, small-towners and city slickers who made up our company was interesting. Kids who had worked in steel mills, coal mines and machine shops. Most, glad to get away from backbreaking work conditions. Some, happy just to get away from home and parental supervision, to be on their own for the first time. All but one or two were happy to be in the Navy and starting their new job of fighting the enemy. You soon learned to be good buddies with Jewish and Italian guys; their mothers sent the biggest food packages, most often. Whatever our differences or ethnic backgrounds, we shared a newly learned common language, a salty English laced with the f*** word.

Within a week, you had it down pat, sounding like a boatswain mate without a good conduct medal. I called home one Sunday after attending Mass. Telephone lines at the PX were long, but finally I got through.

"Hi, Mom, it's me!"

"Hello, son, how are you?"

"Fine mom, fine, how are you. How's Dad?"

"Oh, he's doing O.K. Did you go to church this morning?"

"Yeah Mom, early Mass."

"Are you having a good time up there?"

"Me, I'm having a f***** good time."

"Raymond! What did you just say?"

"Ehrr, Mom, ehrr, ehrr, ducking, ehrr yeah, it's...a good time here. Say how's my little sister, Dolly?"

I was beet-red, tongue-tied and so embarrassed that I had said f***** while speaking to Mom. It was the first and last time Mom ever heard the "f" word from me.

Our barracks bully, a taxi driver from Brooklyn, was a fat Tony Galento type who was older, balding and aggressive as hell. He thought he could bull-drive over everyone. I watched closely, saw how he was cheating the yokels at cards and called him on it. He exploded: "I'll kill you, you dirty little bastard."

"Whenever you're ready, Fatso," I said, sizing him up. He had me 200 pounds to 150, but I had no fear and knew he was more mouth than muscle and that I could take him with a solid punch to his gut or chin.

"You're a cheat, a crook, stacking high cards on the bottom, cheating these kids, you f***** shithead."

"You punk. Yer lucky I don't want to get us all in trouble. I'd kill yer right now. You wait, I'll get yer later."

"Any time, Fatso, anytime."

This put a halt to his nightly stealing, and we had the inevitable show-down a couple of days later. I was in the evening chow line, which stretched single-file, up to the broad steps leading into the mess hall. Fatso was working his way up from the back, pushing, shoving, getting in front of everyone. I saw him coming, waited on the landing above the top step, right fist cocked, at the ready. He started to shove me aside as I uncorked a solid right, brought up from the deck with my full butt behind it, square on his jaw. Ass over tea-kettle he tumbled down the dozen steps. Getting up mumbling: "I'll kill yer if I ever get yer off the base. Yer dead meat!"

I stood there with a full adrenaline flush and clenched fists, waiting for him to make a move. But he was a coward, no balls, all mouth, and now everyone knew it. They smothered him in derisive hoots, hollers and taunts. Fatso never threatened me or anyone else again. Scratch one bully.

Boot camp lasted less than two months. On June 10, 1943, I started a seven-day leave, with orders to report back to Sampson's Out Going Unit (O.G.U.) for testing and assignment.

Once home, after seeing Mom, Dad and Dolly, I couldn't wait to display myself in uniform. First stop was Boris, the local photographer, for a portrait. This guaranteed display, along with other local servicemen, in his storefront window. I asked him to place my photo next to that of my pal Bob Lavery. Bob and I had driven Boris nuts when he was trying to get us to sit still for our senior yearbook photos. (There was also a a slight hint of bodily harm, if he failed to place my picture there. He did.)

The people I met walking around town were all full of good will and good wishes. Most had at least one family member in the service, and their gratuitous-sounding comments were sincere.

Ray Stone, first leave photo.

One of my favorite high-school teachers, besides Joe Page, who was now also in the Navy, was "King"Arthur Combes, my English teacher. Mr. Combes earned my respect and admiration both as a teacher and a fine human being. Also, he was one of the few high-school teachers who tolerated and even appreciated classroom pranks...if they were creative and carried out with style. I visited him during recess at the local grade school where he was now the principal.

There he stood: erect, towering over and surrounded by tiny first and second graders. When he saw me, he greeted me warmly, commenting in his basso stentorian tone:"Raymond, you are certainly a new dimension in your Navy uniform. Welcome!"

"And you Mr. Combes, surrounded as you are, resemble Gulliver about to be tied down by the wee people."

We had a good chuckle and as we talked I felt closer to him. The former teacher-student relationship was different. More man-to-man now. However, as we corresponded throughout the war, Mr. Combes returned my letters with corrected spelling and punctuation. Always my teacher, always my friend and, reading between the lines of his letters, always wishing he, too, was involved in the war as a warrior.

Since I wasn't exactly going steady when I enlisted, it took a few phone calls before locating a high-school heartthrob who hadn't promised to be true to some departed serviceman and was delighted that I called.

Fortunately, Betty was great fun, a good looker, good necker, good dancer, a great date to take to New York City for dancing and a night on the town.

The big bands appeared regularly at major hotels or the Paramount Theater: Tommy Dorsey at the Astor Roof, Jimmy Dorsey at the

Paramount Theater, Jimmy Dorsey or Glenn Miller at the Pennsylvania, Benny Goodman at the New Yorker, Harry James and Vaughn Monroe at other hotels.

You could still have a wonderful night on the town for under $20, which I could afford while working for Dad in the diner. Dinner for two at the Hotel McAlpin's Marine Grill–about $8 or $9, including tip. Drinks for two, plus tip, at a hotel ballroom about $10. (At this time, buck privates in the Army, and apprentice seamen in the Navy were paid about $50 a month).

After dinner, we strolled up Fifth Avenue, turned east at 42nd Street to the Commodore Hotel where Old Muscle Throat, Vaughn Monroe and his big band were performing in the grand ballroom. As we arrived, he was crooning his theme song, "Racing With the Moon." Very romantic, especially after a couple of rum and cokes and when we started dancing cheek to cheek. We hardly left the floor, dancing every set, slow fox trots and some lively Lindys. We just made the last train to Cedarhurst and I was able to get Betty home slightly after her midnight curfew.

A kiss good night at the front door and I was off for a nightcap at Bob Wright's, a local hangout for servicemen on leave. The place was nearly empty, except for the first Miss Rheingold who was sitting on a barstool near a large poster filled with her smiling face.

Rheingold, then a popular New York beer, was conducting it's second annual Miss Rheingold contest. Bar patrons cast votes for their favorite among six or eight pretty, young candidates. The lucky winner was crowned Miss Rheingold and reigned for a year.

My smoothie opening line was: "Gee honey, did anyone ever tell you that you're a dead ringer for that pretty gal in the poster?"

Her icy reply: "Now isn't that strange, since it is me."

"Well, er, shouldn't you be drinking beer, not a highball?"

"Shouldn't you be at sea and not bothering me, sailor boy?"

I couldn't think of a smart retort, so I mumbled: "Loose lips sink ships...so do loose hips...honey!"

End of conversation. I took a barstool opposite her and couldn't keep from staring at her. She was quite beautiful.

While sipping a rum and coke, I tried to look sophisticated by blowing smoke through my nose. I don't remember who the movie star was, but he sure looked sophisticated as he stared into the eyes of his leading lady with smoke drifting from his nostrils. So I tried it, staring at her, thinking surely it would impress her. It didn't, so I drove home. Tomorrow was another day with another night in New York City.

Wartime New York was as full of energy as it was of young servicemen venturing into big city nightlife and entertainment for the first time. Some approached it with fear, having grown up in rural areas; some with bewilderment, overwhelmed by New York's diversity and people.

New Yorkers treated servicemen with warmth and respect, as did most of the country then. Most – but surprisingly not all. New York's Stage Door Canteen was one of the finest in the nation, an oasis for so many lonely or broke servicemen. Here they found a listening ear and understanding doled out by female volunteers, some young, others matronly. They found entertainment provided by Broadway stars. Many a serviceman fell in love and ended up lamenting, as in the popular song: "I left my heart at the Stage Door Canteen, I left it there with a girl named Eileens."

Another place of wartime legend was Sherman Billingsly's Stork Club, which was beyond most enlisted men's resources. However, it was a mecca for officers who could afford to rub elbows with celebrities, or just be in the same room with them.

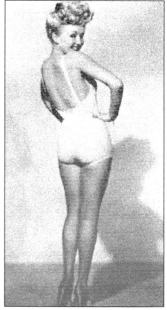

I had a drink at the Stork one night and ended up arranging a date with the pretty cigarette girl. She was a nice kid from the Midwest who hoped to get into show biz, and we had a wonderful night on the town.

When I happened to intentionally mention my date with the cigarette girl from the Stork Club, my buddies reacted as if I had landed a date with a movie star like Betty Grable.

Betty Grable was probably the most popular pinup girl in the Navy, outranking the voluptuous drawings of the Petty and Varga Girls by more than two to one.

Betty Grable's picture was pinned up in lockers throughout the ship.

Broadway's famous Paramount Theater was home to big-name entertainers like Old Blue Eyes, Frank Sinatra, who held court on its huge stage. I disliked Sinatra. To me he was a draft dodger and I was annoyed by the way young teenaged girls, bobby soxers, swooned en masse when he sang. Still, I kept my word to Dolly, my 13-year-old sister, and off to the Paramount we went. She, absolutely thrilled and properly attired in sox and saddle shoes. Me, in my uniform and quite pissed.

The huge Paramount theater was packed, mostly with hordes of young teenyboppers who screeched, sighed, fainted and probably wet their pants as Frank crooned, "All or Nothing at All." They danced in the aisles, seemingly entranced. My sister loved it; I couldn't wait to get away from this disgusting display of bobby soxer mass hysteria, dragging Dolly with me into the nearest saloon when the show ended.

My sister Dolly, a typical 1940's bobby soxer.

The last night of my liberty was spent back in New York with Ilsa, a former high school cheerleader, dancing to Benny Goodman's wonderful music at the Hotel New Yorker. Swing, the driving, exciting music of the time was at its most popular period. After jitterbugging to "Stomping at the Savoy," you could catch your breath while holding a pretty girl tightly in your arms, swaying to "I Can't Get Started With You. "This was a young sailor's dream, making the most of a special moment, enjoying life to the fullest while you could.

Who knew what future tomorrows would bring? You thought about the pros and cons, but certainly didn't dwell upon them.

With my first leave over, it was time for another emotional farewell to the family and to head back to Sampson's O.G.U. for what I hoped would be a combat assignment onboard a ship in the fleet..

During the three weeks spent in O.G.U., I was tested and evaluated, hoping no one knew about my short-order cook skills; I wanted a fighting ship and most assuredly didn't want to end up in the Navy's school for cooks and bakers. My record showed good grades in high-school art classes, so they sent me to try out at the base art studio. Damn, I thought they had me.

The petty officer in charge told me to sit at a drawing table, bringing over some large illustration boards, speed-ball pens and India ink. I was told to lay out and letter tabular charts. I protested about my lack of experience, which was true. He countered that I would be taught and learn quickly. No way was I going to get stuck here. My lettering looked like it was done by a spastic and for good measure I spilled a bottle of India ink on my sample. It looked more like a Rorshach test than a chart. That took care of that problem.

Next, some ensign, who bought my story about not being able to letter charts, thought it would be nice if I did a 60-foot-long mural in the drill hall. I said, "What? Sir!"

He replied, "Washington crossing the Delaware would be nice. "I didn't want to say *no* to an officer, so I said, "That would be nice, but I'm not sure I can do it."

"Well, think it over and make some sketches," he ordered.

"Yes, sir, get right on it."

Fortunately, I never had to face the moment of truth, never seeing him again. The ensign must have shipped out, as I also did a couple of days later, boarding a troop train headed South for the main naval base on the East Coast in Norfolk, Va..

The troop train from Sampson to Norfolk was made up of long-retired, resurrected railroad cars. Everything that could still roll on rails was used.

The dining car was a converted boxcar with a standup counter running its length. About 50 or 60 of us filed in and lined up in front of paper plates. A booming voice bellowed, "You've got five minutes to finish your meal and move out to make room for the next batch of hungry swabbies."

Mess cooks piled mounds of spaghetti and tomato sauce on the paper plates. A major SNAFU, (Situation Normal All F***** Up) had occurred: no forks or spoons, making it a formidable challenge to eat more spaghetti than you ended up wearing. At 18, you were adaptable and took things in stride. Wearing spaghetti wasn't a big deal. It wasn't good, but I figured it was far better than dining on C rations, like the poor Army G.I.'s.

One reason I had such positive feelings about the Navy, over the Army, had something to do with food and clean sheets. I knew cooks would be there in the the ship's galley, clean sheets would be on your bunk, and you would never have to dig a foxhole to sleep in. Besides I loved boats and ships and the lore of the sea.

I was young, adaptable, and also perceptive.

Norfolk/Virginia Beach

Norfolk's Naval Operations Base was a sprawling, but well organized, old Navy base. Upon arrival, we cleaned up, ate a civilized meal and were handed orders: report to Fleet Radar School at the Cavalier Hotel in Virginia Beach. To me, "fleet" was a sweet sounding word; it meant ships. I didn't know much about "radar," but that sounded good, too.

Those damn boots were now stowed in the bottom of my sea bag, to be worn only upon drawing Shore Patrol duty. The hammock, issued initially, which I never slept in, was discarded at Norfolk (at this time, there were very few old U.S. Navy ships that still slung hammocks in berthing compartments).

When the elegant Cavalier was transformed into a Navy school, they stripped it of stylish prewar decor, substituting basic furnishings and bunk beds. However, it still oozed elegance with the setting, the size of the rooms and the manicured grounds. Also, the chow was the best I ever ate in the Navy, which could have been because either their chefs enlisted en masse and were still in the kitchen, or more likely because enlisted men and officers were fed from the same kitchen, in the same dining room. The Cavalier Hotel was, and remains, one of the finest, most elegant hotels on the beach.

Mornings started with everyone marching down the wide brick steps to formal gardens as a band played "The Star-Spangled Banner," followed by French, British and Polish national anthems. Our allies had small contingents of men attending radar school, and the morning muster ceremony made you feel connected to them as allies.

In daily classes we learned to operate different air and surface search-radar sets, and how to plot and apply the math used in figuring speeds and courses of ships and airplanes. We learned to work as a team:

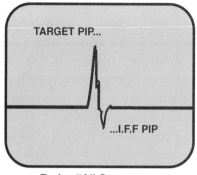

Radar-"A" Scope

radar operators, plotters and the fighter-direction officers honing skills in tracking and vectoring fighter pilots in mock interceptions ending in destruction of "bogeys" (unidentified enemy planes).

In 1943, the SK model radar was our state-of-the-art air-search radar. It could pick up a single plane or group of planes 150 miles away. (Even further, under ideal atmospheric conditions.) After a couple of bearing and distance plots, you could determine the speed and course of a target–but not the altitude, which was guesstimated based on distance and size and signal-strength of the pip.

Radar could also identify friendlies, using I.F.F. (Identification Friend or Foe), which triggered a downward pip from the transmitter in friendly airplanes.

SG Radar, with its PPI Scope, was used in tracking ships and had a normal range of about 26 miles, or to the horizon. It was great as a navigation aid, especially when operating within a task force where ships had to maintain station (a specific relative range and distance from other ships), while steering a zigzag course to confuse any submarines that may be tracking a ship's course.

Learning what was then a "high-tech" weapon, was fascinating and I worked hard to become proficient operating different types of radar. Surprisingly, I also mastered the math used to solve Earth/Ground/Movement equations (E.G.M.s), quickly and with ease.

Attending radar school at the Cavalier was so-called "four-point-0 duty," (4.0–the Navy's highest score).

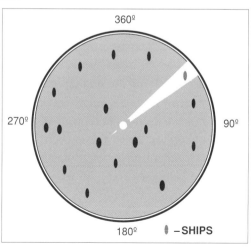

Radar "PPI" Scope (Plan Position Indicator)

Norfolk/Virginia Beach

Virginia Beach attracted a plethora of vacationing, single girls–there to party. Nearly everyone flocked to a roadhouse on the beach that featured a loud juke box and a small dance floor. You worked up a thirst from marathon jitterbugging and hoped the current girl of your dreams would nurse her beer or Coke, especially close to pay day when you couldn't afford another round. (Men usually didn't allow women to buy them drinks back then, and women didn't offer, either).

One night, after being overserved, I paused to rest on the lawn of the Princess Anne Hotel. My slumber was interrupted by the whack of a club across the soles of my shoes. The S.P.'s loaded me in the back of a Jeep, next to Ensign Eddie Duchin, the famous band leader, who had hitched a ride. After unloading at the Caviler, he told the S.P.'s: "I'll turn him over to the duty officer. Thanks for the ride."

Once inside, in the lobby, he said: "Good night sailor. Sleep it off. See you in the a.m."

As much as I liked this 4.0 duty, after completing training I turned down an offer to remain as an instructor. I wanted a ship. I wanted action.

I got my wish when we returned to N.O.B. for assignment and by late afternoon, three of us – Smitty, Doc and I – were on the way to theNewport News Receiving Station, assigned to some ship named the U.S.S. Intrepid. On the ferry ride to Newport News, a wise-ass sailor told

---

Radar–a unique WW II weapon. The British scientist-inventor Sir Robert Watson-Watt pioneered experimental radar. In 1935, he proved that an airplane could be detected by radio waves as they reflected back from the plane's surface. By 1936, his radar was able to detect an airplane as far away as 75 miles. When war broke out in 1939, Britain's string of radar stations along the east coast helped save England; they were able to detect enemy raids and send fighter planes to intercept. This allowed the British to use their limited number of fighter planes for maximum effect.

Early on, the Brits shared their secret with us and the U.S. soon had 150 M.I.T. scientists developing additional and more sophisticated radar for ships, airplanes and gunnery batteries. Meanwhile, Japanese radar was primitive and in the experimental stage throughout the war. Radar gave the U.S. Navy a vital strategic advantage, notably as used by Combat Information Centers (C.I.C.s) on aircraft carriers.

us it was a new garbage scow. We were thrilled when we found it to be a huge new Essex Class aircraft carrier, the third in its class, following the Essex and Yorktown, which were completed several months before the Intrepid was commissioned..

The Intrepid joined the fast-carrier striking force which was also considered a "high-tech" weapon because it

1943–A cluster of the Intrepid's radar antennas that rotate on masts, high above the ship's island structure.

was highly mobile and could bring its planes within range to attack any enemy target, anywhere in the wide Pacific.

Excerpt, from the *New York Daily News*–Aug 14, 1945

U.S. Gives Radar Secrets, 'Major Reason' of Victory–By Reuel S. Moore, Washington, D.C., (U.P.)–The Army and Navy tonight unfolded the long secret story of radar, second only to the atomic bomb as the war's most revolutionary scientific development, the margin of victory in the Allies' darkest hours and a springboard to the perfection of television and other far-reaching changes in postwar living.

Radar is an amazing "seeing eye" electronic device capable of cutting through the blackest night and thickest fog unerringly. It enables fighting men to track down, chart and destroy a target they never see.

Obscured by the atomic bomb in sensationalism, radar possibly has been more valuable because it was at work for the Allies when they might have lost the war without it. It turned the tide in the Battle of Britain, helped win the long struggle against German submarines, made possible the precision blasting of German industry and helped U.S. ships and planes drive the Jap Navy from the seas.

Newport News Receiving Station

The Intrepid's future crew was assembling at Newport News Receiving Station, one of the oddest Navy facilities I ever experienced. It consisted of three two-story barracks and a combination mess hall-administration building. No fences, no guards, no muster, no officers, no rules.

"Find an empty bunk, stow your gear there, get your chow and collect your pay here," said a civilian secretary who seemed to be in charge.

Across the road from the base was a sea of tiny houses, mostly occupied by shipyard workers. At least one was a house of not-so-hot repute with a young lady and her auntie making a fortune by keeping up sailors' morale. It was common for hookers to talk young, horny, naive sailors into marrying them for the monthly subsistence check and a chance of collecting the standard government $10,000 death insurance payoff, if they were, alas, widowed.

With time on our hands and the weekend approaching, Smitty and I decided to head up to New York for a couple of days, figuring no one would miss us. Smitty lived up in the Bronx, my home was out in Cedarhurst, on the south shore of Long Island.

Taking the Old Point Comfort Ferry to catch a train to New York

ATTACHED To U.S.S. INTREPID
BACK To RADAR School
FOR SPECIAL TRAINING
AUG. I TO AUG 14, 1943

WENT ABORD SHIP —
AUG. 15, 1943

SHIP COMISSIONED —
AUG. 16, 1943
CAPTAIN - T. R. SPRAGUE
EXECUATIVE OFFICER -
R. K. GAINES (COMMANDER)
AIR GROUP 8
OUT IN CHESSEPEKE BAY
QUALIFYING PLANES

City was easy with no S.P.'s checking papers. We had nervous moments on the train where S.P.'s and M.P.'s spot-checked passes.

The train was packed to the gunnels, with servicemen standing, sitting in the aisles, even stretched out in overhead baggage racks. Luckily, we made it both ways without a challenge from S.P.'s, returning late Sunday night. Good thing too. Monday morning a sailor said: "Hey, aren't you guys radar? There's an officer looking for you, over in the admin building."

Leon "Smitty" Smith

We headed there on the double.

"Good morning, sir. Understand you're looking for Intrepid radarmen, looking for us. I'm Ray Stone; this is Leon Smith."

"Hi. I'm Ensign Smith, one of the Intrepid's fighter direction officers."

We shook hands, and batted around some small talk about this base, and Smitty started expounding on how great it was back at the Cavalier. Smitty was laying it on thick about ambience and so forth, prepping Smith before he switched gears.

"Sir, I know it would benefit all of us, and the ship too, if we could go back to radar school for a while to practice, to work with you, working as a team with our officers, tracking bogeys, doing interceptions."

Ensign R. H. Smith, a former schoolteacher back in Pennsylvania, was no dope, but by the time Smitty finished his masterful *con,* Smith saw the benefits. He departed saying he would look into it and get back to us shortly.

Two days later, Smitty, Doc and I, along with a couple of others, were headed back to the Cavalier Hotel in Virginia Beach to sharpen our radar skills, working with planes from the nearby Naval Air Base at Pogo Pogo.

The food at the Cavalier was even better than I remembered. After a hearty breakfast, we would go to the roof, watch dolphins swimming off the beach and then assemble in a room with radar sets at the ready; first, we'd try to establish radio contact with pilots and planes at Pogo Pogo, and after a couple of futile hours of no contact, we would give up and work on simulated raids and interceptions.

Our days of frustration were compensated by nightly liberty, enjoying Virginia Beach's friendly, lively nightlife

Not all towns and cities in the Norfolk area were as friendly to sailors. Even with the nation at war, you still saw this denigrating sign, "Sailors and Dogs Not Allowed," posted outside an inn or restaurant. It made me and my buddies madder than hell; we wanted to kick ass, but didn't want to end up in the brig.

Norfolk's Market and Gramby Streets were cesspools, filled with sleazy bars and tattoo parlors. The streets were wall-to-wall Navy uniforms, ebbing and flowing like tides from bar to bar. Sailors were most welcome in bars here, especially on payday.

One of our favorite saloons had a chunky waitress named Ginger, whose response to a passing sailor's goose was a short left hook. I suggested she add a good right uppercut and gave her a boxing lesson between rounds of beers. Ginger was an apt student, far tougher than most of the young, drunken sailors who were copping feels. Her athletic skill was demonstrated a couple of days later when she put down her tray, threw two quick jabs and delivered a solid roundhouse right to a sailor's jaw, knocking him out cold. Pleased by her first KO, Ginger popped for a round of beers on the house.

The more you drank, the more you thought about getting tattooed. "Death Before Dishonor" was a popular tattoo, illustrated with a dagger piercing a heart, sometimes with dripping drops of blood.

Fortunately, while satisfying my curiosity, I never liked the looks of the parlor or the tattoo artist. Both were filthy. Back on board ship, you saw evidence on many sailor's arms: ugly, infected, oozing tattoos.

One of my married buddies got loaded and tattooed with the "Bluebirds of Happiness" emblazoned across his chest with a single bluebird flying above each breast,

Another version of a Death Before Dishonor tattoo.

46

One labeled "sweet," the other "sour." He worried about how he would ever explain the Bluebirds tattoo to his wife. He never had to; he was killed in action.

While at the Cavalier, we found Ensign Smith to be the first of a few good officers we served under. He knew what he was doing: he treated enlisted men evenly and fairly, not like a pompous ass, as some officers did...especially the 90-day wonders who were turned out like Spam during the war. Some *ninety dayers* felt that by acting superior and distant they would impress the enlisted men and obtain our respect. No way.

Sailors were quick and savvy when sorting out those "gold braids" who were real, from those who were empty suits. On the flip-side, most officers could spot "gold bricks" among enlisted men too – unless they were wallowing in the adulation of their personal ass-kissers. And there were many of them with puckered lips at the ready. Aptly designated "brown-nosers," they were despised by their shipmates.

Reporting On Board Ship

Aug. 15, 1943, four months after being sworn into the U.S. Navy, I finally was climbing the gangplank of *my* ship, the U.S.S. Intrepid.

Snapping a smart salute, first to the flag, then to the officer of the deck, I requested: "Permission to come aboard, sir?"

He returned the salute. "Permission granted."

As I stepped on deck, I felt a surge as my new life on this mighty ship began.

Finding my living compartment was easy, only a few steps from where we boarded, starboard, aft on the hangar deck. Down one ladder, and there you were, one deck below the hangar deck. All upper bunks were taken, so I picked a middle, rather than lower, sack. Like the bunks, lockers were stacked three high; I got a middle locker, right next to my bunk. With gear stowed, locker full, I wondered aloud, "What are you supposed to do with the empty sea bag?"

"Shove it up yer ass."

"Send it to sea."

"Sleep with it."

And finally, "Stow it under your mattress." As time passed, under the mattress became a growing storage bin. The mattress was encased in a slick green fireproof cover.

ANNAPOLIS, MD. ———
SEPT. 10 19 & 20, 1943
AND BACK TO N.O.B.

SHAKEDOWN CRUISE
OCT 7, 1943

REACHED TRINIDAD — OCT. 12
PRACTISE OPERATIONS —
IN GULF OF PARIA
LIBERTY IN PORT AU SPAIN
BACK TO STATES —
NOV. 1, 1943 (PORTSMOUTH N.Y.)
VIRGINIA

3 DAY 17 HR. LEAVE
NOV 1 TO NOV 5, 1943

You learned to place dress blues between the fireproof cover and the mattress bottom to more or less press them– sleeping on them – rather than in them.

I asked, "Smitty, got yourself squared away yet?"

"Yeah, no problem. But the guy in the bunk below looks like a snorer; got a helluva big snozzola. Let's find the head."

"I saw a guy wrapped in a towel coming outta there."

The head was equipped with showers, sinks and urinals. The potty, a separate compartment, had a 20-foot-long v-shaped metal trough with seats, formed by two planks that could be adjusted to fit the width of anyone's bottom. A continuous stream of seawater flowed from one end to the other, flushing the refuse.

Almost instantly, some joker figured out how to provide amusement when a downflow slot was occupied by an oblivious, intense reader. A ball of crumpled newspaper was ignited and floated toward the unsuspecting reader's ass; upon reaching the butt, it would catapult him upward, roaring a stream of profanity.

Jokesters also sent innocent seamen for left-handed wrenches and sky hooks, or as lookouts for a mythical mail buoy in the middle of the Pacific Ocean.

Smitty and I spent the next couple of hours exploring, getting lost except when we were on the 880-foot long deck (nearly three football fields), where you had an unobstructed view since our planes were not yet on board.

Below decks it was easy to lose your way in the maze of compartments. The ship was a densely populated small town with all standard services: butchers, bakers, cooks, chaplains, barbers, shoemakers, electricians, plumbers, carpenters, mechanics, along with the laundry, library, "gedunk" stand (ice cream–plus other goodies), mess hall (restaurant), sick bay (hospital) and so forth. A town populated mostly by teenagers supervised by a few experienced elders who directed, taught and shaped them into naval warriors.

It didn't take long for the young crew to make the passage from teen to adult. As we got to know one another, we became family, taking on responsibility for our new brothers and our ship. The evolution was painless, natural and prompt. Suddenly you were no longer just a bunch of kids, except when we got to California, where the legal drinking age was

21. This pissed us off: old enough to fight, to die, but too young to belly up to the bar for a beer. At this time, our country was as united as ever it would be against our enemies. The pride and patriotism of the Intrepid's crew was shared by all, starting with our skipper, Captain Thomas L. Sprague, whom all revered and respected, to our lowest apprentice seaman, whoever he was.

As "plankowners," Intrepid's first crew, we were especially proud of our ship. It was a pride that grew daily as we worked our tails off to get this fighting lady ready for battle. We were on board when the umbilical cord was cut at the commissioning, bringing the ship to life. This crew soon became Intrepid's heart and soul, and for good measure, we added 3,000 pairs of balls onto our fighting lady.

Later, during the ship's baptism by fire and in ensuing battles, we fought and kept our wounded ship alive. Each man earned the right, the honor of calling Intrepid, *"My Ship!"* – through the blood, sweat and tears that were shed later for our buddies who were killed in action.

Crews that followed us had similar pride and special feelings about the Intrepid. Ships are like that, like former sweethearts. Postwar crews did many heroic things during the Intrepid's long service as an Apollo recovery ship in the early 60's and later during three tours of duty in Vietnam and Cold War service tracking Soviet submarines.

When Smitty and I found our battle station in C.I.C., (Combat Information Center), we were elated. Then, C.I.C. was located just aft of the flag bridge in the island, the ship's superstructure that rises above the flight deck..

We shot the breeze with a radarman who was on guard duty. When in port, a radarman packing a .45 pistol, was always on guard duty in

---

Cigarette smoking and cursing became habitual. Cigarettes were five cents a pack, 50 cents a carton. Popular brands were Lucky Strikes after changing the background color on their pack from green to white, their slogan became (Lucky Strike Green has Gone to War); Camels (I'd Walk a Mile for a Camel); Chesterfield's (They Satisfy); Old Golds (Not a Cough in a Carload). At these prices, it was easy to develop the habit, and the cough too, and a carton became a great gift or persuasive bartering item, along with chocolate bars, chewing gum and silk stockings.

C.I.C. to protect the radar equipment from spies and saboteurs.

The sound of a bugle blowing chow call set us in motion. "C'mon, Stoney, we gotta find the mess hall. It's forward on the port side. Hope we've got good cooks."

Climbing down a ladder to the hangar deck, we saw a long line forming, growing, growing and growing. But it was moving quickly, and soon we descended a ladder to the mess hall where our trays were piled with meat, potatoes, vegetables, bread and dessert. Not bad, as a matter of fact; our cooks were good and the bakers even better. The ship's commissary officer, Cmdr. Henry Karp, cared; he knew how to feed over 3,000 men three meals a day, every day. I liked most everything, except powdered milk and powdered eggs. My favorite breakfast, served Wednesdays and Saturdays, was canned figs in syrup, baked beans, cinnamon buns and black coffee. I suspect the beans were loaded with saltpeter, which was supposed to suppress your sexual desire.

THE CHIEF PETTY OFFICERS

AND CREW OF THE

U.S.S. INTREPID

REQUEST THE PLEASURE OF YOUR COMPANY

ON THE HANGAR DECK FOLLOWING

THE COMMISSIONING

PLEASE PRESENT THIS CARD

(Fifty years later, I served this breakfast, sans saltpeter, to my shipboard buddies Botts Alexander, Jack Norton, **Crewmembers, as well as the ship's officers, invited guests to the ceremony** *Winston Goodloe and Polack Vogrin and their ladies. The verdict: the ladies, not too bad; the guys, still pretty good!)*

That night, crawling into the sack, hearing taps echoing throughout the ship for the first time, was a religious experience. It still is, especially since taps have sounded for so many of my buddies. The hair on back of your neck curls in sync with the chills running through your mind and up your spine.

Reveille was something else. Time to hit the deck; make a mad dash for the head; get good position for your morning ritual. Even with a chin covered in light red hair, I had to shave every day to pass inspection at muster. Sharing a sink and mirror with another shaving swabby produced many nicks from the old Gillette double-edged razor blade.

Extra care was taken shaving this morning, Aug. 16, 1943, because it was the Intrepid's commissioning day, the day the Navy officially

Commissioning Day, August 16, 1943: After the acceptance ceremony, officers and their guests gathered at a reception on the hangar deck. (Note:
The uniform of the day for ladies – hats and gloves.)

accepted the Intrepid from the Newport News Ship Building Company.
The Intrepid's full crew of officers and enlisted men, lined up on the flight deck in precise rows, white uniforms sparkling. The ship's band played Sousa's spirited, patriotic music. Captain Sprague accepted the ship in a tradition-rich ceremony, including an invocation by one of the Intrepid's chaplins, Lt. Cmdr. Eric Ahrendt. This ritual was formal, dignified and triumphant and, at the same time, jubilant.

We soon found shipboard amenities, including the barbershop and its four clipper-wielding barbers. Haircuts were free, but you usually tipped a quarter. Laundry was collected and returned the same day and your name had better be stenciled on everything if you expected to get it back. Shoemakers fixed worn shoes; dentists fixed aching teeth; doctors, surgeons and corpsmen fixed sick and broken bodies. A Catholic and Protestant chaplin conducted daily religious services and counseled troubled sailors. Their office, in the ship's library, was next to our sleeping compartment.

The library was stocked with regular books and the then–new Pocket Books, whose pages opened horizontally rather than in the current vertical paperback format. (Aptly named, a pocket book it was… a snug fit in your dungaree hip pocket.)

In ship's stores you could purchase skivvies, etc., with money from your clothing allowance of $12 a quarter, $48 a year.

The "gedunk" stand was the place to go for goodies like ice cream, Hershey Bars, Milky Ways and those five-cent packs of cigarettes. At this price, just about everyone smoked, and most had a Zippo lighter, too.

After-shave lotion, another big seller, was filtered for its alcohol through a loaf of bread by really desperate sailors. (There were also a couple of unauthorized stills operating aboard ship.)

Adventurous alkys would swipe some "torpedo juice" (100% grain alcohol), mix it with canned grapefruit juice pilfered from the ship's storeroom, and party. Occasionally they would be found the next morning passed out on the storeroom deck.

Warnings were issued about the danger of drinking aviation antifreeze: it would either blind or kill you.

My buddies and I smuggled whiskey aboard by tucking a bottle in our sock, which was covered by a bell-bottomed trouser. It usually worked, except when some hard-nosed Marine guard at the shipyard gate took delight in tapping your ankle with his club. (Bell-bottoms were originally made for swabbys to pull up over their thighs while swabbing the decks.)

The precious cache of smuggled whiskey was stowed in a pea-coat locker in our living compartment, to be withdrawn on special occasions – a birthday, anniversary or arrival of a newborn baby, for example. Surprisingly, not one bottle was ever swiped from our secret supply. Our special, secluded place to celebrate was an unused cat-walk, aft, just under the flight deck. This is where we gathered at night to share a few sips for those special occasions. It was our oasis, with a brilliant star-filled sky above and a glowing phosphorescent wake 90 feet below. Usually, four or five of us would gather there, and after a few sips and affable conversation, we would sit staring at the wake with thoughts of home and loved ones.

Red Jones and C.J. King-our two best, or luckiest, at poker.

The after-con in the island structure was an emergency station, used to control and steer the ship if the captain's bridge got blown away. Just inside was a small compartment with backup radar for emergency use We turned it into the radarmen's poker parlor. Stakes were usually nickels and dimes, with an occasional two-bits limit. C.J. King and Red Jones, a couple of good old boys from Georgia, spent most of their off-duty time playing poker there. Pinochle was also popular, but it was played for boasting rights and relaxation, not money. If a hand was interrupted by the call to general quarters, cards were slipped into shirt pockets; when general quarters secured, the game resumed.

Intrepid's crew numbered about 3,300 men, including the attached air group's pilots and crewmen. The number of planes: about 100, with 16 Torpedo planes – TBM or TBF's; 24 dive bombers–first, SBD's and later, SB2C's; 60 fighters – F6F's and F4U's. Fuel to power ship: over 65,000 gallons per day. Aviation gas: about 35,000 gallons per day. Daily freshwater consumption was nearly 85,000 gallons; some was used to brew the 300 pounds of coffee in the galley and throughout the ship in Silex pots, (we had a 4-burner Silex in C.I.C.) When spuds were served, it took one ton per meal.

October 2,1943, the Intrepid's crew, lined up by division on the flight deck for inspection by Admiral Durgin. Four days later, the Intrepid departed on its shakedown cruise through the Windward Passage to Trinidad.

Reporting On Board Ship

The first time our division lined up together on the flight deck, we were near the island structure, below the captain's bridge. V3 Division was comprised of radarmen (V3R), photographers (V3P), aerographers (V3A). The senior V3 division officer was Lt. Cmdr. F.T. Thompson, the aerological officer, or weatherman.

He was the most nonmilitary-looking officer I had ever seen; from his sunken chest and shifty eyes to his rat's-tail, scrubby little moustache. Visually, repulsive. Vocally, offensive. His opening speech burned into my memory.

"I'm Lt. Cmdr. Thompson, your division officer. My wife just gave birth to a baby today, over at the N.O.B. Hospital. I'm not going to see her because it is not my regular liberty day. I'll wait until tomorrow; so don't any of you ever ask me for a special favor."

Smitty whispered, "Boy, Stoney, we've got us a real shit here."

Just then, one of the radarmen, Henry, who was always coughing, started violently hacking away, spitting up blood all over his shirt.

Thompson lashed into him, accusing Henry of being a goldbrick, faking illness. "Stop that coughing. You're not going to get away with this. You are not sick, and you can't fool me."

Henry must have either fooled the ship's doctors or died. We never saw him on board ship again.

After securing from muster, our radar officers seemed as stunned and disgusted by Thompson's tirade as we were. They shook hands all around, and extended friendly welcomes, seemingly to assure us that this martinet would have nothing to do with radar or us.

Which was true for most, but not for me. Thompson later proved to be what Smitty aptly observed, "a real shit," lying to me at an important and crucial time in my life, when my father was dying.

Years later, I couldn't believe it when I learned that Thompson was an Annapolis graduate, class of 1936.

One day, while assembled at quarters in Portsmouth, the ship was about to get under way and Captain Sprague called down to Thompson from the bridge: "Commander, go aft and report on the tugboat's position."

After looking, Thompson returned and reported to the captain: "It's on the back end, sir."

Astonished, the captain roared: "Where? The back end? Come now, commander, is the tug at Mr. or Mrs. Stern? MacGregor, you go aft and report."

MacGregor's report was delivered with a snappy salute: "Captain, the tug is secured, aft on the port quarter, sir."

Fortunately, and in total contrast to this sad-sack aerographer, in radar we had the good fortune of having Fighter Direction Officer, Lt. (soon to be Lt. Cmdr.) MacGregor Kilpatric as our superior officer. He was new to intercepting Jap Zeros via radar and directing fighter planes to intercept and shoot them down.

On his previous tour of duty while on board the U.S.S. Enterprise, MacGregor was a distinguished fighter pilot, a member of the famed "Grim Reapers Squadron" that destroyed many Jap planes.

Captain Sprague persuaded him to accept this key nonflying assignment on the Intrepid to help make the ship battle-ready. He was assured, soon after his promotion to Lietenant Commander, that he would be back flying, in command of his own fighter squadron.

Lt. Cmdr. MacGregor Kilpatric

The following brief account is from a story by Joel Shepard, whose father served with Kilpatrick on the Enterprise. This action took place exactly one year before Intrepid's first taste of battle.

"During operations off Rennell Island, Jan. 29, 1943, the Enterprise directed six Wildcats, commanded by Lt. MacGregor Kilpatrick, to intercept 11 unidentified aircraft approaching Task Force 16. The fighters split into two groups: Kilpatrick and Lt. j.g. Robert Porter on the left flank, the other four on the right. With a 4,000-foot altitude advantage, Kilpatrick and Porter dove on the bombers, splashing two.

They attacked again. Kilpatrick's guns downed a third plane, while Porter's target was hit and fell out of formation trailing smoke." The Grim Reapers were harvesting Japs.

Reporting On Board Ship

Cmdr. Richard Gaines, our executive officer, and MacGregor had served together on the U.S.S. Enterprise, a most gallant aircraft carrier, one of five carriers that were fortunately on maneuvers when the Japs attacked Pearl Harbor. The Hornet, Lexington, Yorktown, Wasp and Enterprise were crucial in first stemming, then turning, the tides of war in early battles.

The Enterprise, heralded as the carrier that fought the most through the end of the war, participated in all but two of the 20 major actions in the Pacific. Her planes and ship's guns destroyed 911 Jap planes, sank 71 ships and damaged or destroyed 192 more. The ship escaped major, disabling damage until May 16, 1945, when a kamikaze blew a huge hole in the Enterprise's flight deck.

Sea Trials & Qualifying Pilots

The expanse of Chesapeake Bay was used to train the ship's crew and our Air Group Eight's fighter, dive bomber and torpedo plane pilots in launchings and landings. As the ship headed into the wind, cruising at some 20-plus knots, pilots manned their planes. Chocks were removed from the wheels by airdales in Orange T-shirts, the pilot revved the engine to high-pitched R.P.M.s, the flight-deck officer flashed his checkered signal flag in a sweeping flourish and the plane roared forward.

Watching the first plane as it finally lifted off, dipping slightly after its wheels left the flight-deck before soaring skyward, was one heck of a thrill. All of us cheered, as we did even louder later when the first plane landed successfully, tail hook catching on an arresting cable and bringing the plane to an abrupt stop, preventing it from crashing into the raised barriers.

It was the first of many thousands of launchings and landings from the Intrepid's deck. When not on watch in C.I.C., I often watched flight operations from the vantage of the after-con. Occasionally, you got more of a thrill than you wanted when a plane came in too fast, too high or wobbly, crashing into the barriers or careening over the side. Regrettably, accidents happened, especially with new and inexperienced pilots or later when planes returned from raids against the enemy, damaged from a dogfight or antiaircraft hits.

Air Group Eight's pilots and radio-gunner crewmen, were a good group. They worked hard at honing their flight skills, and they were generous in compliments to the Intrepid's crew.

This power-packed airborne armada, of nearly 100 planes, was ready to deliver... ready, willing and eager to start kicking Jap ass from one end of the Pacific to the other.

Feeling the gentle vibrations of the ship's steel decks through the soles of your shoes was exhilarating. Tasting salt air while thinking how this huge, powerful ship was cruising along effortlessly at 24 knots or more, blew your mind. (About .29 M.P.H.)

The crew was improv- **The little red drone was an evasive target.**
ing in daily practice drills, correcting or eliminating kinks and bugs, cutting minutes and shaving seconds from the time it took to launch and land planes and man battle stations.

The ship's guns fired away at a plane-towed target sleeve or at a nasty, evasive little red drone plane that was virtually unhittable.

Damage-control crews worked at developing their skills to extinguish fires and plug bomb or torpedo holes. Each day was conducted as a full dress rehearsal for the opening performance under battle conditions.

Competition between divisions was healthy. Everyone in the crew shared pride when our planes were launched or catapulted seconds quicker or when gunners accidentally, or purposely, shot off the tow sleeve cable during gunnery practice.

Goofs and foul-ups were now less frequent. The crew members forged by determined spirit and shared pride were evolving into true shipmates, each feeling that the Intrepid, this beautiful ship, was *my ship*.

One day, while heading into the wind to ride out a Chesapeake Bay nor'easter, I picked up an unknown target on the air-search radar, heading right for the ship at about 75 knots. Lt. Kilpatrick reported to the bridge over the squawk box: "Bridge from C.I.C.: We have an unidentified flying object bearing down on the ship at about 75 knots. Over."

"C.I.C. from Bridge: Nothing flying in this weather. What do you think it is? Over."

"Bridge from C.I.C.: Have no idea. Maybe a flock of geese. Over."

"C.I.C. from Bridge: Did you say geese?"

As his voice trailed off in disbelief, we heard the loud honking of a flock of geese in the background.

I never knew if the goose incident enhanced or diminished radar's reputation on the ship.

With radar so new, some old-line naval officers still preferred and trusted handheld optical range finders over radar. At radar school, they told us about one stubborn old captain who refused to accept the accuracy of radar reports and thereby ran his ship aground.

The laws and regulations that govern the U.S. Navy or "Rocks and Shoals," is required reading to all crews and includes the 11th commandment of the sea: *Thou shall not cause thy ship to run upon rocks and shoals.*

Casey, Intrepid's chief boatswain's mate, was a one-man cohesive force who helped shape up the green crew. A robust, short Irishman with an equally short temper, Casey was all over the ship, ordering, directing, threatening and cajoling the uninitiated. He was good at his job, but didn't have gold (good conduct) hash marks on his sleeve. His hash marks were red, because of his inability to drink without fighting. One drink put a lilt of tenderness in his eyes; two or more ignited his short fuse.

In Portsmouth one day, we watched Casey as he went ashore on liberty. The closest bar was a short walk away, just outside the shipyard's gate. Seeing him leave, we formed a pool, each putting in a buck. The winner: whoever guessed the number of minutes before Casey was returned to the ship in the custody of S.P.'s.

Eighteen minutes later a Shore Patrol wagon screeched to a halt and two huge S.P.'s escorted a flush-faced, profanity-spouting, disheveled Casey up the gangway, turning him over to the officer of the deck. The O.D. had Casey removed to his cabin for a sleep-it-off, and the winner, Polack, was now seven bucks richer.

The bar Casey had enlivened was opposite a raunchy dance hall that we called the Gonorrhea Race Track, which, because of the number of nightly fights, should have been called Madison Square Garden South.

While in port, large ships supplied crew members to supplement the regular Shore Patrol. My fellow radarman and good pal, Leaky Evans, drew S.P. duty at the Gonorrhea Race Track. His account of the night at the "track" follows:

"The regular S.P.'s were huge ex-policemen. They told us, that when a fight started for us (135-pound me) to rush right in. Get in the middle and break it up. Real easy.

Later in the night, when everyone got loaded, fights were starting everywhere. I was scared stiff, not trying to stop them but trying to stay away from them.

A fight would break out on one side; I would head for the other side. I'd run right into another and have to change course again.

Enos "Leaky" Evans-1943

I could imagine one of those 250-pound marines throwing my 135-pound ass through the plate-glass window."

Leaky didn't want to get tossed through a window, but if it was my ass about to be tossed, Leaky wouldn't hold back. He'd jump right in without hesitation, kill or get killed, trying to save me, as I would for him. This was an unspoken given: you knew you could totally depend upon your buddies in any situation on ship or ashore.

One of our liberties in the Norfolk/Portsmouth area was a so-called Cinderella liberty: the crew had to be back on board ship by midnight, ready to shove off at dawn.

Fifteen minutes before 12, quite a few of the Intrepid's crew were lined up at the bar in the sleazy clip joint just outside the shipyard gate, having a last drink before boarding ship.

A sailor started yelling, shaking his fist at the bartender. "Hey, this dirty bastard just stole my money from the bar. This rotten bartender bastard stole my money!"

Response was instant. About 30 of us gripped the bar top-rail and, with a mighty heave, tore the bar loose and dumped it over.

It felt good to have delivered a small kick in the ass to these parasites who cheated sailors. Feeling somewhat virtuous and vindicated, we added a bit of a swagger to our step as we staggered back to the ship.

A break in Chesapeake Bay training exercises came with a two-day trip to Annapolis, Md., home of the U.S. Naval Academy. The Navy first opened the academy 98 years earlier with 40 midshipmen in the first class.

Prior to that time, during the 1812 war at sea, the famous U.S.S. Constitution, *Old Ironsides*, was outfitting for battle at Annapolis with a crew of mostly green hands who had signed on for two years at a monthly salary of $12. (In 1943, we green hands were paid $50 a month.)

My WWII enlistment in the U.S. Navy Reserve was for the duration of the war, plus six months. A regular hitch in the U.S. Navy then was four years.

The Intrepid's Captain, Thomas Sprague and 17 of the 170 ship's company officers graduated from the Naval Academy.

> ANNAPOLIS, MD.
> SEPT. 19 & 20, 1943
> AND BACK TO N.O.B.
>
> SHAKEDOWN CRUISE
> OCT 7, 1943
> REACHED TRINIDAD - Oct. 12
> PRACTISE OPERATIONS -
> IN GULF OF PARIA
> LIBERTY IN PORT AU SPAIN
> BACK TO STATES -
> NOV. 1, 1943 (PORTSMOUTH N.H.)
> VIRGINIA
>
> 3 DAY 17 HR. LEAVE
> Nov 1 TO Nov 5, 1943

Intrepid's Assistant Flight Deck Operations Officer, Lt. Charley Devens, was a former major league baseball pitcher who played with Babe Ruth on the 1932-34 New York Yankees. It was good to have Devens on our team because that's what it was all about – teamwork. Devins threw nothing but strikes as he helped direct Intrepid's rapid plane launchings.

One-by-one, each plane's wings were lowered and locked in place by the airedales, the flight-deck crew of plane handlers who manuvered the planes into position.

After taxiing to the take-off spot, the pilot revved his engine to a high pitch and gave a thumbs up signal. The Fight Officers flag was lowered in a swift, flowing, downward motion, sending the plane roaring down the flight deck, gaining speed and becoming airborne a few yards from the end of the flight deck. You held your breath as some planes dipped down, almost hitting the water before soaring skyward.

Practicing launches and landings, whenever weather permitted, paid off when the stakes were high. Especially when precise, quick fighter plane launchings were necessary to intercept incoming Jap attacks. Then, and until decommissioning in 1974, the Intrepid was always best, or nearly best, at launching planes. During the Vietnam operations, the

Sea trials

Intrepid earned the "Best Carrier" award for its skill.

Planes were "spotted" on the flight deck by type: fighter, dive-bomber and torpedo plane, according to the scheduled take-offs in the plan of the day. One day, as I watched, one of our F-6F's crashed immediately after takeoff. The pilot was barely able to escape, inflating his Mae West life-saver vest while standing on a half-submerged wing, as his plane slowly sank. An anticipating destroyer raced up, plucking the pilot from the sea in less than two minutes.

The plane captain, a second class petty officer responsible for all the pre-flight checks on this F-6F fighter, had missed the fuel capacity check. The gas tank was all but empty. He was demoted to apprentice seaman and spent the remainder of his time on the Intrepid in the mess hall, diving for pearls – washing dishes.

Shakedown Cruise

The ship returned to Norfolk from Annapolis and on Oct. 7, embarked on its shakedown cruise to Trinidad. More drills, more intensive training for the crew and air group, both enroute and in the Gulf of Paria, when we arrived in Trinidad.

The gulf was dotted with a group of tiny islands that looked like rock outcroppings, just barely sticking their peaks above the water. Some had attractive beach houses on them. When anchored, the ship was close enough for us to see what looked like wonderful, nightly cocktail parties; and when the wind was favorable, you caught the lively sound of the Calypso music. A favorite Stateside Calypso song at this time was, "Rum and Coca-Cola:"

"If you ev er go to Trin i dad
They make you feel so ver y glad
Ca lyp so sing and make up ryme
Guar an tee you one good real fine time
Drink in' Rum and Co ca Co la"

A TBF, torpedo bomber making a soft-landing on Intrepid's flight deck

Fortunately, my watch section was granted a liberty in Port au Spain, Trinidad, to attend a special recreation party. This was our first foreign liberty port and we were ready and full of high hopes for a typical Hollywood-movie-type, tropical island liberty.

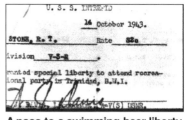

A pass to a swimming-beer liberty.

The plan of the day called for the liberty party to assemble on the hangar deck, board small craft and reassemble at the air station for a talk by the chaplin, Lt Cmdr. Eric Arendt. He advised us first, about the availability of cheap rum and how it would ignite our prurient desires to pursue native women, further warning us that venereal disease was rampant on the island.

"I implore you, before you take a second rum-drink, put on a rubber."

This advice, coming from a man of the cloth, was quite startling, especially to those of us who had our very first rubber stashed in our wallet. We all had seen the scary, official Navy, Mickey Mouse syphilis and gonorrhea films. We also had gleaned rubber wisdom from a few old salts: pull a rubber over your wallet to waterproof the contents if you ever have to abandon ship.

While ashore, we could tour the local Angostura Bitters plant and the city, and be back to the designated place at 1500 hours to proceed to Scotland Bay for a swimming and beer party.

Skipping the cultural trip to Angostura, my group started meandering around town. For starters, each of us purchased a bottle of Red Cock Rum, with a large crowing rooster on the label, for 79 cents. A few sips of rum, without Coca Cola, went a long way and stimulated those prurient thoughts the chaplin had mentioned.

Whenever we headed down an unauthorized street, a Jeep full of S.P.s intercepted and redirected us. With time to kill, we decided to shop for souvenirs to avoid the throng of pursuing street beggars and their persistent chanting, "Penny for bread, penny for bread." Hearing native shopkeepers speak with crisp Noel Coward British accents was delightful relief from the beggars' insistent supplications..

Arriving back at the meeting place for departure to our combo swimming-beer party, we found the sidewalk littered with a long row of passed-out sailors. The trucks arrived to shuttle us to Scotland Bay and

Mc Elroy, Stoney, Griffith, Hudson and Brother Hughes, with a native boy who was paid five cents to pose with us in Port au Spain, Trinidad.

we stacked bodies in the trucks cordwood style and left. The bodies were unloaded, placed in the shade under palm trees and the beer, hamburger, hot dog, swimming party got underway. As the beer party progressed, the number of under-the-palm-tree bodies increased.

Our return to the ship was a noisy melee of singing, cursing, puking drunks. Cargo nets were lowered, bodies stacked, and those who could stand rode up on the outside of the nets to resounding cheers and hoots. The scene was pure slapstick comedy and provided marvelous entertainment for the onlooking sober sailors.

The unconscious bodies were unloaded on the hangar deck and hauled away on stretchers to sick bay. This was the only liberty party from the Intrepid that was permitted while the ship was in Trinidad and it was a real doozy.

On the serious side, the shakedown cruise, with all its emergency drills, gunnery and flight exercises, brought the ship and its crew closer to being in sync. Kinks were being eliminated and the practice was paying off. Routine duties were starting to be carried out with care and by rote. We were a better crew. The ship was a better ship.

More Sea Trials

When the ship returned to Portsmouth, we received a three-day leave, so I headed home to Cedarhurst with my good pal Leaky Evans.

When we got to the house, Leaky knocked on the door while I hid in the bushes. "Hello, Mrs. Stone, is Red home?"

"Oh, no, he's on his ship somewhere. Won't you come in?"

I jumped from the bushes scaring the hell out of Mom. "Here I am Mom, and this is my good pal, Leaky."

Later, when Mom recovered, she took me aside: "Ray, I can't call him Leaky. Doesn't he have another name?" I didn't know, I had to ask. He told me it was Enos, which Mom was able to handle.

We hit the local hangout, Bob Wright's, for dinner and a few drinks. Leaky, with his Southern gentleman drawl and pleasant style, charmed the local beauties, ending up kissing them all before we faded and headed home.

The next morning, Mom loaded us down with goodies, and we were on our way to the ship, back in Ole Virginny.

Early on Thanksgiving Day, the Intrepid got under way from Portsmouth, heading north for Booth Bay, Maine, to engage in 4 days of turn and speed-trial drills.

NOV. 25, 1943 (THANKSGIVING DAY)
LEFT PORTSMOUTH, VA.
FOR MAINE —— THANKSGIVING
DAY MEAL ON THE ATLANTIC
OFF COAST OF VA. ——
ARRIVED AT BOOTH BAY, MAINE —
NOV. 26 — PRACTISE TURNS AND
SPEED IN BOOTH BAY—(NO LIBERTY)
NOV. 29 LEFT FOR NORFOLK
NOV 30 ARRIVED AT N. O. B.
DEC. 1, 43 - LEFT N.O.B
DEC. 8 - DOCKED AT COLON —
ATLANTIC SIDE OF PANAMA
CANAL ——LIBERTY IN COLON
WENT THROUGH CANAL
DEC. 9 —RAN AGROUND IN

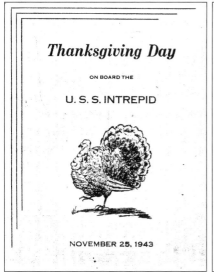

Thanksgiving Day

ON BOARD THE

U. S. S. INTREPID

NOVEMBER 25, 1943

MENU

Fruit Cocktail

Consomme — Saltines

Roast Chicken

Whipped Potatoes — Sage Dressing

Giblet Gravy

Buttered Asparagus — Celery Hearts

Mixed Sweet Pickles

Cherry Pie — Mixed Olives

Hot Parker House Rolls

Mixed Fruit — Fresh Milk

Bread — Butter

Coffee

Cigars — Cigarettes

Cover and menu for Intrepid's first Thanksgiving dinner in 1943.

The following Thanksgiving prayer was on the menu's back page: "This day we render thanks, O God, for the many blessings and gifts received. To us, Thou hast entrusted a great and mighty nation in which we enjoy the inalienable rights of life, liberty and the pursuit of happiness. Grant us, O loving Father, the daily strength of body and soul to preserve these rights, to overcome our enemies and to honor thee ever in justice and charity. Amen."

Dinner was served while the ship was off the Virginia coast. It was a carbon copy of the one served at home: turkey and all the trimmings, from those candied sweet potatoes – through mince and pumpkin pie. The big difference was that we didn't hold hands and say grace; we just dug in and ate. But I was thankful to be with my new family of mostly a great bunch of guys. Like other families, it had a couple of certifiable pain-in-the-ass members, too.

One that surfaced early was Wilkins, radar's leading petty officer, a title handed him simply because he was older than most. A former assistant manager of a cafeteria in Cleveland, he loved to lord it over the less-educated Southern mountain boys.

We didn't have foxholes, as Army soldiers did, but I would rather be in a foxhole with any one else than him.

Wilkins, a pompous, balding porker, liked to put down people, especially the defenseless. He didn't like me and I didn't like him, but he never messed with me. He knew that if he gave me an excuse, he was going to have to fight. Still, I intervened to keep him from being killed, on two separate nonaction occasions. Each time, it was a different mountain boy (first Dingy and then Compton) who threatened him. I got involved because I knew they would be court-martialed and executed if they killed him.

Our second leading radar petty officer was Polack, affectionately called, *Ve-leepe-dup-ya pu-pulski*, (Our phonetic Polish for *big assed Polack*). George Vogrin was totally different from Wilkins. He worked in a machine-shop in Youngstown, Ohio, before enlisting. He didn't have a pompous bone in his big-assed body, treating one and all evenly and fairly. He was my good buddy; then, it was not unusual to hang what may now be considered derogatory nicknames on your shipmates. Even though some may sound like ethnic slurs, they were regarded more as affectionate, pet monikers for someone you liked. Polack, Daigo, Shanty Mick, Jew and Kraut blended in with Pee-Wee, Dingy, Doc, Mother, Pappy and Big Daddy.

Big Daddy was certainly complimentary; he probably had the longest penis in the Navy, some 10 to 12 inches down to his knees, when hanging at ease.

Cavalieri's label was the Boot, even though he was a battle-tested old salt compared to us. The Boot and Zimmy were blown off the aircraft carrier Lexington when it was sunk in the Battle of the Coral Sea.

Some Southern boys didn't have regular first names. My buddy C.J. King was always asked: What's your first name?

Fifty years later: Polack Vogrin approached me on board ship at the Intrepid's 50th birthday reunion.

"Scuse me sir, can you tell me where I can find Red Stone?"

One look and I knew it was Polack.

"You dumb, Ve-leepe-dup-ya-pu-pulski. It's me, Polack. My red hair turned grey."

Laughing he said:"Stoney, I gotta tell you something. I'm really not a Polack; I'm a Croatian."

"A Croatian? Why in hell didn't you tell us?"

"Polack was easier. No one knew where Croatia was, back then."

He'd reply, "C. J."

"Your name, not your initials."

"I told you, it's C.J. That's all there is."

I was either Red or Stoney and to this day I have no idea what the full or actual names were of some of my good buddies. I had to dig to find Mother Stefanich's first name. He was Mother to us because he was like a hen with her chicks, always concerned, caring and advising us on rights and wrongs and proper behavior. Still, everyone loved our self-appointed shipboard mom from Kankakee, Illinois.

John (Mother)Stefanich

Officers usually addressed us by last name, and we them, either by rank and name, or simply, sir.

S hortly before leaving the Norfolk area for good, a ship's dance was planned and held at a large downtown auditorium.

On the day of the dance, radarmen were scheduled for another eye examination by an optometrist at the Norfolk Naval base. We must have been part of a test group for Navy research, to determine if staring at a radar scope in a darkened room had any negative effect on our vision or psyche. Visits to an optometrist and a psychiatrist were frequent.

Drops were put in our eyes to dilate the pupils, which made everything look real fuzzy. Whatever they used this day was more powerful than usual. After the examination, I ran shouting: "Hold that bus. Wait for us. Hold that bus!"

The bus we were running for turned out to be not a bus, but a red brick house that wasn't going anywhere. After getting back to the ship, we donned our dress blues and eventually arrived late at the dance.

S urprise, there were still a few unclaimed females standing around. I latched onto one and my buddy Mack, her girlfriend. I could see my date was blond, but everything else was blurry. She had a soft voice and turned out to be a good dancer. At midnight when we parted I still couldn't really see her face. Back on the ship, Mack was bragging, telling everyone about his beauty.

Two days later, when I showed up for a date, my vision was back to 20/20. My cute blonde was twice my age and had a son half as old as me. I was trying to figure out how the hell I was going to get out of this predicament when she, while looking out the window, said: "Oh, here comes my husband."

"Your what? Husband! I don't mess with married ladies. Where's the back door."

"It's O.K. We're separated, getting a divorce. Don't go."

By then I was in full motion, passing through the kitchen and out the back door running like the wind.

Back on ship, while taking some abusive teasing about my cute blonde, especially from Mack, I noticed the tip of a snapshot sticking out of his jumper pocket. Trying to shift focus from me, I said: "My date may have been older, but she wasn't a two-ton Tessie."

Vehement denials, mixed with counter-accusations, were bantered about until I snared the picture from his pocket, holding it high for all to see. "Well, lookie here. She's more than twice as much woman as mine. You were tripping the light fantastic with a baby hippo."

Everyone had a good laugh then, and retold enhanced and belabored ship's dance stories, whenever eye exams were scheduled.

U.S. Navy Aircraft-Recognition Silhouettes

The Intrepids lookouts and gunners studied and memorized these silhouettes of our planes to make sure they had positive identification. Recognition of friendlies was aided by the addition of a symbol or design. One of our squadrons used a big white slash on the perpendicular tail wing.

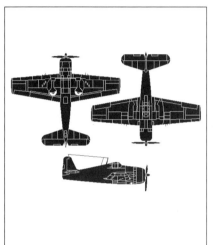

F6F HELLCAT
Our first fighter that surpassed the Jap Zero's agility in combat.

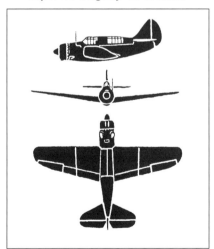

SB2C HELLDIVER
A two-man crew, pilot and radio-gunner flew this dive bomber

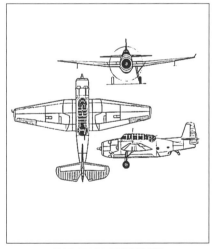

F4U CORSAIR
A mean looking, gull-winged fighter that was truly mean (my favorite).

TBF/TBM AVENGER
A three-man crew, pilot., radioman and gunner flew this torpedo plane

U.S.S. INTREPID, CV 11, 1943 The U.S.S. Intrepid, third of the then-new Essex Class carriers was built by Newport News Shipbuilding in Newport News, Va. at a cost of $44 million. The keel was laid Dec. 1, 1941, six days before the Japanese attack on Pearl Harbor.

It is the fourth United States Navy ship named Intrepid. The first was the Tripolian ketch Mastico, was captured during the War of 181 and renamed Intrepid. Built in 1874, the second Intrepid, a brig-rigge iron-hulled vessel, was 170 feet long. It displaced 438 tons. The third Intrepid was built in 1904, a bark-rigged steel-hulled vessel, 176 feet long, weighing 1,800 tons.

The fourth Intrepid was put into commission on Aug. 16, 1943, w Admiral John H. Hoover's wife as sponsor.

- 1943: Original displacement–36,000 tons (fully loaded)
- Length–898 feet
- Height–waterline to top of mast–131 feet
- Hull Beam–103 feet
- Flight Deck Beam–152 feet
- Max Draft–31 feet

Power Plant:
- 8 Steam boilers, 4 steam turbines
- 4 Propellers–each 15 feet in diameter
- Maximum speed–30+knots (approximately 36 M.P.H.)
- Ship's crew–about 3,000, with 300 additional pilots and
  air crewmen in the Air Group assigned to the ship.

INTREPID'S V3 DIVISION ENLISTED MEN– on the flight deck, with a po
of the ship's battle scorecard above. 72 Radarmen, 12 photographers, stil

In 1943, RADAR was a new, high-tech weapon of war. On board s
Combat Information Center, (C.I.C.) was the control center for planes w
launched from the flight deck, until they landed back on board.

In C.I.C., radarmen manned the air and sea search radars and were res
sible for detecting and plotting "bogies"– enemy planes. Fighter Direc
Officers vectored the fighter planes in our Combat Air Patrol, (C.A.P.) to i
cept and destroy them. Another function of C.I.C. was to aid our ship in n
taining station at a specific bearing and distance from other ships. The Intr
and two or three other Carriers were in the center, flanked by a couple of
tleships, cruisers and an outer circle of destroyers.

movie cameramen, and 6 aerologist, weathermen.The V-3 division also had about one dozen officers who are not shown in the picture.

PHOTOGRAPHERS served on board ship and were airborne on special reconnaissance missions.They were a good bunch, brave and valiant as they documented the Intrepid in action, under attack and burning after kamikaze hits.

The photo division also processed footage from our planes' wing cameras for evaluation and intelligence about enemy activity, providing visual proof of pilots' kills, their "shoot downs" and enemy ship hits or sinkings.

AEROLOGISTS were our ship's weathermen, providing valuable information to our squadrons for daily flight operations.They obtained their data about wind velocity and direction by tracking huge balloons launched aloft.

Pacific Bound

The first leg of our voyage to the Pacific Ocean began when we left Norfolk on Dec. 3, 1943, bound for the Panama Canal and arriving at Colon five days later. Luckily, my watch section was scheduled for liberty and I went ashore. Four of us chipped in, hired a horse drawn-carriage and went on tour with our driver proudly pointing out the sights.

"U.S. government, hospital."

"U.S. government, school."

"U.S government, this. U.S government, that."

He ended the tour dropping us off in the red-light district, as did all taxi drivers, no matter where you wanted to go. As we walked the streets looking for a bar, a bevy of ugly, pathetic-looking whores grabbed at our crotches. "Two bucks, two bucks." They were ugly enough to motivate one to a pledge of celibacy.

Stopping in a small bar, we ordered rum and coke all around. Enter two huge, six-foot-plus M.P.'s in what appeared to be tailor-made uniforms, knee-high riding boots, wide leather belts, pistol holsters and long whips that hung down to their heels. With a sweep of their clubs, the drinks that were lined up on the bar were smashed. One of the M.P.'s said: "This joints a filthy whore's hole. Unless you want to catch something, get out."

Get out we did, thanking them. As we later found, Panama M.P.s protected servicemen from civilians, rather than vica versa. Also, that's why we were advised to travel in small groups, never alone. Lone sailors invited mugging, and at least one was stabbed and robbed every night.

Our next stop was right out of a Grade B Hollywood movie: a smoke-filled dive with a loud band and a sweaty trumpet player blaring away.

Our tails hadn't hit the chairs when four girls joined us. They were young, friendly, sort of attractive in their cheap long gowns and wanted to join us for a drink. Why not? A rum and coke was cheap, from two bits to 40 cents, according to the ambiance of the joint. Without being told, the waiter brought them each a Blue Moon, served in a shot glass, and they tossed it down in one quick motion.

"Four bucks," the waiter said, sticking out his greasy paw.

One of us anted up the money. By this time the girls were sitting on our laps, squirming and chatting merrily. When my squirmer asked if she could have another Blue Moon, I said, "Sure."

What else do you say to a girl squirming on your lap?

I intercepted the shot glass as the waiter was handing it to her. I wanted to taste this expensive elixir.

"Damn, it's tea!" I shouted.

Caught, and in tears, she told me about Blue-Moon girls, they were good girls, not whores. Each, it seemed, had a younger sister in need of either an operation, schooling or salvation. These Blue-Moon girls were even younger than us, just kids, hustling to make a living from their 25-cents-a-drink commission. They earned it by putting up with a lot of grabbing and fondling.

The Intrepid passing through a cut in the Panama Canal.

The next morning, the ship got under way, entering the first lock, which was then flooded, raising this huge ship up to the level of the next lock. Being off duty allowed me to observe all this from the after-con, which afforded a great view of everything.

It was a tight fit, looking to me like less than a foot clearance between the hull and the side of the lock. Occasionally the ship scraped and groaned as it passed through.

A scaffolding had been erected on the flight deck, perpendicular to the bridge, to enable the canal pilot to guide the ship through the bends and turns in Culebra Pass from amidships. He must have been paying more attention to Chaplain Hurley's running narration over the ship's P.A. system: "If you look carefully, you may see crocodiles on either shore."

Shortly thereafter, all hell broke loose.* The canal pilot's miscommand for a full right rudder (instead of full left) was executed, and the ship headed for the right bank. Crewmen assembled forward, rapidly scrambled aft as I watched, frozen in total disbelief.

Orders were shouted.

"Two thirds speed astern! Drop the port anchor!"

Somehow, the starboard anchor was dropped instead of the port anchor, making a bad situation worse.

Even though the ship was proceeding slowly, there was no stopping 36,000 tons of Intrepid as it plowed into the rocky shore, ripping a hole in the bow. Later, with watertight hatches secured and order restored, the ship proceeded on to Balboa on the Pacific side of the canal.

*(This is how I remember the running-aground occurence; there were a few different versions about the cause. However, when a Navy board of inquiry reviewed the incident, it eventually exonerated everyone.)

CULEBRA PASS, DAMAGE
DONE TO BOW -
DEC. 9. DOCKED NEAR BALBOA.
LIBERTY IN PANAMA CITY-
ONE LIBERTY WITH STAN
CROCKER (LANGLEY)
LEFT FOR SAN FRANCISCO
ON DEC. 14 ———
ARRIVED - DEC. 22
DRY DOCK AT HUNTERS POINT
DEC. 23 — CHRISTMAS
EVE. AND DAY ASHORE
IN SAN FRANCISCO ——
NEW YEARS EVE AND DAY
SPENT ABOARD ——
MET RED ROCHE AND

During the five-day stay in Balboa, the bow was patched and we had a couple of days liberty in Panama City, which rated a couple of notches below Colon. You had to be careful as you walked filthy, cesspool-smelling streets to keep from being soaked by a chamber pot being emptied from a balcony above.

Panama City also had a large red-light district with, if possible, even uglier whores than Colon's beauties.

We found a cheap bar, next to the Troc, a nightclub that featured a beautiful, well-built singer who was billed as "Queen of the Tropics." The trick was to drink a couple of 25-cent rum and cokes in the adjacent bar and move next door, have one 40-cent drink in the nightclub while you caught the floor show; then return to the sleeze bar and drink cheaply until the next floor show.

One night, feeling generous, we decided to have a Blue Moon girl join us for only one drink. I was chosen to make the selection and picked the most pathetic, most underselected-looking girl. Her name was Alicia, from Lima, Peru. She had the standard younger sister whom she wanted to rescue from poverty and as we talked, my buddies were all hands, all over her. Curious, I asked: "Alicia, you don't seem to mind the errr...hands. How come?"

Her reply, which I never forgot: "Oh! Ramon, the sailors, they took all the tickles out of me."

We laughed, and feeling guilty, popped for one more Blue Moon for Alicia.

Heading back to the ship, we got lost and asked a Panamanian cop for directions. He apparently didn't speak English and began to act excited. I tried my high-school Spanish and must have not rolled my r's sufficiently, which infuriated him to the point of pulling his pistol, shouting, waving wildly and threatening us with his gun.

Two M.P.s in a Jeep came to our rescue, and just in time. Someone was about to get hurt, most probably one of us. The M.P.s calmed the cop down and sent him on his way.

They also calmed us down and sent us on our way back to the ship, since we were still madder than hell that this little bastard was going to shoot us. Panamanian cops had a bad rep when dealing with sailors; we were advised, "They'd just as soon shoot you as not."

The toll from the Intrepid's passage through the canal was more than a battered bow. An unusually high percentage of the crew left Panama infected with gonorrhea and syphilis. When we got to beautiful San Francisco, they would be denied liberty. Fortunately for them, the new wonder drug, penicillin, was available to treat and help cure their venereal diseases.

The daily routine, as we headed for San Francisco, was more launchings, landings and gunnery practice. One drill was particularly startling. Our own torpedo planes launched dummy torpedoes at the ship. Duds or not, you had a queasy feeling watching a torpedo wake close in on the ship, hit it, and then bounce harmlessly off the hull.

Our dive bombers also made practice runs on a wooden sea sled towed by a destroyer. Watching them go into a sharp-angled dive and pull up after releasing the bomb was thrilling. They even scored a few hits, along with many near misses, on this relatively small, 10-foot-by-10-foot target.

I had the luxury of watching some drills from the flag bridge with Admiral Davis, who was on the Intrepid, travelling as a passenger to San Francisco.

The admiral's flag bridge cabin had a backup radar set, and a couple of us drew standby duty there. The admiral, one of the Navy's earliest pilots, was very democratic and interesting, sharing his coffee and spinning yarns about piloting early bi-wing carrier planes. His tales painted him as a real seat-of-the-pants pilot.

Early-skilled pilots were qualified to fly fighter, scout and dive bombers. They flew from the decks of the Lady Lex and Sister Sara, the Lexington and Saratoga, two of the Navy's first big aircraft carriers. All radarmen wanted to be assigned to what was basically keeping this wonderful passenger, Admiral Davis, company. I wondered why the admiral hadn't at least been assigned one the ship's marines to act as an orderly.

Eventually, I could almost, but not quite, be semi-relaxed while almost one-on-one with this splendid Admiral.

As the ship was passing Mexico's lower Baja Peninsula, the admiral described pristine hunting and fishing trips he had been on to lower Baja, when it was a wild and wooly place, frequented by celebrities like Jack Dempsey. All I could think was, my God, here's this admiral talking to me, an enlisted man, like I was an officer in the ward room.

During those eight days of drills, etc., on the way to Frisco, as we called it, much to the dismay of the city's natives, I read Jack London's book on the city's wild Barbary Coast days. His splendid narrative was stimulating, conjuring vivid images of forty-niner nightlife in this untamed, robust city.

Views of beautiful, raven-haired, bare-breasted saloon waitresses in velvet vests danced in my head. Anticipation peaked when the pilot boat was sighted off the Farallon Islands. A huge yacht, under full sail, appeared out of the pea-soup fog, lowered a dinghy and transported the bay pilot over to the Intrepid.

He boarded, made his way up to the bridge and helped guide the ship under the beautiful Golden Gate Bridge, past Alcatraz, to a berth at Alameda Naval Air Station, where Air Group 8's planes were unloaded by the ship's cranes.

That evening, the silhouette of San Francisco, across the bay, was backlighted by a beautiful sunset.

San Francisco

The morning of Dec. 23, 1943, the ship sailed five miles across the bay to the Hunters Point Shipyard for dry docking and proper repairs to the bow. It amazed me how easily the ship was maneuvered into place, and when the water was pumped out, the keel came to rest precisely on a row of huge, pre-positioned concrete blocks. 36,000 tons of steel balanced like a prima ballerina on her toe.

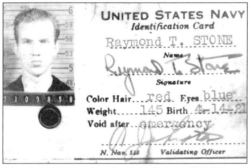

UNITED STATES NAVY
Identification Card

Raymond T. STONE
Name

Signature

Color Hair....red. Eyes.blue
Weight......145 Birth .4-14-21
Void after...emergency

N. Nav. 548   *Validating Officer*

My photo-I.D. card with altered year of birth.

While preparing for San Francisco's legal drinking age of 21, I was busy altering I.D. cards so my underage buddies and I would be served in Frisco bars. My actual date of birth, 4-14-25 was typed on photo print paper, covered in thick cellophane, with open sides, secured by a grommet just below the portrait. By lifting the cellophane carefully, I was able to erase the last numeral, 5, and change it to look like a typed-in number 1. Those, formerly under the drinking age were reborn, all in 1921. Even little Pee Wee Wildes was two years beyond legal drinking age, at twenty-three.

Now for that first, most eagerly anticipated, Frisco liberty. Somehow, we were in luck finding a couple of rooms in a not-so-hot hotel, one at the other end of the spectrum from the famous Fairmont or Mark Hopkins hotels. But getting a hotel room in any class hotel in San Francisco was lucky, since it was almost impossible.

Our group decided to split up into duos, figuring it would be easier to pick up two girls than four, six or eight. The strategy worked for me. I met an attractive gal who knew the town. We started with a cable car ride out to Fisherman's Wharf and later came back to a Market Street nightclub called the Bohemian Gardens.

It wasn't exactly a Barbary Coast-type gin mill, but it was lively, noisy and packed with sailors and marines plus a few Army guys. The floor show was awful: in one act, the doorman doubled as a snake charmer, with a stuffed cloth snake and gilded spittoon, while wearing pantaloons and a turban. His performance was riddled with jeers and he was finally hooted off the stage.

A short woman, built like a Siamese fireplug and with a large sheriff's badge pinned over her left boob, was the official I.D. age-checker and bouncer.

A staggering, protesting soldier was being ushered out by Sheriff Shorty when he made the mistake of resisting, pushing her away. She hit him with a short right, or two, dropping him to his knees. Then, assisted by the snake dancer-doorman, the groggy G.I. was propelled through the door onto the pavement.

It was about midnight when Frisco bars closed, so we headed for bacon and eggs at a nearby cafeteria. En route, we ran into my buddy Doc, who joined us. As we were finishing our late-night snack, a huge sailor, with two buddies flanking him, stopped at our booth and for no reason whatsoever smashed Doc's face with a vicious punch.

It was a stunning bolt from nowhere. It took a few seconds to recover and realize what had just happened. Doc looked dazed. I jumped up telling him, "Don't worry, Doc, I'll get that dirty bastard."

Doc said, "No, Stoney, he's mine, all mine!"

Chasing after, we caught up to the bastard and his two buddies just outside the restaurant door. Once again, Doc emphatically stated, "That bum, he's mine!"

I grabbed the other two sailors, knotting their kerchiefs together with one hand and shoving them up against a plate-glass storefront window with the other. They were neutralized, and my right fist was cocked and at the ready: "First one of you bastards moves, he goes through the window."

Doc was doing O.K. against this giant, boxing, landing solid blows and ducking wild roundhouses. One he ducked caught an onlooker

Jack (Doc) Swartz, pre-fight photo.

in the crowd, who looked like the youngest baby-faced sailor in the entire Navy, full in his face. He spurted blood and teeth.

Following this, Doc slipped, going down on one knee. The giant kneed him, full in the face, sending him sprawling flat on his tail.

I released my grip on the kerchiefs and ran over to help Doc, whose right eye was now shut closed. His left didn't look much better, just a narrow slit. Blood was flowing freely from cuts above his eye and from his nose and mouth.

"Doc, Doc, are you all right? Can you see?"

"I can see enough. He's still mine. Where'd he go?"

The baby-faced, blood-spouting sailor pointed, yelling: "That way. There he goes. Let's get him!"

As we worked our way in pursuit, through the huge crowd that had gathered to watch the fight, I repeated my plea: "C'mon Doc, you've had enough. Let me take him on."

"No way Stoney, he's still mine. One more shot. Just one more."

Baby-face yelled again, "There he is, over there, on the other side of the street."

As we waited for the traffic light to change and to cross over, I pleaded with Doc again, but his pulverized lips kept repeating, "Mine, mine, one more time, Stoney, one more."

Crossing, we caught up with the trio, one sailor supporting on each side of the giant, who was saying: "I guess I showed you guys how tough I am. Right?"

"Yeah, Moose, you sure did, you..."

At that instant, Doc tapped Moose on the shoulder while bringing one up from the pavement that landed square on the button of Moose's jaw. Moose went down like a fallen tree.

As his buddies were bending over, imploring him to get up, I banged their heads together as hard as I could. The three lay in a heap on the sidewalk. Doc stood silently over them – no words of triumph, no bravado, just standing. I grabbed Doc saying, "Let's haul ass and get the hell out of here while we can." S.P. whistles were blowing, coming closer, as we slipped into the crowd and hastened down the nearest side street.

Back at the hotel, ice packs were applied to Doc's face, which looked as if he'd been battered in a Pier 6 brawl–which he had. During the fight, he lost not only a couple of teeth but his I.D. card too, which meant no more liberty for him in Frisco during this stay.

Me, I just lost my first Frisco date.

The liberty turned out to be a semi-Barbary Coast-type night, rough but without a tumble with one of the beautiful, raven-haired, bare-breasted waitresses that I had read about.

In the morning we found other shipmates also had rooms on the same floor and by the way they were acting, chasing chambermaids all around, you would have thought they just returned from years at sea. Above the clamor, I heard someone yelling: "Intrepid. Hey! Help! Intrepid, help!"

Bounding toward the call for help, down a wide stairway, I found a lone U.S. sailor slugging it out with four British sailors. Jumping onto them from above, I caught two Brits pretty squarely, knocking them over, down the stairs. Six more Intrepids responded to the call for help, and it was a rout with the Brits in full retreat.

It was not uncommon for U.S. and British sailors to battle one another, usually over women or after copious alcohol consumption. Sailors and Marines also had their fair share of fisticuffs for the same macho reasons, as well as for upholding service pride.

For most of us, it was the first time we were ever away from home at Christmas. You could feel homesickness in the air. Some talked about it; some didn't.

I had spotted a Christmas tree, complete with lights, outside an office in the shipyard. I mentioned it to our division officer, Lt. MacGregor Kilpatric, saying: "The office workers won't miss this tree over the weekend. We could borrow it for a while, maybe a week or so. A Christmas tree sure would look great here in C.I.C."

His reply: "Sounds good to me. Do you have a plan?"

"Yes, sir, I do."

"What do you need?"

"One man to help me get it over a fence. That's all, sir."

"Stoney, let's go get it!"

Operation Tree went smoothly, and the large vertical plot board in C.I.C. was decorated with festive green grease-pencil drawings of holly surrounding a large, bright red, "Merry Christmas Intrepid," filling the center of the plot board.

The holiday spirit kicked in, and MacGregor invited Captain Sprague to C.I.C. Someone started singing a Christmas carol and pretty soon all of us, including the Captain, joined in. His presence helped cheer us up.

Our Captain was admired and respected by all the officers and enlisted men in his crew. On a capital ship of the line, like ours, the social gap between officers and enlisted men was wide, traditional and accepted. Officers lived in small cabins, forward in the ship's forecastle area. Meals, in their wardroom, were served on china plates by black steward's mates.

During WWII, blacks had little opportunity to serve in other Navy jobs. During G.Q. some of the Intrepid's steward's mates manned a 20-millimeter gun tub. In action off the Philippines in 1944, 10 were killed, while strapped in to their guns when a kamikaze hit the Intrepid, spewing flaming gasoline on the men in gun tub #10.

One who survived the attack, Alonzo Swann, was finally awarded the Navy Cross for his bravery and valor by President Reagan some 50 years later.

The gun captain of gun tub #10, Alfonso Chavarrias, a Hispanic who was killed in the same kamikaze attack, was awarded the Navy Cross for his valor and bravery posthumously by President George W. Bush in a presentation to Chavarrias' sister, in the Oval Office on July 2002.

Midnight Requisition: An unwritten, non-existing document which entitles the bearer to borrow anything permanently, (a license to steal Navy property but not personal belongings). You could leave a wallet on your bunk, while in the shower, and no one would touch it.

The Intrepid's shipboard cranes however, hooked onto everything they could reach, including Jeeps and a captain's gig, which was quickly repainted, renumbered and stashed aloft in the hangar bay.

An organ pilfered from the officer's club in Panama by Air Group 8's pilots was returned after S.P.s arrived with orders from the base commander. Later, another organ was given to the ship as a gift. A talented pilot from Torpedo Squadron 8 always played the organ during happy hours. His rousing rendition of "The Hawaiian War Chant," soon became the ship's fight song.

Christmas Eve dinner was ashore with Smitty and Botts at a French restaurant where you ladled soup from a large tureen in the center of the table. This was a new experience for us, as much soup as you wanted, and we savored it and returned frequently. After roaming up and down a couple of San Francisco hills, we went to Market and Third to catch a ride back to the ship. Transportation was provided by a stream of old Packard limos with pull-down jump seats in the rear and, at 25 cents a head, they crammed in as many sailors as possible. The usual haul was ten or twelve at a time, with all laps occupied. I don't know how they managed, but one night the count went up to 16 sailors

Back on board ship, the altar and folding chairs were set up port side, forward in the hangar bay, for Christmas Day Catholic and Protestant religious services. The chaplains found a few spruce trees to form a backdrop behind the altar.

Father, The Rev. Timothy Herlihy, a lieutenant, was in good voice Christmas morning, singing the High Mass in Latin as I followed in English with my missal. All masses were said in Latin then, and during the war Catholics had a special dispensation from fasting and abstinence.

"All Catholics of the armed forces of the United States are dispensed by the Holy See from the law of fast and abstinence on all days of the year except the vigil of Christmas, Ash Wednesday, Good Friday and Holy Saturday until noon."

After mass, Christmas greetings were exchanged, and I drifted off by myself for a smoke and a stroll on the flight deck with a mind filled with back-home thoughts of family and friends.

The Intrepid's band serenaded us with traditional Christmas music as we gathered in the chow line on the hangar deck, waiting for the mess hall to start serving.

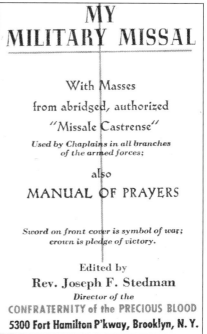

MY
MILITARY MISSAL

With Masses
from abridged, authorized
"Missale Castrense"

Used by Chaplains in all branches of the armed forces;

also

MANUAL OF PRAYERS

Sword on front cover is symbol of war; crown is pledge of victory.

Edited by
Rev. Joseph F. Stedman
Director of the
CONFRATERNITY of the PRECIOUS BLOOD
5300 Fort Hamilton P'kway, Brooklyn, N. Y.

First page of my Prayer Book.

San Francisco

After the usual Christmas Day meal, from soup to nuts, I was back in our compartment shooting the breeze with Polack, preparing to go ashore, when I heard someone say: "Who'd you say you're looking for, Stoney? He's back there."

What a surprise! The visitor was Jim Roche, my boyhood pal from home. I hadn't seen Jim since we got together in boot camp.

Jim was attending the Radio Material School at Treasure Island and had drawn S.P. duty the previous day when he noticed some of Intrepid's crewmen were on the arrest list of those pulled in. (This list was a reliable roster of ships in port, usually with at least one or two crewmen from every ship on it).

That Jim found me in my compartment was surprising; that he was allowed to board the ship was remarkable. Jim was not scheduled for liberty; therefore, his I.D. card was being withheld. He needed one to get off the base and on liberty. The I.D. he borrowed bore the picture of a very dark black sailor. Even a blind man could see this wasn't Jim's lily-white face.

Jim first presented the bogus I.D. to the officer of the deck at the forward, officers-only gangplank. Then, after being sent aft to the enlisted men's gangplank, Jim showed it to the O.D. and was granted "Permission to come aboard." So much for our tight, wartime, in-port ship's security. After a brief tour of the ship, we went up to C.I.C. where I proudly showed Jim how we operated.

His visit was like a special Christmas present from home and it was the first of a few liberties we shared in Frisco.

Jim had relatives in the area and we decided to visit his uncle, who tended bar at Solari's, an excellent San Francisco restaurant located off the beaten track in Maiden Lane. I wasn't hungry, but managed to down a few Old Grand Dad bourbons on the rocks as we, the only sailors in the place, sipped, smoked and chatted with civilians. This was a nice change of pace; with friendly San Franciscans, you could relax and not have to worry about arguments and fights.

Solari's became one of my favorite watering holes in Frisco, not just because drinks were usually on the house, via Jim's uncle, but because you rarely saw more than a few servicemen there. There was something refreshing about escaping from the usual sea of sailors that surrounded you everywhere you went.

90

It was easy to fall in love with San Francisco, which I did, returning many times after V.J. Day. The city was like a stylish, well-turned-out woman who seduced you and your mind. The only knock I remember about Frisco during WWII was that the movie houses were loaded with fleas. On nights when you could, and didn't feel like going back to the ship, a 25-cent seat in an all-night itch house was a cheap option.

Pepsi Cola operated a dormitory where you could get a clean bunk for four-bits. But you had to check in early to get one and if you did, you slept with your wallet tucked safely in your skivvies. Sound-sleeping, over- indulged sailors often awoke to find the pillow case had been slit with a razor and their wallet liberated.

My last liberty before we sailed from Frisco was followed by an early-morning appointment with a Navy dentist in the Hunters Point Shipyard. On the previous visit, when he told me all four of my wisdom teeth were to come out in one session, I asked, "Are you a drinking man, sir?

"I most certainly am."

"It's my last liberty. Would you mind if I happen to have a few in me when I arrive in the morning?"

He had no problem with my imbibing; so I smuggled a pint past the guards at the gate, and we each had a good belt before he loaded me up with Novocain.

This dentist had strong wrists and hands, good for the task of extracting my four wisdom teeth. I don't remember feeling much pain then, but I do remember that for a couple of days after, I couldn't open my mouth wide enough for anything but thin soup.

That afternoon, the Intrepid crossed the bay once more, to Alameda, and loaded Air Group 8's planes back on board.

Pearl Harbor

WENT ON LIBERTY TOGETHER.
JAN. 5, 1944 LEFT
DRY DOCK - DOCKED AT
ALAMETA AIR BASE.
JAN. 10, 1944 ——— ARRIVED
AT PEARL HARBOUR
JAN. 12, — LEFT PEARL HARBOUR
FOR TARGET PRACTISE —
JAN. 14 — BACK IN PEARL HARBOUR
JAN. 16 — LEFT PEARL HARBOOR
IN TASK FORCE FOR RAID
ON MARSHALL ISLANDS ——
JAN. 22 — CROSSED THE
EQUATOR AND INTERNATIONAL
DATE LINE SIMANTANIOUSLY —
TIME-APROX- 5:45 A.M.

On Jan. 6, 1944, the Intrepid left San Francisco, arriving at Pearl Harbor four days later. Diamond Head loomed large to starboard as the ship made its way to Ford Island in Pearl Harbor. The ship glided slowly past some remaining shoreline debris, but most of the wreckage and destruction had been cleared.

Tugs helped guide the Intrepid to a dockside berth, one occupied by the Tennessee during the infamous attack. The submerged hulk of the Arizona lay visible with an uppermost portion of the bridge tower poking above the surface to complete the eerie, grotesque image. Seeing this once-mighty battleship in its watery grave was sickening.

At Pearl Harbor's U.S.S. Arizona Memorial, the names of those 1,177 gallant men who died on the ship now cover an entire marble wall in the shrine room. A simple tribute proclaims:

TO THE MEMORY OF THE GALLANT MEN

HERE ENTOMBED AND THEIR SHIPMATES

WHO GAVE THEIR LIVES IN ACTION ON

DECEMBER 7, 1941 ON THE U.S.S. ARIZONA

Those of us looking down on the Arizona from the edge of the flight deck stood wrapped in solemn silence, thinking about the brave men who lost their lives defending their ship. The magnitude of these reflective moments was amplified at sunset by the lonely notes of a bugler sounding taps as the ship's flag was slowly lowered on a dockside mast.

Amidst those thoughts of the 1,177 Arizona's crewmen killed that Sunday morning, I felt a surge of anger and resolve to avenge, to get even, to kick ass!

On liberty the next day, we headed for Honolulu's world-famous Waikiki Beach. It was beautiful, an impressive sight, but I got my chest laid open by some coral while riding the waves. My lily-white Irish skin was not meant for sun bathing, so I repaired to a shady bar and applied an indirect medical alcohol treatment to my scrapes.

Everywhere you went in Honolulu there were the ever-long lines of sailors waiting – for a bus, bar, restaurant or whorehouse.

Whorehouses were government controlled, operating on the basis of the number three. Three bucks for three minutes.

One buck for the government, one for the house and one for the wench who operated from one of three cubicles. One for getting ready, one for doing it and one for having done it. Judging from the length of the serpentine lines meandering throughout downtown Honolulu, the three partners were doing O.K., operating their assembly line at peak wartime efficiency.

Air Group No. 8 was replaced by Air Group 6's planes and pilots, lead by Cmdr. H.L. Miller, and we left Pearl for a

Jack (Doc) Swartz and Leon (Smitty) Smith, Waikiki Beach, January 1944.

day of gunnery practice and qualifying launchings and landings. Upon our return to Ford Island, we stocked up on provisions and fuel prior to sailing to join the fleet and Admiral Marc Mitscher's Fast Carrier Task Group 58.2.

Target: The Marshall Islands

Captain Thomas L. Sprague

Now, as part of the most mobile and powerful naval armada ever assembled, the Intrepid headed for its first action. Target: the Marshall Islands, Japan's important central Pacific base.

Underway, on Jan. 16, 1944, Captain Sprague addressed his crew: "Now hear this: To all hands of the Intrepid, this is the captain speaking. The greatest force of carriers, battleships, cruisers and destroyers ever assembled in the world, and the greatest number of auxiliary vessels ever assembled in the Pacific, will strike Japanese bases in the Marshall Islands, commencing January 29. The Intrepid is proud to be in a task group of this force, which includes the carriers Essex and Cabot, the battleships North Carolina, South Dakota and Alabama, the antiaircraft cruiser San Diego and 10 destroyers. Many other powerful task groups will also participate in the total operations and will be in the area.

"The Marshall Islands, together with the Mariana Islands and the Caroline Islands, were given to Japan under the League of Nations mandate of 1920. It was provided that an annual report be made to the League and that the islands be kept unfortified. No League observers, however, were allowed in the mandated islands, and very few white men went there, and so they gradually became known as the Islands of Mystery. We know all too well that the nonfortification rule was not observed.

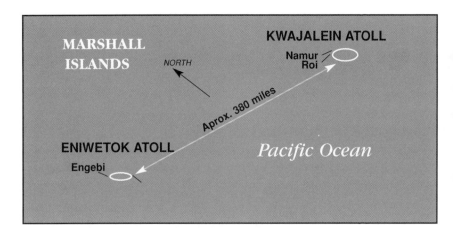

"The Marshalls are a group of coral atolls and are located at the easternmost end of the mandated island lying about 2,500 miles southeast of Japan and 2,100 miles from Pearl Harbor. These islands form the eastern anchor of the outer screen of bases protecting the Japanese Empire. Although most of the islands are only a few miles in any dimension and have little commercial importance, they are of primary importance both to Japan and the United States as stepping stones. Capture of the Marshalls will remove the stony barrier to the Japanese base of Truk, which lies 1,000 miles to the west. Until we have captured the Marshall Islands, the United States task forces will not be free from air attacks in the move to the western Pacific.

"The Marshalls differ from the Gilberts to the south, only recently captured by our naval and marine forces, in that the Gilberts were only taken by the Japanese from the British in 1942, after war was declared. The Japanese having had over 20 years longer to strengthen the Marshalls, it is accordingly felt that they may prove a tougher nut to crack. This undoubtedly accounts for the tremendous force we are throwing against them at this time. This will be the first time we are making a large-scale attack at the pre-Pearl Harbor Japanese Empire. Landing operations are scheduled, in which our ship will play an important role in air support for the invading marines

"There are six island land-plane bases in the Marshalls, in addition to numerous seaplane facilities. There is an important sub base in the southern portion of the islands. There are excellent fleet anchorages in the many lagoons, protected by the islands and coral reefs of the various atolls. Charts will be posted for all hands to inspect.

"Our targets will be Kwajalein Atoll, the world's largest atoll, being 66 miles in a northwest-southeast direction, and which has a maximum width of 18 miles. More than 80 islands and inlets lie along the reef, which surrounds a lagoon with an area of 655 square miles, providing more anchorage than any other atoll in the Marshall group. Kwajalien Atoll is the most important Japanese military and naval base in the Marshall Islands. Roi is the target for the Intrepid planes."

Enroute to the Marshalls on Jan. 22, at 0545 hours, the Intrepid crossed the Equator and the international date line simultaneously. Shellback and Golden Dragon initiation ceremonies were delayed until a future date.

A key to the mobility of the fast-carrier task force was the "sea train" of oilers and cargo ships that refueled ships every four or five days. Ships were coupled with lines and oil hoses while they continued cruising, on course, at about 10 knots. The people who orchestrated this highly mobile supply chain should have received Navy Crosses. The oilers also delivered equally valuable commodities – mail and new movies, precious moral builders for home-starved sailors. There was a rush of letter-writing when the crew knew refueling was scheduled, with all of us trying to get those promised letters homebound. Most didn't make it in time, that day, since all letters were censored by assigned officers, and some looked like Swiss cheese after sensitive information was cut out. An officer was heard to comment: "I can't believe it. (Censored) Wrote the exact same letter to five different girls. And I had to cut each by more than half."

Movies were frequently swapped, mostly with destroyers that would come alongside, shoot a monkey's-fist line over, make the swap and go back on station. On occasion, one of our planes would even land on another carrier just to pick up and bring back hot reels for the night's showing on the hangar deck.

I wondered what tomorrow would bring when we engaged in our first action as part of Adm. Marc Mitchner's mighty Task Force 58 with air strikes in support of the invasion of the Marshall Islands.

I was also thinking about tomorrow for another reason. It was also my father's birthday. I thought about him and his experiences in

Target: The Marshall Islands

WWI. Dad was a cook on the S.S. Mongolia, a merchant ship on the Atlantic Run, where German U-Boats prowled, sinking many of the cargo- laden vessels bound for England.

T he Mongolia was among the first "Q" ships to sail for England from New York. It had a U.S. Navy gun crew that manned a three-inch cannon, covered with fake cargo crates, on the fantail.

To save torpedoes, German U-boats usually surfaced when they found unprotected merchant ships, ordered the crew to abandon ship, and sank them with shells fired from their deck gun cannon.

When a U-boat surfaced and ordered the Mongolia's crew to the lifeboats, the gun crew whipped off the camouflage from its cannon and fired off a couple of quick rounds before the startled Germans knew what was happening. It was probably the first "Q" ship kill in WWI.

The Mongolia proceeded on to Liverpool, England, docked and started unloading cargo. That night, they were part of another first – the first bombing of an English city in WWI. German dirigibles dropped hand-launched bombs on the ships in the harbor. The Mongolia wasn't hit, but later Dad, in an interview in The New York World, described the German air raid as "the most horrible thing I have ever experienced."

Upon returning to New York, Dad experienced one more adventure: he was slugged, mugged and robbed of his pay by a couple of thugs.

Planes being catapulted for an early morning strike against enemy targets.

U.S.S. INTREPID (CV11)
PLAN OF THE DAY Saturday 29 January 1944.

The preparations are over, and we are now steaming at high speed for our launching point tomorrow morning. To the best of our knowledge, the presence of our force is still undetected by the enemy. We arrive at a point some 150 miles to the west of Roi in time for the ESSEX to launch the first strike of the day – 20 Fighters and 6 Torpedo planes – at 0545. We hope to destroy any aircraft on the field at that time.

At 0600 the INTREPID launches its first strike–21 dive bombers and 8 Fighters. At 0715 we send off 12 Torpedo planes, each loaded with a 2,000-pound message. These will be dropped on runways to render them unserviceable for any Jap planes. At 1115 10 VF, 2 SBD and 2 VF will take pictures which will be of great assistance to the eventual operation. At 1200 the torpedo pilots go again, this time with four 500-pound bombs apiece. At 1345 the dive bombers carry 27 1000-pound bombs to their targets.

All of the above strikes will be escorted by our fighters, in addition to which F6F's will maintain a continuous combat air patrol over the tar gets at Roi and Namur. There will also be a continuous anti-submarine patrol from dawn until dark and fighter protection of this force.

At the same time we are plastering Roi and Namur, one of our Sister Task groups will be doing the same thing to Kwajalein Island, 44 miles away at the south tip of Kwajalein Atoll. The other Jap air bases in the Marshalls will be getting the same treatment simultaneously from other Carrier groups and our land based planes in the Gilberts. We aim to knock out the Jap air strength in the Marshalls completely tomorrow and the next day.

On the third day, the Marines land on our end of Kwajalein Atoll and the Army on the South End. Our flyers will be called on all that day and the next to bomb and strafe in supporting their landings. The battleships in our Task Group, the South Dakota, Alabama, and North Carolina, bombard on the second day. Other battleships are also arriving to bombard on the third and fourth day. Kwajalein and its Japs will get a good going over.

We have an exciting schedule to meet–one which is timed to the minute with those of the ESSEX and CABOT. This is the chance we've been waiting for. LET'S GO INTREPID!

R. K, Gaines
Commander, U.S. N.

"Operation Flintlock"

The night before the Marshall Islands operation began, we picked up blips on the SG surface radar: four ships about 26 miles distant, proceeding on course away from Kwajalien. A destroyer was dispatched, investigated and sank all four Jap merchant ships. I was on a watch break and not operating radar, so I popped outside and back to the after-con trying to see flames from the ships. No luck. Couldn't see anything except the Southern Hemisphere's brilliant canopy of stars and thought: "Well, this is it. Drills are over. Tomorrow we'll be tested, our ship, pilots and crew. May God be with us."

An hour before dawn, the ship was at general quarters. Three thousand men choreographed into action: pilots to ready rooms or in their planes, airedales (plane handlers) to their stations on the hanger and flight decks, gunners to the five-inch, 40 millimeter and 20 millimeter cannons. Below decks: damage-control parties to assigned stations, cooks to the mess hall to make battle-ration sandwiches, doctors and medical corpsmen at the ready, musicians standing by with damage-control parties or stretchers. Each man had a job to do and each depended upon the other to perform at his peak. At stake: the life of the ship and its crew.

The Intrepid's flight deck was lively with activity as plane directors maneuvered aircraft into position for takeoff.

Different colors–different duties: The men in blue T-shirts were plane handlers who helped move and unfold a plane's wings. Those in purple placed or removed the wheel chocks, green designated arresting-gear handlers. Red, was for ordinance personnel, arming with bullets and bombs; also fire fighters. Yellow shirts helped maneuver planes.

The Combat Information Center (C.I.C.), had responsibility for planes, from the moment the wheels lifted off the flight deck, until they landed back on ship. Its duties also included detecting bogies on radar, plotting them to determine course and speed and vectoring our fighter planes to intercept and destroy them.

If one of our planes was hit or had engine trouble or couldn't make it back to the ship, our fighter direction officers directed the pilot to the closest submarine or destroyer stationed on rescue duty. If the pilot had to ditch in the ocean before he got there, we transferred the latest plot, where the plane disappeared from the radar screen, onto a D.R.T. (dead reckoning track) chart, which showed both the ship's and the downed plane's position when we lost contact.

This information was relayed to the submarines, search planes and destroyers deployed on rescue duty. Many of the pilots, forced to ditch in the sea, were rescued and eventually returned to their ships.

AIR GROUP 6
JAN. 29, 1944 — First raid made on Roi - Continuous bombing by our planes until FEB. 3rd when the islands were completely captured by land forces. Also four Jap merchant ships sank by a destroyer.
FEB. 4th I anchored in the lagoon at Manjuro atoll - (Fueling)
FEB 12th - Left Manjuro atoll for a raid on Truck.

A pilot rides in a breeches chair as he is transferred back to the Intrepid from the destroyer that rescued him after he crashed into the sea.

Special-delivery love notes on bombs were sent to Tojo and his cohorts.

Bombs were covered with chalked messages from the Intrepid's crew. It was a way of delivering personal expressions of hatred and loathing to the unseen enemy.

"Take this Tojo!"

"This gift is for Hirohito or Tojo – from the boys from Flatbush!"

"Hope Hirohito gets a big bang out of this one!"

The fleet was poised, about to deliver its lethal one-two-punch. Battleships and cruisers moved in to bombard Roi and Kwajalein with devastating salvos. .

Six of the older battleships, that had been either sunk or severely damaged in the sneak attack on Pearl, were back in action for the first time. Refurbished and full of fury, the California, Maryland, Nevada, Oklahoma, Pennsylvania and West Virginia unleashed salvo after salvo from their 14-inch guns on Jap fortifications. It was the long-awaited payback time for these mighty ships and their crews

"Operation Flintlock," the code name for the Marshall Islands campaign, was under way. Our task group first concentrated most of its devastating firepower on the causeway-connected islands of Roi and Namur, home of Kwajalein's main air base, to soften them up for the Fourth Marine Division's landing on Jan. 31. First strikes by our planes caught the Japs by surprise and destroyed most of their planes while they were still on the ground.

L ed by Gen. Holland Smith, the Marines advanced quickly on Roi but met stiffer resistance on Namur. The Japs launched a counterattack on both islands that first night, but were repelled. There were also landings by troops from the Army's 27th Infantry Regiment on lightly defended Manjuro, which was easily captured.

Carrier operations, bombing and strafing continued against targets on Roi and Namur, and on Feb. 1 Gen. Corlett's 7th Infantry Division troops landed on Kwajalean itself and had control of one-third of the island by nightfall.

The next day, occupation of Roi and Namur was completed and Adm. Ginder's TG 58.4 carrier planes attacked Eniwetok in support of landings there.

The few Jap planes able to get airborne were picked up by radar, tracked and, after heading for our ships, were either turned away or splashed by Combat Air Patrol fighter planes.

The Intrepid's crew was called to battle stations several times during each day, usually only for short periods. However, General Quarters didn't interfere with the scheduled launchings or landings, which went off smoothly. And any of our crew's initial prebattle fears were being replaced by confidence, which was enhanced by personal action reports from returning pilots..

Pilot ready rooms were portside, opposite C.I.C., and some pilots spent their down time observing operations in C.I.C. They particularly liked watching while an interception was in progress, being recorded with x marks on the plot board until the pilot's voice blared an excited "Tally Ho!"–followed by a jubilant "Splash! One bogey."

Some shared their air-combat experiences with our fighter-direction officers. It was interesting to listen in on these firsthand accounts, especially as a fighter pilot told how he splashed two or three Zeros during dog-fights in one air battle.

By Feb. 4 (my diary says Feb. 3, but the date, as the mis-spellings throughout my diary, is in error), all organized Japanese resistance on

Operation Flintlock

Kwajalein Atoll was over. Almost all of the 8,700 defenders were killed, with only 265 captured, mostly Korean laborers or Jap wounded. Of the 41,000 Americans involved in the landings, 370 were killed and 1,500 wounded.

Mopping up pockets of resistance on these islands continued as major bombing and bombardment assaults were made against Eniwetok and Engebi by carrier planes.

On Feb. 4, we entered and anchored in Majuro's vast lagoon. Here we were, in the midst of this former prized enemy anchorage. The view, at sunset, of carriers, battlewagons, cruisers, destroyers, destroyer escorts and supply ships was awesome. One helluva armada, hundreds upon hundreds of the Navy's finest fighting and support ships stretching as far as you could see

The only thing about liberty on an atoll was that it was on land, if you call coral land. Each man was issued two cans of beer, or Coke, and you were ferried over in an L.C.P. (Landing Craft Personnel) and put ashore with your, by then, warm beer. There were no palm trees; they were leveled in bombardments. No huts, no natives, nothing. Your two cans of beer were quickly recycled as perspiration and there was nothing to do. I saw a sailor scrounging around in the corral and asked him what he was doing.

"Gathering monkey fist shells."

"Why?" I asked.

"To make a bracelet for my girlfriend." He then explained how easy it was to stuff the cavity with cotton and glue as you ran thread through to connect the shells. That sounded great, and soon a dozen sailors were hunting these small monkey-fist shells.

With no shade, you soon marched fully clothed into the water, after tucking your wallet and cigarettes into your hat, and sat there submerged up to your chin. It was a ludicrous sight, hundreds of heads with white hats barely above the surface.

An announcement would be made from a dockside bullhorn, "Now hear this, hear this. The liberty party from the battleship New Jersey, assemble on the dock. Your boat is here."

A hundred wet sailors emerge, board a landing craft and head for their ship. In the few minutes it took, they would be bone -dry by the time they arrived.

Ships were refueled, this time by tankers tied up alongside. Stores were replenished from cargo ships; and for the first and only time, I was put in charge of a work party of radarmen assigned to unload food from a merchant cargo ship. As we were waiting for a L.C.T. to shuttle us to the cargo ship, I noticed that Compton looked green around the gills.

"Hey, Compton, you feeling O.K.? You look like shit."

"Not as well as I should. Got a fever, Stoney."

After touching his forehead I told him: "Go down to sick bay. Get some aspirin, or whatever. Get a medical pass and hit the sack."

A couple hours later, we returned with a load of canned food and there stood Compton with a hangdog look on his face.

"You still look like sad sack; why aren't you in your bunk?"

"I did like you told me, Stoney, and after sick bay, I lay down in my sack. When Wilkins saw me, he lashed into me, ordered me up, calling me, a dumb, goldbricking, hillbilly son-of-a-bitch"

I told Compton that Wilkins outranked me, but I'd go find Ensign Smith and settle this.

"Don't bother, Stoney. It will only make things worse for us. He's always on our case, lording it over us. Just no way does he like us ridge-runners and mountain boys."

Wilkins treated Southern mountain boys like dirt, with no respect; and early on, word spread through their grapevine that Wilkins was an antagonist. Word that I was a friend of country boys must have spread, too. There were nights when I'd be stretched out in my sack before lights out, and three or four good ol' boys, one with a guitar, would appear and without a word of explanation proceed to serenade me with country and folk music.

From them, I learned about "Nancy Brown," "The Judge Talkin' Blues," "Freight Train Blues" (Lordy, Lordy, Lordy, got 'em in the bottom of my ram-bil-lin sho-ho-ho-hoes) and other wonderful folk songs.

I liked these guys; they were straightforward, truthful and compassionate. You knew where you stood, and you knew you could count on them when things got rough. They may have had a bit less schooling, but they had more common sense than most and also had a most colorful manner of expressing themselves.

"Never get in a pissing contest with a skunk."

"That old whore, she was a soup bowl with arms."

"I'm as happy as a hog wallowing in slop."

A couple of weeks after Wilkins' derisive treatment of Compton, I was heading for C.I.C. when I came upon Compton and Wilkins in the passageway. Compton was shouting and had Wilkins pinned against the bulkhead, with the tip of his six-inch sheath knife under his chin. I shouted: "Hey, Compton. What in the hell are you doing?"

"I'm going to kill him, Stoney. Tired of his crap."

"Hold on. Put down that knife. Let's think this out."

I was stalling for time, wondering what to do. Wilkins was sweating like a pig and Compton's knife remained at his throat as he raged on. I don't remember what I said but I got Compton's attention when I started talking about his after-the-war dream of raising the biggest, goldarnedest vegetables ever, up thar in Alaska.

He started to lower his knife and stopped, saying, "I'm in big trouble, even if I don' kill him."

"No way, I'm the only witness and Wilkins is scared shitless. He won't say anything. He'll suffer a loss of memory, like me. Won't you, Wilkins?"

He tried to speak, couldn't, but nodded his head affirmatively.

Compton, with tears of rage streaming down his cheeks, let go and hurried away. I followed, after advising Wilkins, "If I were you, I'd seriously think about changing your attitude before one of those Southern boys skins you alive."

Surprisingly, and for whatever reason, there weren't any repercussions. Wilkins didn't put Compton, or me, on report. He didn't learn though, he was soon back to his usual rough treatment of the mountain boys.

Target: Truk

After Operation Flintlock, Adm. Chester Nimitz, the brilliant Pacific war strategist, decided not to have his forces return to Pearl Harbor before embarking on their next major operation.

Admiral Nimitz had the bigger picture in mind. The Pacific was a huge ocean, not a land mass, and the most prudent, surest, quickest strategic way to victory–with the least losses–was to utilize nullification and isolation.

Truk was to be nullified. There was no need to invade it; just render it inoperable and proceed on from there.

Fast Carrier Task Force 58 was quickly readied for its next action, on Feb. 12 we left Majuro bound for Truk. For years, the Japs had been secretly building up their fortifications on Truk. It was one of their most formidable air and naval bases. Strategically positioned some 770 miles west of the Caroline Islands, Truk was Japan's key defense link to the central Pacific.

They should have known Truk would be attacked next, but when T.F. 58 arrived at dawn, it was undetected; they were caught with their pants down.

This task force packed an awesome wallop, provided by its 9 carriers, 6 battleships, 10 cruisers and 29 destroyers.

FEB-16 - DAWN ATTACK ON TRUK
FEB 17- 1207 A.M. GOT ONE TORPEDO IN STARBOARD QUARTER FROM SINGLE JAP TORPEDO PLANE- LARGE HOLE, 20'×30'- STEERING ENGINE ROOM- RUDDER KNOCKED OUT- HAD TO STEER WITH SCREWS
FEB 25 - PULLED INTO PEARL HARBOUR
FEB 26 - WENT INTO DRY DOCK - CUT RUDDER OFF.
FEB 29- LEFT DRY DOCK AND STARTED FOR STATES - COULDNT MAKE HEADWAY

Target: Truk

The first strike by the Hellcat fighters shot down 30 enemy planes, strafed, damaged and destroyed many more on the ground. Over 300 planes from the nine carriers bombed and strafed while battlewagons and cruisers blasted the island targets with deadly salvos. The nullification of Truk was underway.

The Intrepid's planes from Air Group 6 worked over Truk's shore installations, including a seaplane base that they completely destroyed along with 15 seaplanes.

Our dive bombers and torpedo planes joined with other planes that were attacking ships anchored and docked in the harbor. One delivered the *coup de grace* with the fifth bomb hit on an ammunition ship, which was blown to hell, dispatching it's crew to meet their ancestors.

Air Group 6's planes were credited with sinking two ships and damaging 10 others. They were also credited with the downing of 16 in air combat and 43 more planes on the ground.

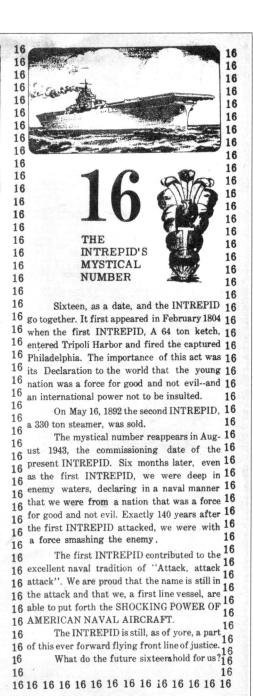

THE INTREPID'S MYSTICAL NUMBER

Sixteen, as a date, and the INTREPID go together. It first appeared in February 1804 when the first INTREPID, A 64 ton ketch, entered Tripoli Harbor and fired the captured Philadelphia. The importance of this act was its Declaration to the world that the young nation was a force for good and not evil--and an international power not to be insulted.

On May 16, 1892 the second INTREPID, a 330 ton steamer, was sold.

The mystical number reappears in August 1943, the commissioning date of the present INTREPID. Six months later, even as the first INTREPID, we were deep in enemy waters, declaring in a naval manner that we were from a nation that was a force for good and not evil. Exactly 140 years after the first INTREPID attacked, we were with a force smashing the enemy.

The first INTREPID contributed to the excellent naval tradition of "Attack, attack attack". We are proud that the name is still in the attack and that we, a first line vessel, are able to put forth the SHOCKING POWER OF AMERICAN NAVAL AIRCRAFT.

The INTREPID is still, as of yore, a part of this ever forward flying front line of justice. What do the future sixteens hold for us?

From an early issue of "Intrepid."

The Task Group's total of 200,000 tons of war and merchant ships destroyed is the most tonnage sunk on any single day in WWII.

Even a routine day in C.I.C. was always interesting. We were fortunate to always be in the know, privy to all sorts of information, including overall objectives, pilots' debriefing reports and confidential and even secret battle plans. These bits and pieces helped you assemble a current, up-to-the-minute picture of what was going on and how it was progressing.

When the plan of the day called for engaging and defending against enemy attack, there was less small talk and strict by-the-book conversation. If problems arose, seconds counted as decisions were made and orders expedited.

Feb. 16 seemed to be an extra-long day: we had been at G.Q. for hours, searching for and tracking snooping bogies that approached, then veered away from ships in our task group. A few of them were shot down by fighters in the Combat Air Patrol (C.A.P.), but none had penetrated our defense. While on a break from the SK air search-radar, I grabbed a cup of joe with Doc.

"Stoney, do you believe in that 16th crap?"

Scuttlebutt had it that today, the 16th of the month was an unlucky one for the Intrepid. Smitty overheard Doc's question; he answered before I could: "I heard a couple of things. Two welders were killed on the 16th when their tanks blew up portside on the hangar deck, when they were building the ship in Newport News. What about you Stoney?"

"Heard that, too. But I agree with Doc. It's all bull-crap. Besides, in a few minutes it will be the 17th, so forget it."

About then, an announcement from the bridge came over the PA speaker: "Now hear this, hear this. The ship will secure from general quarters and switch to condition one easy. Those not on watch may return to their compartments, and sleep fully dressed with the fireproof covers on their bunks."

"Ever hear of condition one easy, Stoney?"

"New to me, Doc. Let's check it out."

C.I.C. was now manned by its normal watch section as Doc and I made our way down to the hangar deck and aft to our compartment. Climbing into my upper bunk, I stretched out on the clammy flash cover.

Target: Truk

Doc was about to bite into a dried-out salami sandwich, "Damn it! These horse-cock sandwiches smell like horse shit!"

"Hey, Doc, hungry? I've got a ham 'n egg sandwich in my locker. Traded with a radioman for it this afternoon."

"How's that, Stoney?"

"I said, I've got a..."

Va- va-boom! A thundering explosion rocked the ship. My head bounced off the overhead, and I landed on the deck with a resounding "Holy shit!"

The ship shuddered violently. Men were scrambling up the ladder from the compartment below, some dazed and wet. They were hurrying along, without panic, climbing up the ladder to the hangar deck.

My feet took over, sprinting the familiar G.Q. path forward on the hangar deck, up ladders to my battle station in C.I.C., arriving in time to hear an announcement from the bridge: "We've taken a torpedo in the starboard quarter. Damage-control parties, lay aft to your stations."

A single, undetected Jap plane, flying close to the water and weaving between ships, sighted his prime target, a big aircraft carrier. Following the wake as the ship veered in a sharp turn, he laid a "fish" into our starboard quarter, just aft and below my sleeping compartment. The torpedo ripped a 20-by-30-foot hole in the ship's surface skin below the water line, jamming the rudder against the hull.

Now, manning the SM air-search radar in C.I.C., I scanned the skies looking for other bogies. I was probably still more excited than scared; fear would set in later when I had time to think about what happened.

The Intrepid was basically uncontrollable, on a wild ride passing through, near and away from the other ships. Somehow, we barely missed a collision with our sister carrier, the Essex. It scared the hell out of both of us.

Finally, after the Intrepid had cleared the other ships and was detached, I started worrying about our vulnerability, the possibility of taking another torpedo and having to go over the side into shark-filled waters.

The light carrier Cabot, two cruisers and four destroyers were assigned to escort us back to Eniwetok.

Later, some steering control was achieved by fast-forwarding two screws on one side of the crushed rudder, while reversing two on the other side. Planes were stacked forward on the flight deck to catch the wind, but when the wind velocity increased above 20 knots, the ship weather-cocked and headed in the direction from which the wind was blowing.

Captain Sprague said:"The ship would weather-cock with the wind. The ship kept turning west towards Tokyo. At the time, I didn't want to go to Tokyo."

The captain and Cmdr. P. S. Reynolds, the ship's damage control officer, met and decided to make a huge canvas sail that would be rigged in the open space between the flight and forecastle decks.

One of our ship's sailmakers who worked on it was Gordon Keith, a West Virginia farm boy. As a lad, he learned to operate and fix what machinery his family had, including his mother's sewing machine, which he also learned to operate.

On board ship, sailmakers made canvas covers for a variety of uses, including the body bags for burying our dead at sea. Much of the canvas in this huge sail came from disassembled body bags.

When hoisted, the sail acted like a jib on a sailboat, catching the wind, helping to pull the bow around toward a desired course and enabling the ship to make quicker turns.

The sail also contributed to erratic and unpredictable zigzag course changes. Ones that would baffle any enemy submarine trying to get a fix on our course. It did the same to our own escorts, which had to be ready to change course as often as we did.

T G 58's scorecard for Truk: Jap losses from air attacks: one cruiser, two destroyers and several other warships, as well as an additional 140,000 tons of shipping; another cruiser and two more destroyers were sunk by the battleships New Jersey and Iowa; 250 enemy planes downed in the air and numerous others destroyed on the ground.

U.S. submarines also scored big, sinking several more Jap ships.

T.G. 58's losses: Less than 30 planes and damage to the Intrepid, with seven crewmen killed.

Truk lay in ruins, its harbor cluttered with sunken ships. Truk was thoroughly nullified.

Under way to Eniwetok, fears of thrashing around in shark-filled waters diminished, as the ship's daily routine of four-on, eight-off watch-es was re-established.

Years later, I learned how some of my best buddies felt and acted during their baptism in battle.

**Jack, (Botts) Alexander
Radarman 2/c
18 years old**
"I was on watch in C.I.C., manning a radar set. We were part of Task Force 58.2, cruising under total darkness, when a lone enemy plane dropped a torpedo that hit and explod-ed in the starboard quarter, the stern of the ship, creating a gaping hole in the ship's hull. We lost use of the ship's rudder. Some of our shipmates were wounded and killed during this attack.

Jack Alexander

"Fear was my initial reaction. Thoughts raced. How badly were we dam-aged? Anyone wounded, killed? Would there be more explosions? Would the ship sink? Negative thoughts flood your mind at a time like this.

"You think of loved ones, of death. Will I survive? See another day? We had our battle stations to man, responsibility to one another, a job to do come what may."

Botts was then, and is still, a sensitive guy. Each of us would have given his life for the other; we were tight. It wasn't called male bonding then, but we had total trust and complete faith in one another. This trust helped us bear, share and face the things of war that we had to deal with during battle.

Torpedo Juice: The fuel that propelled torpedoes doubled as fuel for unauthorized cocktail parties. It made a drink with the kick of a mule, even when amply diluted with canned grapefruit juice. Party "guests" were usually found the next morning, passed out, with tell-tale purple circles from the 100 proof torpedo juice ringing their lips.
Where there's a will, there's a way. And those serious drinkers, who needed a daily jolt, had two secret stills operating on the ship. They either really needed to have a drink, or they just enjoyed bucking authority. Probably both.

Winston S. Goodloe

Winston S Goodloe
Aviation Machinist Mate 3/c
21 years old

"This was the first front-line action for most of the men aboard the U.S.S. Intrepid, and though we were all very patriotic, we had often wondered just when we would get our chance to release this pent-up anger that we harbored for the "Japs." Little did we realize that in precisely three minutes a Japanese aerial torpedo would crash through our ship's hull and, in one devastating blast, demand the lives of some of our gallant buddies.

"Twenty hours had passed since the first pre-dawn attack had been launched from our pitching, rolling flight deck – to crack the pillboxes and tremble the reefs of Truk's atoll's. We had worked feverishly and silently during that 20 hours, remaining at our battle stations until there were no more bogies left on our ship's radar screens.

"The bugle sounded "Secure from battle stations" and we headed for our ever-waiting bunks, the cool night air seemed to caress our tired nerves. Chief Petty Officer Elmer Graves came down the flight deck. We spoke of the day's action and he asked if I would like to come down to the chief's quarters for a cup of coffee. As we walked towards the hatch leading down to cheif's quarters, I told him I was out of smokes, would stop by my compartment, get some and join him in a few minutes. (The time was 12:01 a.m.)

"I reached into my locker and in the dark found my cigarette carton; it was empty. Someone bumped into me. It was Roger; I knew he smoked Luckies, too. Seconds ticked away. "Roger, can you let me borrow a pack of butts?" (12:02.) "Thanks, buddy." I stepped through the hatch into the next compartment and my foot found the deck, but the deck moved. I steadied my balance.

"The airplane motor overhead was definitely not one of ours. Spinning around, I started for the flight deck, and the ship listed as it went into a sharp turn. The battle-stations gong sounded over the P.A.'s and was emphasized by a deafening explosion. Silence followed, broken by the clamor of anxious, frightened men rushing to their stations.

Target: Truk

"Captain Sprague was speaking into the bridge microphone: "Men, we have been torpedoed. The ship's rudder is jammed, and we are turning east through the task force. Stand by for a possible collision."

"Topside, I could make out the silhouette of our huge sister ship, 36 thousand tons of the U.S.S. Essex bearing down on our bow. Seconds later, she sped past our fantail. We severed paths on the wake of what seemed to be the entire task force.

"At noon the next day, I stood on the hangar deck, head bowed, hat over my heart while taps sounded and our detachment of marines raised their rifles and fired a salute as the bodies of Chief Graves and others gently slid from beneath American flags and into the sea."

Nearly 59 years passed before I caught up with Gerry Goguen and his remembrance of the night the Intrepid was "Off Truk," on Feb. 16, 1944.

Gerald Goguen

Gerald G. Goguen
Aviation Ordinance Man 3/c
18 years old

"I remember that night very well. I was at my G.Q. station on the flight deck, in back of the 5-inch .38 big guns. My division was V7A, aviation ordinance and my duty-to man the head phones and the bomb elevator that brought bombs up to the flight deck from the ammo magazine.

It was close to 2400 hours when Chief Bill Naylor asked: "How are you doing?" "O.K.," I replied. "Good. You can secure your watch and go catch some shuteye."

"Three of us were there: Joe Penner, (named after the famous comedian from the *Do you wanna buy a duck?* era) and Max Marion, a wonderful native American who was an AOM 1/c in V7 division.

"Out of the darkness, and alongside the ship, came what sounded like a misfiring lawn mower. Joe said, "What the hell is that?" I said, "It's one of ours, a SBD bomber." Max said, "SBD hell!" and started running forward. Looking to starboard, I could see the planes fiery exhaust and silhouettes of the pilot and radioman were illuminated by the eerie green light from the plane's instrument panels.

"The plane veered left and flew over our flight deck, forward, so close that it must have ruffled Frank Doria's hair before it disappeared.

(Frank was at his G.Q. station just forward of the 5-inch gun turrets.)

"Seconds later, all hell broke loose. The Jap had laid a torpedo in our starboard side aft. What to do now? There was a 1,000 pound bomb lashed on a transport skid, next to the bomb elevator, which was locked tight. My chief warrant officer told me, "The bomb has to go."

"Where sir?"

"Over the side."

"Aye, aye, sir."

"I used all of my 150 pounds to push the bomb forward into the wind, dumping it over the port side; being careful not to get caught on the skid handles and unceremoniously catapulted into space.

"It was a dark night. You hardly could see anything and I later thought maybe I should have jettisoned the bomb aft. I don't think I would have made it through the maze of planes that were lashed down on the deck back aft. Besides, forward on the port side was clear of any catwalks and there, the deck extended out further from the ship's hull.

"To me, it was sad to think this 1,000 pound bomb was wasted, ending up tossed into the deep-six, instead dropped off on a Jap target."

The funeral ceremony next day was conducted by the Intrepid's two chaplains, with shipmates and a marine honor guard. The bodies were lined up in a row, each in a canvas shroud with a five inch shell at their feet to weigh down the body.

Burial at sea had all the deep, sorrowing impact of a solemn funeral mass in St. Patrick's Cathedral. Even more, since it was compounded by lamenting many deaths, not just a single passing of a member of your ship's family. Shipmates were truly family with some like brothers, others like cousins.

Transforming Lowly Polliwogs

"Now hear this! Hear this! All lowly polliwogs, lend an ear. The Royal Party from the Domain of Neptunis Rex, including the Royal Baby, is coming alongside. Prepare to welcome them on board!"

On Jan. 22, 1944, when we crossed the Equator and the International Dateline simultaneously on our way into action, there wasn't time for indoctrination into the Ancient Order of the Deep.

Now, we lowly polliwogs were summoned to prepare a welcome for the Royal Party that was coming alongside in one of the Intrepid's longboats. The members were piped aboard and held court on the hangar deck: Neptunis Rex with his crown and trident, the Queen with a mop for her hair; and the exceedingly plump Royal Baby, decked out in nothing but diapers.

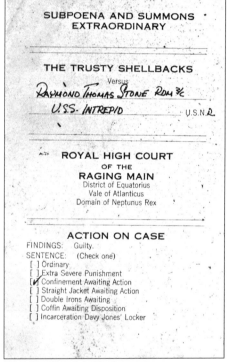

The Shellback initiation subpoena accused me of being a wolf, a known chowhound, and flirting with mermaids.

This was prelude to a well-organized, traditional hazing that took place on the flight deck later. There were probably only 200 certified Shellbacks in the crew to carry out the initiation of nearly 3,000 polliwogs into the mysteries of the deep.

Crewmen not on watch assembled at quarters on the flight deck in the normal, formal way, with division officers lined up in front of the enlisted men. A boatswain's pipe signaled the start and Shellback Cavalieri, the Boot, stepped forward with a half-pound can of grease.

Our division officer, Lt. Cmdr. Thompson, attired in a brand-new pair of starched khakis, started to say something as the Boot approached him, wearing his most lascivious smile.

"Quiet, you lowly polliwog. Stand at attention!"

As Thompson started to protest, the Boot smeared grease over his face, then all over his uniform, finishing by wiping his hands on Thompson's chest. We stood there in stunned, joyful disbelief, watching the Boot do what we would have loved to be doing.

Spared a grease job, we waited for the next phase of indoctrination. Earlier, I asked the Boot to see if he could arrange to get me initiated among the very first. He did.

The scene as he escorted me portside, amidships, to where you started, was a bit bizarre for a U.S. Navy ship. The Royal Party was holding court, surrounded by various royal torturers, some with lethal electronic prods. There also was a holding cage for those especially despised polliwogs who deserved, and got, extra-special treatment.

After kissing the Royal Baby's grease-smeared belly-button, I proceeded crawling on my hands and knees through a 100-foot-long canvas tunnel into the force of water from a fire hose, with my head down and ass up. Whatever body part stuck up was whacked.

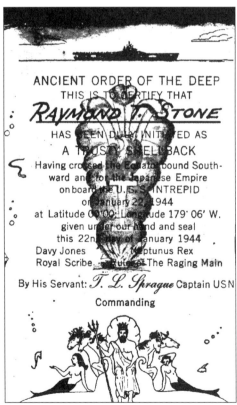

The Trusty Shellback card issued to all lowly polliwogs after initiation.

Out of the tunnel, I started running the gauntlet, with everyone whacking the hell out of me with their stuffed canvas batons. I made it to the end with only minor bruises. (The day's casualties, included a couple of broken arms and legs, plus a broken back.) I believe all serious injuries were unintentional, coming from accidental falls on the wet deck.

After the last ordeal, they anointed me by smearing a big red spot on my forehead. Now, I was a Trusty Shellback, ready and able to dish out prompt justice by nailing Thompson as he ran the gauntlet.

Comdr. Richard Gaines, was unable to produce his Shellback card. He was re-initiated, wearing boots, and scanning the horizon using Coke bottles for binoculars.

When I explained what I wanted to do and why, a Shellback gave me his stuffed canvas baton. I lined up on the curve, where runners slowed down.

It was a while before a soggy, woeful-looking Thompson stumbled his way toward me. His ass was whacked with such savage force that he flew skyward, bounced off the deck and was propelled onward by more vicious blows. Staggering away, battered, but without serious injury, he probably wondered why he was among those singled out for electric prod-stings and extra measures of punishment. I'll never understand how someone like him could be such a bastard and not have a clue.

Later, while on watch in C.I.C, I delighted in detailing Thompson's whacking to my jubilant buddies, making sure the officers overheard and shared the visual picture I was

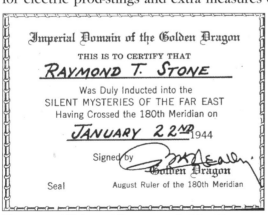

Imperial Domain of the Golden Dragon

THIS IS TO CERTIFY THAT

RAYMOND T. STONE

Was Duly Inducted into the
SILENT MYSTERIES OF THE FAR EAST
Having Crossed the 180th Meridian on

JANUARY 2 2ND 1944

Signed by

Golden Dragon

Seal   August Ruler of the 180th Meridian

Equator + 180th meridian = one Golden Dragon.

painting verbally. I could see by their suppressed smiles that they were tuned in and enjoying it.

"He looked like a soaked sewer rat, dragging his tail after a bout with a tough alley cat."

Scuttlebutt had it that Thompson was later transferred to an obscure weather outpost in China. I hope so. However, it was not before my worst dealings with him were to unfold.

Pearl/Under Full Sail

As far as I know, the Intrepid was the only carrier ever to come into Pearl Harbor *under full sail.*

We were met by a couple of tugboats that took us in tow to a dry dock for repairs. All Captain Sprague wanted was a quick patch over the hole so we could return stateside for permanent repairs. However, the port captain, who had the authority, insisted on also having the crumpled rudder removed.

While the ship was being repaired, we had a couple of liberties in Honolulu and downed a few at the Enlisted Man's Beer Garden in The Royal Hawaiian Hotel. The Navy used the hotel for R&R (Rest & Rehabilitation) for submarine crews between their long voyages.

I was not that fond of liberty in Honolulu; there were too many sailors, the lines were too long and there was too much coral at world-famous Waikiki Beach.

George Vogrin, Ray Stone and Jake Fegley hamming it up at Honolulu's Royal Hawaiian Hotel.

Wally Schultz, getting a hug and a photo.

Others liked it, especially Gordon Keith, one of the ship's sailmakers. His daughter Rhonda later told me of his fondness for Honolulu and said that one of his treasured souvenirs was a pair of doll-size pink panties with "Remember Pearl!" printed across the front.

Some of the longest lines in Honolulu were those at the whorehouses; they stretched out onto the sidewalk and around the corner. However, they moved relatively fast since they operated on the three factor. $3 for three minutes. Each girl had three cubicles; one for doing it, one for the guy she just did it with, and one for the guy she was about to do it to.

The $3 fee was also split three ways; one for the house, one for the girl and one for management-control by the Army's Provost Marshall. According to reports from my buddies, the girls rated a notch above the whores in Panama – slightly younger, slightly better looking. Like most of my buddies, I was never curious enough to go and find out for myself.

On Feb. 29, with temporary repairs completed and with tugboats guiding, the Intrepid put to sea, escorted by two destroyers. After the tugs headed back into Pearl, heavy winds and high seas came up. The Intrepid was soon bouncing around like a cork. Forwarding and reversing screws had little effect, since there was no crumpled rudder for the force of the screws to work against. Captain Sprague was right, the port captain wrong.

Given the weather, it was too dangerous to try bringing the Intrepid back into Pearl. Over the next two days, bobbing around offshore, we listened to Tokyo Rose's nightly broadcast. She played music from a collection of big band hits and, between songs, she taunted her listeners.

Typically, in a soft modulated voice, Tokyo Rose would say something like this: "Are you sailors lonely tonight? Don't you wish you were home with your sweetheart and could cuddle up with her? Don't worry, she's all right, probably out having a good time with a local 4-F guy, one of those home front wolves. You know the type, a real lady's man. Or maybe she's out with her boss from work. You don't mind do you? Don't worry, I'm sure she thinks of you, sometime. I hope you don't get a Dear John letter from her," etc.

During those two days offshore, we were amused and also startled to hear Tokyo Rose say: "This next song is for those lonesome sailors on that carrier offshore Oahu. We know where you are and will send our submarines to sink you. Be sure to say your prayers before you close your eyes tonight."

Hearing this crap usually produced a round of expletives, followed by laughter. Tokyo Rose's attempts at demoralizing the Intrepid's crew didn't work.

When the seas calmed, tugs returned, took us in tow and once again eased us into dry dock, where a jury rudder was affixed. On March 15, the dry dock was flooded and the Intrepid prepared to leave Pearl for the States. We got under way next morning, again escorted by two destroyers. It took seven, rather than the usual four, days to reach Frisco.

MARCH 6 - WENT BACK INTO DRY DOCK AT PEARL HARBOUR - HAD A JURY RUDDER RIGGED AND HOLE TEMPORAIRLY PATCHED.

MARCH 16 - LEFT PEARL HARBOUR FOR THE STATES.

MARCH 22 - ARRIVED AT SAN FRANCISCO AND WENT INTO DRY DOCK AT HUNTERS POINT.

JUNE 10 - LEFT ALEMEDIA FOR PEARL HARBOUR WITH TROOPS, TRUCKS, PLANES

Tokyo Rose was portrayed by 20 different women. One, Iva Ikoku Toguri, an U.C.L.A.-educated Japanese-American went to Japan to take care of her sick aunt five months before the war started. She worked as a typist for Radio Tokyo and was selected to read scripts. She had no broadcast experience, and her voice was not very compelling. At the war's end, she gladly returned to the United States not believing she had done anything wrong. However, interviews with the press led to her trial and conviction of treason after false testimony by two of her Japanese-American radio-station supervisors. Iva was sentenced to 10 years in prison and a $10,000 fine. After she served more than six years, investigations and articles in The Chicago Tribune eventually resulted in her being pardoned by President Ford.

San Francisco—Here I Come

Seeing the Golden Gate Bridge looming in wispy fog was an enticing illusion. Whoopie! Back stateside, soon back home on a 20-day leave, but first, liberty. There'll be a hot time in Frisco tonight.

While the ship was easing into dry dock, I started getting ready, pressing my dress blues and putting a spit shine on my shoes and a gleam in my eyes. Polack wanted to tie into a big steak and I wanted to pick up a babe and go dancing.

In the morning I'd be be on leave, heading cross-country for New York on the San Francisco Challenger.

"Now hear this, hear this! Liberty for Watch Section 4 is cancelled. Only Watch Section 2 has liberty today."

"Damn it! Polack, did you hear that? What's this all about?"

"Your guess is as good as mine, Stoney."

Polack took it in stride, as he did everything. Shit just happened. Not I. After much mouthing off and beating my gums, I finally calmed down. While heading back to our compartment to change into dungarees, we heard loud, excited voices.

"Come a 7, come 11! Baby needs a new pair of shoes."

Twenty guys surrounded a blanket on the floor, the dice were flying, and the green stuff was exchanging hands. It was a wild scene, and I decided to try my hand with the $20 I had planned to spend on liberty that night. My gambling knowledge was limited to poker and black jack, but Polack said he knew the bets in craps. I gave him my money, and while I rolled the dice, he covered the bets.

Luck was not my lady this night. I kept returning to my locker for more and more money and losing it, until I was down to my last five bucks. I felt sick, stupid and ashamed. How was I going to get home on leave?

Train fare on the Challenger was 75 bucks, round trip. I didn't know what to do. Getting home to see my parents and sister was urgent. But how? Things were tight financially at home and I didn't want to tell them I lost all my money in a crap game. Finally, I decided to fess up and sent a telegram: Have 20-day leave. Lost all my money in a crap game. Need to borrow $75 for train fare. Sorry. Love, Ray

The next morning I picked up $85 at Western Union and found a couple of my buddies waiting for the train gates to open when an announcement was made: "The Challenger will start boarding in a couple of minutes. Women with children first. Women next and then servicemen followed by civilians."

The gates opened and, after the women and children boarded, a mad rush followed with everyone trying to get to the best remaining coach cars. Railroads were using every passenger car that had wheels and we ended up in one of the oldest. It must have been of Civil War vintage; it was illuminated by gas lights and had straight-back facing seats, covered in red-plush, itchy, upholstery.

Prospects of the long train ride and being able to see the country as we crossed it were appealing. Within hours, the appeal wore off, tarnished by stiff backs, sore butts and foul smoke-filled air. An old salt, who made the trip a couple of times advised: "When we get to Cheyenne, one of you run down the main drag to the Chinaman's butcher shop, about six blocks on the left, get a couple of pounds of pepperoni and some bread. The other hit the liquor store, about three blocks on the right, get a couple, or more, bottles of booze. Keep it out of the S.P.'s sight. Take a couple of bites of pepperoni with some bread; wash it down with a couple of shots of booze. Nap and nip. Every time you wake up, repeat the procedure. It will get you all the way to Chicago with less pain."

Payday! Payday!: When the bugle sounded, you checked the payroll list, saw how much you had on the books, and withdrew what you needed. At sea, you didn't need much money and you let your money ride, drawing a couple of bucks, just enough to keep you in cigarettes, (five cents a pack), shaving cream and Milky Ways.

One of our older chiefs had $6,000 on the books, his life's savings. His nest egg, his future chicken ranch. He lost it all, one afternoon, in a crap game on Mog Mog.

Sightseeing in Cheyenne was limited to my six-block run to the Chinaman's, but I'll never forget seeing the imposing beauty of a majestic mountain at the far end of the road.

Back on the train, Polack and I practiced what the old salt had preached. Nap, pepperoni, bread, nip some booze, another nap. It was not a cure-all, but it sure helped. We made it to Chicago in decent shape, despite awakening one night to the smell of gas from extinguished, but not turned-off gas illumination fixtures.

A bright spot along the route was when we were cheered on by the good ladies of Council Bluffs, Iowa. They met every train with goodies like homemade pies, cakes and cookies for the servicemen who were passing through. These women looked as if they just stepped out of a Norman Rockwell illustration for a Saturday Evening Post cover: pink-cheeked, plump, kind and cheerful. The warmth and generocity of the good ladies brightened our spirits as the train went on to Chicago, where, at last, we could shower and shave at the U.S.O.

Refreshed and decked-out in dress blues, I boarded a clean, comfortable New York Central train for New York City. The individual, adjustable seats were real luxury. A middle-aged woman, who looked like a talker, plumped down next to me. I wanted to catch up on some sleep and decided to feign deafness to escape her probable prattle, pointing to my ear while shaking my head, no. It worked until a pretty girl, seated in front, turned and asked me a question. My reply generated a smile from her and a dirty look from my portly seatmate, whom nevertheless remained mute.

The days at home went by quickly. I didn't want my parents to know that my ship had been torpedoed and merely told them, "needed to have the rudder replaced." Mom bought it, but I could tell by Dad's questions that he didn't. Dad and I exchanged knowing looks that mutually implied, you and I know it isn't the rudder but the less said, the better for Mom.

Score: one goose downed.

San Francisco–Here I come

In addition to nights spent dancing to big-band music in New York, I went duck hunting with a borrowed shotgun. For a first-time hunter, I was lucky, and bagged a Canada snow goose.

Dad said, "You pluck it, I'll cook it." My first plucking took two days to complete. Being a novice, I didn't leave the goose submerged in hot water long enough, and it made feather-plucking extremely difficult.

Dinner on the last night of my leave featured roast goose, served with Dad's special Champagne sauce. It was superb, and I packed some pieces the next morning before I left for the train trip back to San Francisco.

Like some meals, roast goose tasted even better the next day, when I met Polack on the train in Chicago. We shared the goose and washed it down with slugs from a bottle of Polack's finest Youngstown slivovitz.

The trip back to San Francisco took five uncomfortable and boring days. Soot from the coal-fired steam engine managed to find and cover you everywhere. By the time we reached San Francisco, we were ready for a long hot shower and 24 hours of sack time.

Another historic crap game occurred later, while the Intrepid was ferrying troops back to the States. One big roller, Felix Novelli, reported: "The game took place in the portside head and it became known as the 11-day crap shoot. Stakes were so high that a "ref" had to be hired. As the game went on for hour after hour it grew more serious. One soldier started bidding high and the pot kept growing. It took three-quarters of an

Felix Novelli AMM 2/C

hour to cover his bet. The soldier rolled a 6 and a four for 10. It was now a $20,000 pot. He tossed the dice again and the bones came up 6 and 4, making his 10 point. But one flaw put it all at stake – the number 4 die lay on the corner of a $20.00 bill. Those who bet against him yelled: "No Dice!" The "ref" got down on his knees, took the thin cellophane from his cigarettes pack and used it as a feeler gauge. He jumped to his feet and called "dice." It was good. The soldier took off his pants, tied the ends of the legs, and stuffed his $20,000 in winnings into the "sack." (Intrepid's cooks also came out big winners in this perpetual crap game. They supplied the food at $25. per sandwich."}

A Plane Captain's Day

STONE: "Tell me what it was like-- your responsibilities as a Plane Captain on the Intrepid and how did your day begin"?

Novelli: "My day started with reveille at four-o-clock in the morning and my job was one of the most important on the carrier, I was assigned to one aircraft, a mighty Corsair F4-U-4 with its highly distinguishable gull wing design. This fast, highly maneuverable, heavily armed war bird stuck fear into many a Jap pilot's heart during combat. They respectfully called it "Whistling Death."

"My responsibility: I held the safety of this pilot's life in my hands. I had to see that this plane was in a hundred percent perfect condition before he got in to take off. Readying the plane for a combat mission took better than one hour. All systems, supplies, fluids, fuels and ordinance were checked and re-checked again. Everything had to be in absolute A-One working order. Only then was the plane brought up on the elevator to the flight deck and no one except the pilot and his Plane Captain was permitted to climb into the cockpit.

"Around 0530 pilots are summoned by the familiar call, "Pilots man your planes". His Plane Captain is waiting, perched on the starboard wing holding on to the plotting board, charts and orders until the pilot enters the cockpit and is strapped in. The engine turns over, and the huge four blades of the of the prop begin spinning. The 18 cylinder Pratt and Whitney engine soon hums to a perfect pitch, the pilot smiles, gives a "thumbs up" signal and the plane begins maneuvering to its take off position on the flight deck. Once there, the Plane Captain is relieved, the plane handlers and Launching Officer take over and this beautiful big bird soon roars down the flight deck and makes it's way skyward, heading for another raid against the Land of the Rising Sun.

A group of Intrepid Plane Captains with Felix Novelli..........▲ ▲ ▲

"Now comes the stressful time, hours of waiting for planes to return from a strike. As the time of return nears, Plane Captains make their way back to the flight deck to await the call from the Air Officer (air boss)–"Standby to land planes." There's nothing more rewarding to a Plane Captain than to see his bird coming back home to roost as he lets out a heart felt sigh of relief.

"After the landing, when the tail hook is freed from the arresting cable, the Plane Captain makes sure that the gas tank is refilled, two and a half gallons of oil are added to the engine, checks and refilsl all hydralic fluids, replaces the oxygen bottle, checks tire surfaces and sees that ordinance men re-arm the six 50 calibre cannons.

"Finally the Plane Captain can call it a day, and its one helluva good day, when his pilot reports:"We got two of them bastards today – one Zero and one Tony!."

Felix Novelli Aviation Machinist Mate 2/C
Serve on the Intrepid from February 1945 – August 1946
during the Okinowa Invasion Campaign and the Fast Carrier
raids against mainland Japan.

Great City – Great People

The more you saw of San Francisco, the more you loved it and during the two and a half months the ship was being repaired, we also discovered San Jose and the De Bello family.

Cavalieri, the Boot, visited relatives in San Jose whom he had never met before. They opened their hearts and homes to him, and at their urging he brought three or four of us along on his visits. We too shared their warm Italian hospitality and ample meals.

The De Bellos treated us as family, and it was always party time. First, ring the necks of a couple of chickens and let the rabbit have one last shot before slitting his throat. Pete De Bello said it made the meat more tender if the rabbit died with a smile on his face.

Meals were presided over by Mama De Bello, the family matriarch, who advised us: *"Mange, mange.* And don't mess with my youngest daughter. She's a virgin."

We didn't mess with any daughter, but *mange* we did. After the first dinner, I learned to skip seconds on pasta; you had to save room for the chicken, rabbit and salad that followed. Every meal was a real feast, in spite of the austere wartime food rationing. The De Bellos' victory gardens provided ample fruits and vegetables. A son-in-law also raised pigs, and we helped slaughter one that weighed over 350 pounds. Slaughtering

The Boot, Mike Cavalieri, bottom row center, surrounded by the De Bello family and some of his shipmates, San Jose, Calif. 1944.

129

and butchering the pig took on the air of a family festival, a chance for another party. I helped cage the pig and lift it onto a pickup truck for transport to another relative's farm.

As tradition dictated, we all gathered around a large round table for a breakfast that included sausage, donated by the previous pig who oinked here.

While waiting for the professional pig killer to show, we filled an old claw-foot bathtub with water and lit a wood fire beneath it, to get the water boiling-hot.

The pro was a lean, long-legged guy who looked like a cowhand. He spoke like one, too, with some howdys all around, as well as a few yups. He went about his business tieing a rope on the pig's hind hoof, which led up to a block and tackle. He then put a .22 bullet from an ancient rifle into the pig's head and hoisted him up. After slitting the hog's throat to drain the blood, he gutted and quartered him.

We immersed the carcass in the hot water, added ashes from the fire and at Mama's direction, started to shave off the bristles. Even with sharp knives, it took a while before we perfected the technique.

The ladies then took over, sewing each quarter into a shroud of clean white sheets. The meat was then hung in the barn for a couple of days before it was butchered into various cuts. Sausage was made...some to be saved and served at breakfast when the next pig was slaughtered.

Wine, music and bountiful quantities of food followed, until we left at sundown to hitchhike back to the ship at Hunters Point.

It was nice to have a family away from home. Especially this wonderful, fun-loving Italian family whom we visited many times while our ship was being repaired.

Being sailors, we also actively pursued what Hollywood said sailors were supposed to pursue. One night, four or five of us decided to hit a Frisco hot spot, a nightclub where, according to the scuttlebutt, there was plenty of action. Even without a tip, the waiter led us to the best table, front and center on the dance floor. We ordered a round of rum and Cokes and waited for the floor show.

When the show started, the star, a well-built tall redhead in a long black evening gown, made a grand entrance, wiggling across the stage with lots of gyrations to loud applause, hoots and whistles from the sailors in the audience.

After a couple of numbers, she slinked her way into a sexy rendition of "I'm in the Mood for Love." Oh boy! She was singing to me.

I was frozen, locked on, when she plopped herself onto my lap, then leaped up and returned to center stage and loud applause as the song ended.

After many bows, she pulled off the red wig, extracted two grapefruit from her bosom, tossed them at me and ran like a bat out of hell.

I jumped up, shouting: "You bastard, you dirty bastard! I'll get you." Before I could take more than two steps, I was grabbed by two, then four, waiters who were standing at the ready. We went round and round, knocking over a couple of tables before they pinned me on the floor. My good buddies sat there doing absolutely nothing to help, laughing their asses off.

I was mad, so damn mad. My redhead-and-freckles temper was fully inflamed. I was embarrassed; the patsy, the sucker who'd been duped by a transvestite, a damn female impersonator. All I could think of was beating the crap out of someone. Anyone would do.

It took a couple of rounds of on-the-house drinks before I calmed down and was able to begin laughing at myself. My shipmates, of course, all swore they knew *she* was a *he* all along. Word about my being bamboozled spread on the ship and I endured a lot of good-natured lambasting.

Red Jones and C.J. King had a good 'ol-boy buddy, a room clerk at the Golden Gate Hotel, who kept a room for them when the ship was in port. Being generous country folk, they told their buddies: "It's there. Room 722. Door's open. Use it any time you want to."

I took them up on their offer one night; so did a lot of other people. When I entered the room, I couldn't believe it. The bed had at least four people on it and there were six or more on the floor. The bathtub had a couple making out in it; the toilet was the only unoccupied space. I thought about lifting a couple off the bed and putting them on the floor, but decided to leave instead.

When I told Red and C.J. how I found the room so fully occupied, they took it in stride, happily proclaiming, "Isn't it nice that we're able to provide hospitality and a roof over the heads of so many of our good buddies right here in San Francisco."

I agreed that it was nice, but never tried to shack up there again.

Great City—Great People

On June 9, 1944, the day before the Intrepid departed for Pearl from Alameda, we had our last liberty and a party with the De Bellos in San Jose. It was the usual feast and fun-filled time that we had grown accustomed to sharing with these special people. We were family. They gave us much, and it was muchly appreciated.

Late in the evening, it turned into an ethnic drinking contest and we moved to one son-in-law's farm kitchen. The farm's previous owner, a Japanese-American, left a cellar full of home-brewed sake.

Seated at the round kitchen table were Joe, for the De Bello's; the Boot, one more for the Italians; Polack, for Polacks; Smitty, for Jews; Fegley, for Pennsylvania Dutchmen; and me, Stoney, for the Shanty Irish.

One by one, Joe brought up the bottles of sake from the cellar. You had to be careful, pouring to within only a couple of inches of the bottom, since each bottle had a flock of flies floating in it.

Our host was the first to go, followed by his Italian teammate. Smitty's last words were, "I'm a Jewish lover, not an Irish boozer." Polack and Fegley went quietly.

I sat smoking and staring at the losers. I was the only one still sipping and was glad the contest was over. It was the first time I ever drank sake and I vowed it would be my last. I was more than *three sheets to the wind*, when I looked at my watch and it dawned on me that first light was approaching...and we were due back by 0800.

Polack, and a splash of water in the face, helped me get the others on their feet. It was going to be close. At this hour we couldn't depend on hitchhiking, so we called a taxi.

The driver put the hammer to the floor and made it with about 10 minutes to spare. We emptied our wallets and came up two-bucks short, telling the driver we'd pay him next time. He wished us luck and told us to forget about the money.

Missing your ship, especially when it was leaving port for the war zone, was a serious offense that usually resulted in a court-martial, followed by a long prison term at hard labor.

At this sailing, the Intrepid had only a few crewmen who intentionally, or not, missed getting back aboard on time.

Japanese Aircraft-Recognition Silhouettes

The ship's lookouts and gunners studied and memorized these silhouettes of Japanese planes to make positive identification before they were fired-on by the Intrepid's antiaircraft batterys.

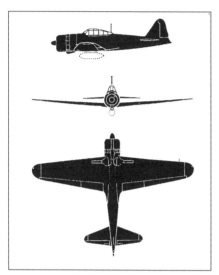

ZERO
Japanese Fighter

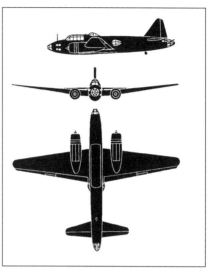

BETTY
Japanese Medium Bomber

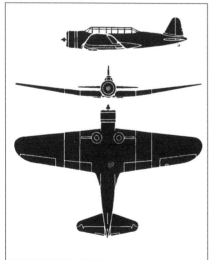

KATE
Japanese Torpedo Bomber

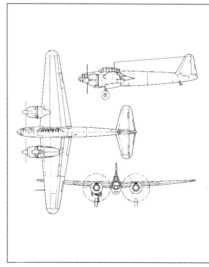

FRANCES
Japanese Dive Bomber

COMBAT INFORMATION CENTER (C.I.C.) 1944-45

After relocation from the island structure to the gallery deck, amidships, under the flight deck

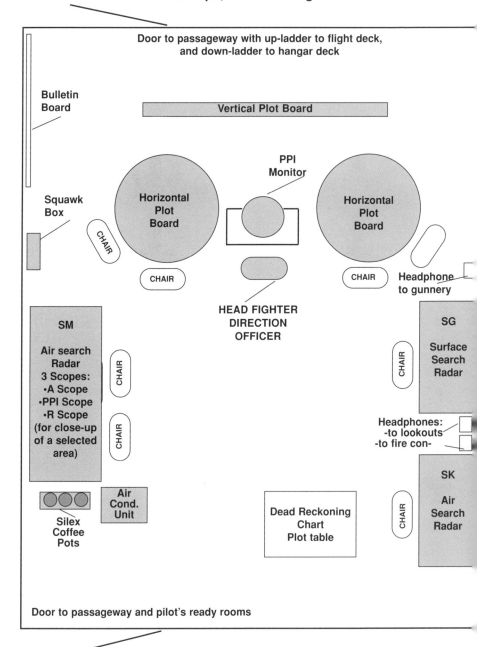

Door to passageway with up-ladder to flight deck, and down-ladder to hangar deck

Bulletin Board

Vertical Plot Board

PPI Monitor

Squawk Box

Horizontal Plot Board

CHAIR

CHAIR

Horizontal Plot Board

CHAIR

Headphone to gunnery

HEAD FIGHTER DIRECTION OFFICER

SM

Air search Radar
3 Scopes:
•A Scope
•PPI Scope
•R Scope
(for close-up of a selected area)

CHAIR

CHAIR

SG

Surface Search Radar

CHAIR

Headphones:
-to lookouts
-to fire con-

Silex Coffee Pots

Air Cond. Unit

Dead Reckoning Chart Plot table

SK

Air Search Radar

CHAIR

Door to passageway and pilot's ready rooms

Now It Can Be Told—Story
Of Radar and How It Works

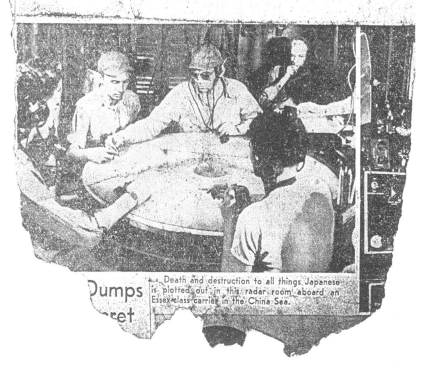

Death and destruction to all things Japanese is plotted out in this radar room aboard an Essex-class carrier in the China Sea.

During a standard 4-hour watch in C.I.C., radarmen rotated every half-hour, from operating a radar set to either standing-by resting their eyes, or swapping places with a plotter. This changed during G.Q. when things heated up. Then, the best, most experienced radarmen manned the radar, working closely with the fighter direction officers, especially when the night-fighters were involved.

C.I.C. operated in a calm, efficient, structured way, even in the thick of kamikaze attacks on the ship. The head fighter direction officer was like the maestro conducting his orchestra; assigning specific raid interceptions to other officers while the sound and percussion of our anti-aircraft guns set the tempo.

135

Some Intrepid Bogey Chasers

Mike Cavalieri

Jack Alexander

Enos Evans

C. W. Hudson

T.C. Greenfield

Red Jones & CJ King

There's a Bogey on the Screen

George Vogrin

Leon Smith

Merle Hossler

Jake Fegley

Jack Swan

All day long the men have labored,
Tired out and feeling mean–
Now sacked off in solid comfort,
There's a Bogey on the screen.

"Get the hell to General Quarters,"
Threats and growls and oaths obscene,
"Bugler: where in hell's that bugler?"
There's a Bogey on the screen.

Dah-dah-dah-da, battle stations,
Breaks upon their sleep serene,
"Hit the deck, there, on the double,"
There's a Bogey on the screen.

A little dot in Radar Plot,
Is the cause of all this scene,
All this running, all this cussing,
There's a Bogey on the screen.

"What's the range, and what's the bearing?"
Shouts the Gun-Boss, wild of mien,
Tousled hair, and pants still drooping,
There's a Bogey on the screen.

Roy Harbour

Charles Casteel
(KIA)

Wally Schultz
(KIA)

Dean Krouch
(KIA)

Lew Arnowitz

Peewee Wildes

Ray Stone

Pappy Hodges

Floyd Turner

ho Lorick

ack Norton

C. Siper

Ski Kozlowaski

Bear Lassitter

'Round the guns the crew is huddled,
Eyes are wild like Hallowe'en,
On the bridge the Skipper's shouting,
"There's a Bogey on the screen."

Up the halyards flags go racing,
Signals flash in red and green,
"At the dip, two-block those Foxes,
There's a Bogey on the screen."

"Distance, twenty, closing slowly,"
Down the deck the planes careen,
Roaring like the Bulls of Bashan,
To blast that Bogey from the screen.

Tally-ho, a snooping Betty,
Streaks of tracers can be seen,
And the dot in Radar Plot,
Is fading slowly from the screen,

Comes the word–"All hands secure!"
In their sacks men sit or lean,
Tired still, but plenty happy,
There's no Bogey on the screen!
                    –*Author Unknown*

137

Ferry Duty/First Anniversary

On Mar. 29, 1944, while the Intrepid was undergoing repairs at Hunters Point, our esteemed skipper, Capt. Thomas L. Sprague received his promotion to rear admiral. First, our executive officer, Cmdr. Richard Gaines, and then Capt. William D Sample assumed temporary command until Capt. Joseph Francis Bolger took over command on May 30.

Three days later, the Intrepid put to sea to test our new rudder and hull repairs. After some additional minor fixes we sailed across the bay to Alameda, where we were packed to the gunnels with troops, trucks, planes and all sorts of cargo that filled the flight and hangar decks. They also filled our sacks when Operation Hot Bunks was implemented. This put a sweaty passenger in my bunk while I was on watch, which always made the sheets hot and clammy. Thank God, it only lasted four days, until we unloaded our human and military cargo at Pearl.

During the passage from the States, the Intrepid suffered steering problems and a burned-out reduction gear on the No. 2 propeller shaft. After a quick, in-and-out dry-dock visit at Pearl, we were back in the ferry business, headed for Eniwetok with a relief air group's planes and pilots plus other critically needed supplies.

BURNT OUT REDUCTION GEAR ENROUTE. ARRIVED AT P.H. JUNE 15. - WENT INTO DRYDOCK TO HAVE REDUCTION GEAR FIXED JUNE 23, LEFT P.H. FOR ENIWETOK WITH RELIEF AIR GROUP AND SUPPLIES JUNE-2 ARRIVED AT ENIWETOK JULY 4- LEFT ENIWETOK WITH SOLDIERS FROM " AND WOUNDED FROM SAIPAN JULY 12 - ARRIVED AT P.H. WENT INTO DRY DOCK TO HAVE REDUCTION GEAR FIXED

The Intrepid, loaded to the gunnels, ferrying cargo and personnel to Pearl Harbor.

After catapulting the planes at Eniwetok, we on-loaded wounded soldiers, sailors and marines... casualties from the battle for Saipan.

Back in Pearl Harbor, and back in dry dock to repair the reduction gear, it took weeks of fixing, adjusting and testing before the Intrepid was shipshape and ready for fast carrier duty again.

During this time, Air Group 18 landed aboard, led by Cmdr. William E. Ellis.

On Aug. 16, we left Pearl for Eniwetok to join up with Task Group 58. Once under way, we celebrated the first anniversary of the ship's commissioning starting with divine services early in the morning and followed by a soup-to-nuts or, in reality, a fruit-cocktail-to-cigars, mid-day meal, provided under the watchful eyes of Cmdr. Henry H. Karp.

One of the ship's airplane elevators, raised to about four feet above the hangar deck, made a good roomy stage for the band and other performers., who appeared to be sober. Folding chairs, set in rows, formed the theater.

The Happy Hour celebration started with a concert by the ship's band with Chief Frederick conducting Sousa's "Semper Fidelis," Romberg's "My Hero," Gould's "Pavanne" and Van Boskerck's "Semper Paratus."

AUG 16 - LEFT P.H. FOR
ENIWETOK WITH AIR GRP.
18 - TO JOIN TASK FORCE
58 - 1ST ANNIVERSARY
OF SHIPS COMMISIONING.
AUG 24 - ARRIVED AT
ENIWETOK - CHANGED TO
THIRD FLEET, PUT IN TASK
FORCE 38.2
AUG 29 - LEFT ENIWETOK
IN TASK FORCE 38.2 FOR
RAIDS ON PALAU, AND
MINDANAO (PHILLIPENES)
SEPT-6 - FIRST STRIKE ON PALAU
BY FIGHTERS - NO AIR RESISTANCE
ONE PLANE HIT BY A.A. ALL

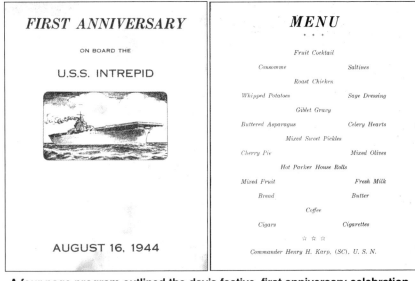

FIRST ANNIVERSARY	MENU
ON BOARD THE	* * *
U.S.S. INTREPID	Fruit Cocktail
	Consomme — Saltines
	Roast Chicken
	Whipped Potatoes — Sage Dressing
	Giblet Gravy
	Buttered Asparagus — Celery Hearts
	Mixed Sweet Pickles
	Cherry Pie — Mixed Olives
	Hot Parker House Rolls
	Mixed Fruit — Fresh Milk
	Bread — Butter
	Coffee
	Cigars — Cigarettes
	☆ ☆ ☆
AUGUST 16, 1944	Commander Henry H. Karp, (SC), U. S. N.

A four page program outlined the day's festive, first anniversary celebration. .

After greetings from Capt. Bolger, the party headed toward a lighter path with Frank Rehor M.C.- ing the "Intrepid Varieties," that featured Steve Maggio doing a Hindu dance, and "Short's Hungry Seven," performed by Bob Short, Nat Amend, Troy Fay, Gene Johnson, Bill Marles, John Schmid and Charley Shaha.

Troy Fay did a solo skit; George Jahn played the accordion. Amend, Shaha and Short were soon back on stage performing their rendition of a fan dance. Frank Rehor's, "Trombone Speciality" was a welcome change of pace, it included one of my favorite songs, "Back Home in Indiana."

Next, a wrestling match between Harry Mathews and Charley Shaha that was refereed by Al De Pinto.

Eugene Lilly, the band's great trumpet player, staged and supervised the festivities.

The ship's swing band, Gene Johnson directing, and with special arrangements by Bill Murphy, added a rousing finale, playing three favorites, "When Irish Eyes Are Smiling," "My Heart Isn't In It," and the foot-stomping hit, "Take It and Get."

In the year past, the Intrepid's young sailors had matured into a disciplined, proficient and experienced crew. We were ready, willing and able to get back into action and kick some more ass.

The U.S.S. Intrepid ship's band, Ulithi, 1945.

The ship's band serenaded us almost daily, as well as at shipboard ceremonies, happy hours and whenever appropriate. They played on the hangar deck, as we filed by in the chowline. It was good, in the groove, either as a concert band, swing orchestra, or as a jazz combo. Most of its members were Navy musicians, but a few were former professionals, like Eugene Lilly, a trumpeter with musical pit orchestras, and Frank Rohar, a trombone play-

Bill Murphy, M/3/c, clarinet & sax player.

er with swing bands. During G.Q. musicians took five, switching musical instruments for duty at their damage-control stations throughout the ship, ready to fight fires, stop leaks and help attend the wounded.

Left: Bill Murphy solos while jamming with the Intrepid's jazz combo.
Above: A pilot from Torpedo Squadron 8, hits the organ keys, playing what became the ship's fight song, the "Hawaiian War Chant."

The Third Fleet/T.G. 38.2

Eight days after leaving Pearl with Air Group 18, we arrived back at Eniwetok, now as part of the Third Fleet in Task Group 38.2. Designation of T.G. 58 or T.G. 38 changed, depending on which admirals were in command during a specific operation.

T.G. 58's leaders were Admirals Raymond Spruance and Marc Mitscher. T.G. 38 was lead by Admirals William (Bull) Halsey, Marc Mitscher and John McCain.

The ships, battle wagons, carriers, cruisers and destroyers were interchangeable under either Task Group designation, 58 or 38..

The ships in T.G. 38.2 were:

CARRIERS: Intrepid CV-11, Bunker Hill CV-17, Hancock CV-19, Independence CVL-22, and Cabot CVL-28

BATTLESHIPS: IOWA BB-61 AND NEW JERSEY BB-62

CRUISERS: San Diego CL-53, Vincennes CL-64, Houston-CL81, Miami CL-89, and Oakland CL-95

DESTROYERS: Cushing DD-97, Miller DD-535, The Sullivans DD-537, Stephen Potter DD-538, Tingey DD-538, Twining DD-540, Yarnall DD-541, Hickox DD-613, Colahan DD-658, Hunt DD-674, Lewis Hancock DD-675, Marshall DD-676, Stockham DD-683, Wedderburn DD-684, Halsey DD-686, Benham DD-796, and Uhlmann DD-867

Leaving Eniwetok on Aug. 29, 1944, T.G. 38 was headed for raids on Palau and Mindanao in the Philippines.

On Sept. 6, planes from all the 16 carriers operating within the 3 different Task Groups attacked Palau, meeting little air resistance.

One of our ship's planes was hit by enemy AA fire but it returned and landed safely.

Strikes by bombers, torpedo planes and fighters continued over the next two days, softening defenses in preparation for the coming invasion of Peleliu Island.

At 1630 on Sept. 8, T.G. 38 shifted course towards Mindanao in the Philippines, proceeding at 25 knots in order to arrive in time to launch early morning strikes against targets in the Davoa Gulf. Again, our planes met with very little air resistance, but the enemy AA fire was intense. There weren't any heavy shipping targets in the area, only 50 small sampans, which were sunk by destroyers.

RETURNED SAFELY.
SEPT-7 STRIKES MADE BY BOMBERS, TORPEDO BOMBERS, AND FIGHTERS
SEPT. 8- SAME AS PREVIOUS DAY - 1630 STARTED ON COURSE FOR MINDINAO AT 25 KNOTS IN ORDER TO ARRIVE IN TIME TO LAUNCH FIRST STRIKE IN EARLY MORNING SEPT-9-10- HIT DAVOA WITH PLANES - VERY LITTLE AIR RESISTANCE - HEAVY A.A. FIRE. NO SHIPPING EXCEPT 50 SAMPANS WHICH WERE SUNK BY D.D.s SEPT. 11- REFUELING - NO

In C.I.C. and throughout the ship, it was more or less routine with four hours on/eight-off as normal watch sections with occasional brief calls to general quarters due to snooping bogies.

On the 11th, we pulled back for fueling, hooking up with the marvelous sea train of tankers that were always near when needed.

After refueling, course was set for Samar, Leyte and the southern tip of Luzon for a dawn air attack against ground and shipping targets.

Results: Some Jap ships hit, left burning and probably sunk. Air resistance still light. One Betty downed by Independence's C.A.P. Another bogey closed within 12 miles and was driven away.

In an attack by planes the next morning during G.Q., one Jap Francis was downed by the C.A.P.

During our routine, predawn G.Q. on Sept. 13, one Francis was shot down by the C.A.P.

The main targets for Intrepid's planes were Negros and Sabu islands. Resistance was heavy this day and we lost 3 planes while downing 6 Japs in the air. We destroyed 28 on the ground, with 18 probables plus 8 more damaged planes. One ship was sunk, 11 were damaged and left burning.

Our pilots' summation: *"Targets were given a good going-over today."*

STRIKES - STARTED ON C's.
FOR SAMAR Is., LEYTE Is, AND
SOUTHERN TIP OF LUZON Is.
IN. N. PHILLIPINES FOR DAWN
ATTACK - ++
SEPT. 12 - PLANES HIT GROUND
TARGETS AND SHIPPING - SOME
SHIPS LEFT BURNING (PROBABLY
SUNK). 1 BT JAP PLANE (BETTY)
SHOT DOWN BY C.A.P. OF.
INDEPENDENCE. 2000 ANOTHER
JAP PLANE CAME WITHIN 12 MI. BUT
44 PRISONERS TAKEN
WAS DRIVEN OFF. OFF CAPTURED JAP SHIP.
SEPT. 13 - DURING MORNING G.Q.
ATTACKED BY JAP PLANES -

ONE (FRANCIS) SHOT DOWN
BY C.A.P. 12 MILES FROM Us.
CHIEF TARGETS FOR STRIKES NEGROS Is
SABAU Is. - RESISTANCE HEAVY - WE LOS
3 PLANES - OUR PILOTS SHOT DOWN 6
JAP PLANES, DESTROYED 28 ON GROUND,
18 PROBABLE ON GROUND, 8 DAMAGED.
SHIPS - 1 SUNK AND 11 DAMAGED AND
LEFT BURNING. TARGETS GIVEN A GOOD
GOING OVER.
SEPT. 14 - STRIKES ON TARGETS BUT
RESISTANCE NULL AND TARGETS SCARCE.
SEPT. 15 - SET COURSE FOR PALAU
FOR RENDEVOUS WITH REST OF TASK
FORCE. TODAY D-DAY ON PALAU.

Strikes launched on the 14th found targets scarce and no resistance.

The next day, Intrepid set course for Palau to rendezvous with the Task Group prior to the invasion. We were on standby duty to provide a few support strikes. Again, no air resistance.

On Sept. 19th, T.G. 38 set course for Manila, launching the first strikes on targets in Manila two days later.

The first day results were very successful.

The Intrepid's fighter squadron shot down 23 planes, and destroyed and damaged more on the ground.

Three ships were sunk; four were damaged and probably sunk.

The next day was stormy, with rain, high winds and rough seas. There were few attacks on the task group by hostile planes. Our C.A.P. downed one bogey and a couple more were downed by fighters from the other carriers' C.A.P.s.

Considering the weather conditions that our planes were operating in, the results of their strikes, which included Clark Air Base, were rather good. Air operations had to be halted at noon as the foul weather became even fouler.

One Jap plane was downed by one of our fighters; 18 planes were destroyed on the ground with 13 more damaged; 3 ships were sunk, 4 more were probably sunk, and 5 were damaged and left burning.

SEPT 16 - 18 - STANDBY AT PALAU, FEW SUPPORTING STRIKES FOR THE INVASION - NO AIR RESISTANCE SEPT 19 - SET COURSE FOR MANILLA. SEPT 21 - FIRST STRIKE ON MANILLA - STRIKES VERY SUCCESSFUL 23 PLANES SHOT DOWN BY OUR FIGHTERS, SOME DESTROYED AND DAMAGED ON GROUND - SHIPS - 3 SUNK 4 DAMAGED 4 PROBABLY SUNK SEPT 22 - WEATHER VERY POOR, RAIN, WIND, AND ROUGH AS HELL. FEW ATTACKS BY JAP PLANES, ONE SHOT DOWN BY OUR C.A.P., COUPLE MORE SHOT DOWN BY OTHER CAPS ON STRIKES PLANES DID VERY WELL

CONSIDERING WEATHER. 1 JAP PLANE IN AIR 18 DESTROYED ON GROUND; 13 ON GROUND — 3 SHIPS SUNK, 4 PROBABLY SUNK 5 DAMAGED AND LEFT BURNING SEPT. 23 - FUELING OFF MINDANAO, ULATOWSKI PICKED UP BY D.D. AFTER 9 DAYS IN LIFE RAFT. SEPT 24 - HIT SABU, CEBES AND CORON BAY - MANY SHIPS HIT SUNK, BURNING. NO AIR RESIST- ANCE. 1 PLANE SHOT DOWN BY OUR CAP. ABOUT 12 MI. FROM SHIP. SEPT. 25 - ON THE WAY TO SIAPAN, FOR SUPPLIES. SEPT. 28 - ARRIVED AT

S ept. 23: while refueling off Mindanao, the task group practically sailed over Ens. Dan Weaver and Ed Ulatowski, an Intrepid photographer. Nine days previously, they had been launched from the Intrepid on a pre-invasion photo-reconnaissance mission.

When their plane developed engine trouble, Ensign Weaver made a water landing, and he and Ulatowski got into the inflatable raft. They had been floating around until a lookout on the destroyer Dortch spotted their raft. The Dortch picked them up and later transferred them back to the Intrepid, where both fully recovered and after a couple of days in sick bay, returned to duty.

Ed Ulatowski, is transferred back to the Intrepid from the destroyer Dortch after 9 days in a life raft.

The next day, strikes continued on Sabu, Cebes and Cordon Bay. Many ships were hit, sunk and left burning, and there was little or no air resistance. One Jap plane was shot down by our C.A.P. about 12 miles away.

It is one hell of a thrill when you've been tracking a bogey on radar and plotting his bearing and distance to establish his course and speed. You can hear the fighter director officer's orders as he vectors a fighter onto the enemy's tail. As the fighter pilot closes in, and sees the plane, you hear his excited report, "Tally ho!" Then comes a short wait, which seems long, until the final jubilant: "Splash! Splash one Betty!"

You, and everyone in C.I.C. cheers loudly, if it was the only bogey on the screen; silently, if you are in the midst of tracking and intercepting additional incoming raids.

One element that made each *Tally ho!* and *Splash!* a vivid experience was the sound, the drama, of those stark, terse radio transmissions as they burst from a crackling bulkhead speaker.

As each triumphant cry pierced the air, your ears and heart were filled with abundant joy and pride in your ship and the brave pilots who flew from it.

One of my most horrible memories was hearing a wounded fighter pilot trying to make it back from a mission in his shot-up plane. Radar plots of his position started about 75 miles out and were closing. Radio contact was constant, and all were listening intently as the the fighter direction officer was talking him in, giving bearings, assurances and a heap of encouragement.

"We have you on the screen, keep on coming, maintain your course, only 40 miles to go. Stay alert. We'll get you home. Your can make it."

The pilot's voice was growing weaker. Suddenly, his woeful voice came blaring over the speaker, "I'm going down, going down, going..."

His dying words reverberated throughout C.I.C., followed by the longest, most agonizing, sorrowful scream. Sometimes, I almost hear it again, and it reminds me of the pilot's valiant courage as he struggled trying to make it back to the ship.

And he nearly did. Our last plot had him only 30 miles from possible rescue by a destroyer. One was dispatched to search the crash area, but didn't find a trace of him or his plane.

With a break in the action, the Intrepid set course for Saipan, which had been under American control since early July when after five weeks of fierce fighting, the Japs finally surrendered.

From the ship's anchorage at Saipan, you could see remains of the sugar refinery on the shoreline. It was the only visible large building; everything else had been leveled during the pre-invasion pounding by carriers' dive bombers and salvos from ship's big guns.

After taking on bombs, the Intrepid shoved off for Ulithi to stock up on food supplies. After two days at anchor, a typhoon struck and the fleet upped anchor and headed for open seas to ride it out.

Riding out a typhoon on a carrier is anything but tranquil, but compared with doing it on a destroyer, it rates as pure heaven. Those poor destroyer sailors – their ship was under water so much of the time that they should have been earning submarine pay. The destroyer's bow would rise up, plunge deeply into a huge wave and disappear, until it rose up again and plunged once more. It was an eerie and frightful sight that aroused deep compassion for the ship and its crew.

The Intrepid wasn't exactly steady as the Rock of Gibraltar: it had erratic hull movements in these churning, mammoth waves. While standing aft on the hangar or flight deck, you could see the bow doing a snake dance, twisting sideways and up and down at the built-in deck expansion plates. Without this give-and-take at the expansion plates, the stress could cause cracks in the ship's hull.

Unusually rough seas also played havoc with maintaining a full compliment of men to staff watch sections. Usually, about half were able to make it, while the other half remained horizontal, either in their sacks with a bucket, or with their head stuck in a trough puking.

I was fortunate and rode out storms, with only a slight headache; and I never got seasick.

147

The Third Fleet/T.G. 38.2

On the dog watch (midnight to 4 a.m.) that stormy night, I sat opposite Ensign Smith trading good-natured barbs – "you're gonna go before I do, sir." Nearly half of our half–watch section had departed, succumbing to green gills and the heaves. I felt a bit queasy, but started chomping away on a greasy horse-cock sandwich (a couple of slices of salami on dried-out white bread), daring Smith to dig in and join me. Being a good sport, he accepted and we both managed to keep it down and remain on duty until relieved by the next watch.

After the seas calmed, the ship returned to Ulithi and continued taking on food stores.

Oct. 6: course was set for the islands south of Japan. The Japanese fleet was reported out of port. There was still no real air opposition. Two planes were shot down early in the morning. These attacks didn't interfere with the strikes launched against Okinawa, sinking many ships.

During daytime, radar screens were relatively free of bogeys. After midnight, we started picking up a few snoopers. They were using harassment tactics, not intending to attack but to keep track of the ships and to keep crews on the alert and deprive them of sleep.

While we were refueling the next day, they kept up the pressure with a continuous stream of snoopers. During this time, five or six were shot down near the task group.

They were learning and using different air tactics, like dropping windows, small strips of foil, which bounced back confusing radar signals, making them look like multiple planes, rather than a single one. We quickly learned to read the window pips, especially on the S.M. radar's R scope, which allowed you to select and zoom in on a specific five-mile area. Being able to read windows was essential when working on interceptions with our night fighters. This was usually a one-on-one combat condition with the Jap pilot trying to evade the pursuing Corsair F4U that was closing on his tail. The Corsair pilot always won!

When they started timing air attacks to hit the fleet while our C.A.P. was landing at sunset, it became standard procedure to launch our night fighters well before the daytime C.A.P. landed.

The closer the fleet got to Japan, the more optimistic we were about finding and engaging the enemy fleet. We were looking forward to catching Japan's Imperial Navy. Confident that we would annihilate it in battle, sending its ships to the bottom of the Pacific.

The next day, our ship's planes hit Formosa's warehouses, hangars, airstrips, docks and shipping, hard and heavy. Our F6F and F4U fighter pilots had a field day destroying a total of 46 planes in dogfights and 10 large freighters and cargo ships, as well as many small ships.

The action was intense, both in the air around and on board ship. In C.I.C. we were picking up a sky-full of bogies, tracking them, and vectoring pilots on interceptions. One pimply-faced pilot, who looked younger than me, usually hung out in C.I.C., always complaining, "I'll never become an ace. How can I, if I don't get to fly?" This day, he was flying – and bagged his first two Zeros in combat.

The following is a portion of the grand total for the day's activity between 1730 and 2100 hours: during this period 11 of the 46 were downed by our C.A.P.; 3 downed by our night fighters; 2 blasted out of the sky by our ship's gunners; 6 shot down by our destroyer screen's gunners; 3 more shot down by other ships in our task group.

Total destroyed by our T.G. during those three-and-a-half intense hours alone: 25. Five minutes after we secured from G.Q. it sounded again and we were at our battle stations until all clear sounded at 0300.

Throughout this time of almost constant attack, the mission of some bogies was solely harassment to create confusion and a diversion from the others that came in to attack. The Intrepid dodged two or three torpedoes, one hit sideways and exploded after bouncing off the hull. But the ship was essentially unscathed, suffering no damage either from torpedoes or strafing runs.

During the night action, our sharpshooting ship's gunners were credited with one more kill for a total of three, making the day's total 49.

On the 13th, our strikes continued despite very poor weather conditions, without encountering enemy air resistance.

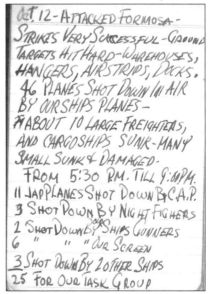

Oct. 12 - ATTACKED FORMOSA -
STRIKES VERY SUCCESSFUL - GROUND TARGETS HIT HARD - WAREHOUSES, HANGERS, AIRSTRIPS, DOCKS.
46 PLANES SHOT DOWN IN AIR BY OUR SHIPS PLANES -
& ABOUT 10 LARGE FREIGHTERS, AND CARGOSHIPS SUNK - MANY SMALL SUNK & DAMAGED -
FROM 5:30 P.M. TILL 9:00 P.M.
11 JAP PLANES SHOT DOWN BY C.A.P.
3 SHOT DOWN BY NIGHT FIGHERS
2 SHOT DOWN BY SHIPS GUNNERS
6 " " " OUR SCREEN
3 SHOT DOWN BY 2 OTHER SHIPS
25 FOR OUR TASK GROUP

G. Q SECURED FOR 5 MINUTES
THEN BLEW AGAIN LASTED TILL
0300. DURING WHICH TIME MORE
PLANES CAME IN, WOULD ONLY
COME IN TO ABOUT 10 MILES AND
GO OUT AGAIN — DURING G.Q. WE
DODGED 2 OR 3 TORPEDOES — ONE
HITTING SIDEWAYS AND EXPLODING
AFTER IT BOUNCED OFF US — STRAFFED
A COUPLE OF TIMES AND SCHRAPNEL
THE 2 PLANES SHOT DOWN BY
SHIPS GUNNERS TONIGHT BROUGHT
THE GRAND TOTAL TO 48 PLANES
SHOT DOWN BY THE SHIP TODAY.
CORRECTION — SHIPS GUNNERS GIVEN
CREDIT FOR 1 MORE TOTAL 49

OCT. 13 — STRIKES CONTINUED BUT
WEATHER VERY POOR — NO AIR
RESISTANCE OVER TARGET — ATTACKED
AGAIN ABOUT 1930. CRUISER HIT BY
TORPEDO IN OTHER TASK GROUP. WAS
TAKEN IN TOW — FEW PLANES SHOT
DOWN BY OTHER TASK GROUPS —
ATTACK BROKEN UP IN ABOUT 1½ HRS.
OCT 14. FIGHTER SWEEP OF 24 PLANES
+ 12 BOMBERS ONLY STRIKE TODAY
VISABILITY OVER TARGET POOR — NO AIR RESIST-
ANCE Ə AT ABOUT 3:30 (1530) 30-40
JAP PLANES ATTACKED OUR TASK GRP.
OUR SHIPS C.A.P. SHOT DOWN AT LEAST
22 OF 34 PLANES SHOT DOWN BY
OUR TASK GRP. BETWEEN 330 & 4:15 (1530 - 1615)

A Jap attack on our task force began at 1930 and lasted for about one and a half hours. A cruiser in one of the other task groups was struck by a torpedo and taken in tow. The other two task groups were getting most of the enemy's attention.

The next day, the only strike the Intrepid launched had 24 fighters and 12 dive bombers. Visibility over the target was poor, and they met no air resistance. Back on the ship, things got lively in C.I.C. around 1530, when radar picked up a large group of bogies. You could tell from the size of the pip that there were some 40 to 50 planes attacking.

The Intrepid's Squadron 18 fighters shot down at least 22 of the 34 planes downed by our task group during the 45 minute air battle.

We remained at our battle stations until midnight because of pesky harassment by snoopers. After securing from G.Q., a night fighter from the carrier Independence splashed a snooping flying boat.

The Intrepid spent the next day refueling, and on the 16th we launched long-range search patrols, trying to locate the Jap fleet. Just before sunset, they were spotted about 200 miles from us. It was too late to launch an air attack, but we hoped to catch them in the morning. They got away, making a high speed retreat to Kyushu in lower Japan. During the day, while searching for the fleet, our air patrols encountered and shot down quite a few planes.

G.Q. CONTINUED TILL ABOUT MIDNIGHT - JAP PLANES WERE USING HECKLING TACTICS AFTER G.Q. SECURED ONE 4 ENGINE JAP FLYING BOAT SHOT DOWN BY ONE OF INDEPENDENCE'S NIGHT FIGHTERS. OCT. 15 - FUELING OCT 16 - SENT OUT PATROLS TO TRY AND LOCATE JAP FLEET WHICH WERE SUPPOSED TO BE OUT OF PORT FOR A CHANGE; JAP FLEET SIGHTED 200 MILES FROM US JUST BEFORE SUNSET - TOO LATE TO SEND AN ATTACK. HOPED TO CATCH THEM IN THE MORNING, BUT DURING THE NIGHT THE MADE KNOTS TO KYUSHU (LOWER JAPAN) AND

GOT AWAY. PATROLS PATROLS DURING THE DAY SHOT DOWN QUITE A FEW JAP PLANES. OCT. 17 - MORE LONG RANGE PATROLS - BUT NO JAP SHIPS SIGHTED. OCT 18 — LAUNCHED STRIKES AT NORTHERN LUZON - JUST T.G. 38.2 - NO AIR OPPOSITION, SOME PLANES DESTROYED ON GROUND - 4 LARGE TRANSPORTS SUNK - NUMEROUS SMALL SHIPS AND BOATS SUNK OR BURNING. OCT 19 - FUELING OCT 20 - STAND BY FOR AIR COVERAGE ON THE INVASION OF PHILLIPINES

Meanwhile, Mindanao, Leyte and Cebu were being pounded by land-based bombers and planes from the 18 escort carriers in Adm. T. F. Sprague's Task Group 77.4 (Part of the Seventh Fleet).

On Oct. 17, Admiral Davison's T.G. 38.4 attacked Luzon while more unsuccessful long-range patrols in search of Japan's fleet were launched by the Intrepid.

On Oct. 18, T.G. 38.2 attacked northern Luzon and in addition to some planes destroyed on the ground, four large transports were sunk, along with numerous smaller ships. The next day, the Intrepid pulled back, taking on fuel and aviation gas.

On the 20th, the Intrepid was on standby duty, taking part in the air strikes provided by all fleet and escort carriers in support of the invasion of the Philippines, which began, this day, on the east coast of Leyte.

Admiral Kincaid's Seventh Fleet, made up mostly of the older battle wagons and cruisers, was providing the heavy naval bombardment and landing ships for the invasion.

There was light fighting on the beaches as the Japs retreated to prepared positions and dug in to await reinforcements.

Later in the day, the supreme commander, Gen. Douglas MacArthur, made good on his famous "I shall return" promise. This was the photo-op the general had been waiting for: MacArthur,

General Douglas, "I shall return" MacArthur, wading ashore at Leyte.

carefully attired in a newly starched uniform, looked elegant as he emerged from a landing craft. The only problem was that the LST got stuck some yards off the beach, and he had to wade through knee-deep water as photographers clicked away, capturing this historic moment.

Another problem was that MacArthur was pissed, and it showed in the photos. He insisted they reshoot him in a fresh uniform. However, when the two photos were compared, his aides convinced the General that his aura in the first picture was much stronger, one of determination, and that picture was released to the press.

The next day's strikes were aimed at the Philippine Islands of Leyte, Negros, Cebu and Sabu: 2 planes were downed in air combat; 19 destroyed on the ground; 3 ships sunk.

On Oct. 22, long-range search patrols for the Jap Fleet were renewed and continued through the next day, but it wasn't until Oct. 24 that the Fleet was finally sighted in the waters off the coast of Mindanao.

Our T.G. 38.2 was operating alone, with only the Intrepid and Cabot supplying the air power. The Bunker Hill and Hancock were temporarily detached.

For much of the day we cruised in the San Bernardino Straits area, within 25 miles of land. Being that close, virtually surrounded by land on three sides, made it difficult for radar operators to pick up any low-flying bogies. It was not only difficult it was scary, too. We were used to being able to scan a full 360 degrees without any close land showing on our radar screens.

However, the Intrepid was in a good position to launch an attack on Admiral Kurita's Central Force ships. The submarines that first reported them had already sent three of Kurita's cruisers down with their torpedoes.

> Oct. 21 – SUPPORTING STRIKES ON LEYTE, NEGROS, CEBU, SABU. 2 PLANES SHOT OUT OF AIR 19 ON GROUND 3 SHIPS SUNK.
> Oct. 22 – CONTINUATION OF LONG RANGE SEARCH PATROLS FOR JAP FLEET
> Oct 23 – SAME AS PREVIOUS DAY WITHOUT ANY RESULTS.
> Oct. 24 AT LAST – JAP FLEET SIGHTED IN THE WATERS IN BETWEEN PHILLIPINE IS. OFF N. COAST OF MINDORO. OUR TASK GROUP WAS OPERATING ALONE. ALSO BUNKER HILL + HANCOCK TEMPORARLY DETACHED, PLANES FROM OUR SHIP MADE STRIKES

We threw everything we had at the enemy force of 4 battleships (two of the Yamato, superbattleship class), 8 cruisers and 13 destroyers.

Our pilots reported the most intense antiaircraft flack ever fired at them. Even the superbattleships were using their 18-inch guns as AA batteries. Many shells contained phosphorous, which was still smoldering in the wings of our planes when they landed back on the ship.

Our ship's AA fire was also intense and accurate, thank God, downing five attacking planes initially, then one more later.

The medical alcohol – scotch – flowed freely in the pilots' ready rooms later that day. There was good reason for celebrating. The results from air attacks on Kurita's Center Force were impressive: 2 battleships hit with multiple bombs and torpedoes. One, the superbattleship, *Musashi,* last seen dead in the water, listing by the bow, later went down. The other battleship was seen with fires burning on the fantail; 1 cruiser, believed sunk; 1 destroyer, probably sunk.

Our Air Group 18's losses: 3 dive bombers and 3 torpedo planes.

At 1600, Admiral Ozawa's Northern Force was sighted, 300 miles north. The initial report indicated that the Northern Force consisted of two battleships and four carriers, accompanied by a screen of destroyers.

There was a second, then a third, report on the number and types of Jap ships. The latest report listed one carrier, two light carriers, one

THE AA FIRE WAS INTENSE & ACURATE - APPARENT RESULTS - 2 BBs HIT WITH BOMBS & TORPEDOES - ONE BB WHEN OBSERVED AT DUSK WAS LISTING IN THE BOW & DEAD IN THE WATER, THE OTHER BURNING ON FANTAIL. ALSO ONE CA BELIEVED SUNK & POSSIBLY 1 DD. - WE LOST 3 BOMBERS & 3 TORPEDO PLANES. 5 JAP PLANES SHOT DOWN. 0830 - TORPEDO DEFENSE / MORE SHOT DOWN. 1600 - ANOTHER JAP TASK FORCE 300 MILES NORTH SIGHTED & CONSISTING OF ABOUT 2 BBs 3 CVs 4 CAs DDs. SO WE SHOVED OFF TO MEET THEM - ENROUTE MEET TURK TG 38.2.

OCT 25. LAUNCHED STRIKES WITH OTHER CARRIERS. AT PRESENT RESULTS BELIEVED AS FOLLOWS. 1 CV HIT W/ TORPEDOES, BOMBS - PROBABLY SUNK, 1 CVL ALMOST SURE SUNK 1 CVL - DAMAGED - PROBABLE, 2 CAs HIT HARD 2 DD PROBABLE SUNK, AS BATTLE GROUP OF OUR BBs CAs DDs MOVED UP TO FINISH OFF THEM GOT ORDERS TO GO SOUTH AND HELP 7TH FLEET WHO WERE BATTLING JAP TASK FORCE. WE LEFT WITH THEM AS BATTLE LINE CARRIER. OCT 26 - BATTLE WAGONS ETC. WENT TO FINISH OFF SOME JAP CRIPPLED SHIPS WHILE WE MADE STRIKES ON

escort carrier, one battleship, two cruisers, one light cruiser and seven destroyers.

The Third Fleet headed north to meet Ozawa's force. At dawn, planes from all the fast carriers launched attacks, with wave after wave of strafing fighters and torpedo and dive bombers hitting and sinking Halsey's special vendetta targets, the enemy aircraft carriers, along with the other ships.

Our air group 18's planes were among the first to arrive and press the attack, scoring torpedo and bomb hits. Initial reports on Ozawa's Northern Force indicated: 1 large carrier hit with torpedoes and bombs – most surely sunk; 1 light carrier also most surely sunk; 1 light carrier, damaged and probably sunk; 2 cruisers, hit hard; 2 destroyers, probably sunk.

(According to a later report, all four of Ozawa's carriers were sunk.)

As Admiral Halsey's Battleline Force–T.F. 34's battleships, cruisers and destroyers were assembled, preparing to chase and finish off Admiral Ozawa's Northern Force of retreating ships, orders were received from Admiral Nimitz directing Halsey's newly formed Battleline Force to head south to aid Kincaid's Seventh Fleet, whose only air support was supplied by Taffy-3, which consisted of three groups of small escort carriers, destroyers and destroyer escorts.

T.G. 38's other ships remained and continued pounding Ozawa's retreating ships, while the Intrepid joined the newly formed group of battleships, cruisers and destroyers as the battleline carrier and proceeded with these big boys at near top speed of 31 knots, south toward the San Bernardino Straits.

Initially, after the devastating punishment it received, Kurita's Center Force had turned away. Halsey believed their withdrawal was permanent and should they resume on their former course, he was confident Kincaid's Seventh Fleet ships could handle them. During the night, Kurita did reverse course and once again headed for San Bernardino Straits.

Describing the Battle of Leyte Gulf, the biggest naval battle ever, would take a book in itself. The following, a short synopsis, tells another part of this historic battle:

Admiral Kincaid ordered Admiral Oldendorf to deploy his battleships at the northern end of Surigao Strait. The West Virginia, Maryland, California, Tennessee, Mississippi, Pennsylvania and seven cruisers took up station and waited for Nishimura's Southern force.

Shortly after midnight, on Oct. 25, P.T. boats and destroyers launched an attack on Nishimura, sinking one battleship, two destroyers and damaging others without any harm to themselves.

Nishimura's undamaged ships continued on their course and were met by the old battleships, executing the classic naval maneuver of "crossing the T," and pouring salvos from their 14-and 16-inch guns onto the enemy's soon hapless ships, forcing the remaining surviving vessels to change course and retreat.

Meanwhile, Admiral Shima's force, which was scheduled to join and support Nishimura, saw what was happening and retreated without firing a shot.

Throughout this entire action, only one U.S. destroyer was hit by enemy fire. This was an especially gratifying victory, won by those old battleships that were put out of action during the attack on Pearl Harbor.

While the Intrepid's task group were attacking Ozawa's Northern force, we intercepted radioed pleas from Admiral Sprague for help. Taffy Three was made up of three escort carrier groups, and it had two Admirals named Sprague. Taffy One, with Rear Adm. Thomas Sprague, the Intrepid's first skipper, had six escort carriers, three destroyers and five destroyer escorts.

Taffy Two, with Rear Adm. Felix Stump, had six escort carriers, four destroyers and five destroyer escorts.

Taffy Three, with Rear Adm. Clifton Sprague, had six escort carriers, three destroyers and four destroyer escorts.

While off the coast of Samar, Clifton Sprague's Taffy Three escort carriers were launching invasion support strikes against targets on Leyte when a scout plane reported 4 enemy battleships, 7 cruisers and 11 destroyers just over the horizon, heading for them.

Soon the seas around Taffy Three were dotted with geysers of water from the salvos of exploding shells. Adm. Clifton Sprague managed to launch his carriers' remaining planes, armed with everything they had – bombs, torpedoes and even depth charges.

Clifton Sprague then took his carriers to cover, behind rain squalls and a smoke screen, ordering his destroyers and destroyer escorts to attack with torpedoes. They raised hell, darting between the Jap ships at close range, laying a fish into a cruiser before one destroyer, Johnston, was hit by a salvo and sent to the bottom.

Jap gunners now had the range and were zeroing in, pounding the little carriers with their big guns. The escorts, converted merchant ships, had no armor, only thin steel-plate hulls. Some shells were passing right through the ships, in one side and out the other, without discharging. Others, though, exploded, sinking one carrier and three destroyers.

Kurita mistakenly thought Taffy Three's attacking planes were from Halsey's more powerful Third Fleet and decided he must withdraw. Had Kurita stuck to the battle, he probably would have been able to annihilate Taffy Three, and then he would have been able to attack the troop transports and landing craft at Leyte's beachheads.

Adm. Thomas Sprague's Taffy One, operating farther south, was being hit by land-based planes from Davao in one of the first kamikaze attacks. One crashed into the escort carrier Santee. The next kamikaze, hit by AA fire while diving on Thomas Sprague's flagship, Suwanee, crashed into her flight deck, ripping a huge hole and causing numerous casualties.

Two hours later, after repairing the flight deck, Thomas Sprague's group fought off two more kamikaze attacks as it was steaming on a northeasterly course to help Taffy Three and launch strikes against Kurita's fleeing force. On the next day, just after noon, another kamikaze struck

Suwanee, causing major damage and a fire that burned for hours before being brought under control.

When Kurita retreated, land-based kamikaze attacks were launched against all the carriers, sinking four. Three of Adm. Stump's escort carriers suffered heavy damage.

These were among the first of the *Divine Wind* kamikaze attacks. The kamikazes, the new Japanese weapon of desperation, were suicide pilots who crashed their planes onto enemy ships for the glory of their Emperor.

While Kurita was retreating back through the San Bernardino Straits with the crippled remnants of his center force, carrier-based planes attacked it continuously until it finally steamed out of range.

Japan's Imperial Navy was battered and decimated by the severe losses: 4 carriers, 3 battleships, and 10 destroyers sunk, plus many other heavily damaged ships.

The Imperial Japanese Navy was no longer an effective force. Its only hope of battling the more powerful U.S. Navy rested in its new weapon, kamikazes.

It has been estimated that some 4,000 kamikazes sacrificed their lives during the 10 months that they operated before war's end.

Back on the Intrepid the next morning, Oct. 26, when Halsey's ships arrived in the San Bernardino area, there was little left for them to do except mop-up duty: sinking the cripples. While T.F. 34's battlewagons and cruisers finished off Kurita's derelicts, the Intrepid's planes attacked Kurita's retreating remnants.

Kamikazes believed they would gain a special place of honor at Yasukuni, the eternal resting place of ancient warriors who died in righteous warfare. Inspired by the legend of the divine wind, which saved Japan from the Mongols 700 years earlier, the first unit was formed on Oct. 19, 1944. They were promised "war god" status, which helped make their suicidal deaths easier to face. Shintoism provided belief that the dead live on as spirits, and Buddhism that life is transient and death is not the end of life. Before taking off, departing pilots would drink a cup of sake while facing the Emperor's palace.

A senior officer flew with them, staying well back to observe and record their loyalty. Some preferred crashing in the water, and were designated "chicken kamikazes."

The following day, while refueling, the carrier Hancock rejoined the Intrepid.

Over the next couple of days the Intrepid launched strikes supporting the Philippine invasion and our C.A.P. was busy downing snooping planes. The morning of Oct. 29 began with the splashing of three Jap planes and shortly after noon, our C.A.P. downed nine more. One kamikaze got through a hail of AA fire and was aiming at the Intrepid's flight deck. Fire from Gun Tub No.10's 20-millimeter battery, directed by Gun Captain Chavarrias, hit the diving plane, deflecting its path, preventing it from crashing onto the flight deck.

However, the plane's wing hit Gun Tub No. 10, enveloping it in flaming gasoline and killing 10 of the brave men who literally stuck to their guns. The flames were quickly extinguished and the dead and wounded were removed to sick bay.

Alfonso Chavarrias, gunners mate 3/c, a survivor of the sinking of the Lexington during the battle of the Coral Sea, was killed with nine of the Intrepid's black steward's mate gunners.

At 1700, while the funeral and burial-at-sea services were being conducted, C.I.C. picked up another raid. G.Q. was sounded, and during the attack, an additional seven planes were downed before we could resume the funeral service and say farewell to our fallen shipmates..

Two of the men in Gun Tub No.10 were eventually awarded the Navy Cross, the Navy's highest award for valor.

Alonso Swan, one of the black steward's mates who survived the inferno, was finally awarded the Navy Cross by former President Ronald Reagan in a ceremony on board the Intrepid on Nov. 3, 1993, some 49 years later.

On June 5, 2002, President George W. Bush awarded the Navy Cross posthumously to Alfonso Chavarrias' sister, in a White House ceremony. Chavarrias died while directing the gunners, strapped-in and firing his 20-millimeter cannon.

Alfonso Chavarrias
Gunners Mate 3/c

Chavarrias Presidential Citation:

"For extraordinary heroism while serving as captain of Gun Tub Number 10 while serving on USS INTREPID (CV 11) on 29 October 1944. Petty Officer Chavarrias was in charge of the 20-millimeter gun tub into which a Japanese suicide plane crashed. He remained at his station directing the fire of the guns until the plane struck, even though, throughout the end of the plane's dive, it was apparent that the plane was going to strike the gun tub. It is very probable that the fire from this gun tub prevented the Japanese plane from crashing into the flight deck. His heroic actions and devotion to duty resulted in his own death. By his outstanding display of decisive leadership, unlimited courage in the face of enemy attack and the utmost devotion to duty, Petty Officer Chavarrias reflected great credit upon himself and upheld the highest traditions of the United States Naval Service."

The Intrepid's fighter planes downed a total of 41 Jap planes this day and their strafing runs left many more enemy planes burning on the ground. They reported that the pilots were the best they had encountered.

> SHIP AND CRASHED INTO A 20MM. GUN TUB. GASOLINE FROM PLANE CAUGHT ON FIRE KILLING 10 OF THE GUNNERS AND INJURING ABOUT 2 X as MANY. DURING FUNERAL SERVICES AT 1700 ANOTHER ATTACK AND 1 MORE JAPS KNOCKED DOWN. THE STRIKES ON CLARK & NICHOLAS FIELDS ENCOUNTERED HEAVY AIR OPPOSITION. OUR SHIPS PLANES KNOCKED DOWN A TOTAL OF 41 TODAY - HIT HANGERS, AIR STRIPS, AND STRAFFED & LEFT MANY PLANES ON GROUND BURNING - OUR PILOTS REPORTED THAT THE JAP PILOTS TODAY WERE THE BEST THEY HAD ENCOUNTERED

A Salute to Air Group 18

The following is excerpted from the "History of Air Group Eighteen." Told in straight-forward, matter-of-fact language by one of them. It is a vivid account of a single day's action, which demonstrates the skill and courage of those magnificent men who flew from the Intrepid's deck.

"Oct. 29, 1944: The air group was depleted and exhausted, but Admiral Bogan had not had enough. The task force headed north for Luzon. On Sunday morning, 29 Oct., we had a total of 67 planes in the air. Clark Field was the objective of the fighter sweep and strike. They ran into a hornets-nest of Jap planes, accounting for 19 Jacks, Tojos, Zekes and Oscars, the bombers getting 4 Oscars. Our fighters lost Naughton, who was seen to water-land near Pollilo Island, and Mollenhauer, who unaccountably disappeared over Clark Field. Naughton was later reported safe.

"The second strike was getting ready to launch when general quarters sounded. All planes had just cleared the deck when the ship received a tremendous jolt. A Tojo came diving at the ship from out of the sun, sliced across the stern and exploded in the 20-millimeter gun tub aft of the No. 3 elevator.

"Our Negro mess attendants were manning these guns and never for an instant flinched. Fearlessly firing until they were hit, 10 of them were killed.

"Damage control soon extinguished the fire and announced that no serious damage had been done.

"Paying tribute to these gunners, the executive officer also spoke of the Air Group: 'It would be unjust not to mention the superb courage and stamina shown by personnel of our Air Group. For almost two months they have operated continuously against the enemy. The flying alone has been tough against strong enemy opposition. It has been magnificent.

"Our second strike ran into some angry Japanese defenders over Clark Field. Elmer Namoski dropped his bomb and then attempted to strafe a Tojo taking off. He was shot down with his rear-seat man, Graham. Pulling up to join the formation after the torpeckers had dropped, Rocky turned out to shoot at a Zeke. Soon after, he called out he was hit and would have to land.

"Returning to the ship, Joe Rubin announced he was wounded and would water-land. His plane had been badly riddled. Assisted by Kingsbury, who worked the controls by hand from the tunnel, Joe made a smooth water landing and he and his crew were picked up.

"Strike Two Charlie was launched at 1400. Bud Williams warned all the pilots in his division to stick together in case of trouble. Blouin, Harris and Van Dyke led the fighter escort and, in purely defensive fighting, they shot down seven Tojos, four Zekes and one Oscar In so doing, they doubtless saved many of our torpedo and bombing planes.

"It was later when Two Charlie returned and, just as the pilots approached the task group, they saw it plunge into a thick squall. While the formation circled on the outside, Blouin went in several times to give the ship directions on how to turn to get into the clear. But the soup got thicker. Finally, Blouin and most of the fighters and Preston and the bombers felt their way in and miraculously landed aboard safely. Clancy and Baker of the bombers didn't make it, but they located a destroyer and, zooming over the bow, they let down through the darkness until they hit the water. They were picked up with their crews, unhurt. It was splendid flying, plus plenty of luck.

"Bud Williams, knowing that his torpeckers would soon be out of gas, told them to line up behind him for a water landing. Bud landed first and waved the others in from his life raft, using oars for flags. All landed safely with their crews and, tieing their rafts up in pairs, they prepared for the night. This Goodyear fleet consisted of Williams, Miller, Dixon, Doyle, Koegler, Royce, Olson, Beeson, Johnson, Spalding, Jesperson, Schnack, St. John, Garber, Schmitz, Ursch, Bonner and Huber. They were wet and most of them seasick, but at 0230 a night fighter from the Independence spotted them. Soon, a destroyer hove into sight and hauled them over the side.

"Back on the Intrepid, there was bedlam. Planes from various carriers were nosing through the driving rain and mist, precariously feeling their way down to the heaving deck to land. One Hancock bomber, piloted by

A Salute to Air Group 18

Lt. John Edmonds, made a pass, badly shot up. He later tried to land, som-
ersaulted over the flight deck and finally hung his plane on one of the
antenna towers aft of the island, up-side down. The plane was burning
furiously, but Joe Riley the rear-seat-man crawled along the fuselage and
got out. Damage control put out the fire, but couldn't find Edmonds.
Soon, a dispatch came from a destroyer. They had seen a light flash in
the water and picked up pilot Edmonds, unhurt.

"Two of our fighter pilots were missing. Ensign Hedick and Lt. Bill
Thompson, one of the outstanding pilots who came to the air group
from VF(N)-78. Searches the following day failed to find them."

Air Squadron 18 fighter pilot, Lt. (jg) James "Buck" Newsome, checking his
F6F-Hellcat's instrument panel prior to take-off.

Five days before the squadron's reported action on Oct. 29th, Lt.
(jg) "Buck" Newsome was flying cover and attacking in the
strikes aimed at the Jap fleet off the North coast of Mindoro. My diary
notes: "The AA fire was intense and accurate." Buck Newsome was shot
down and was among the missing for 40 days before he was rescued
and returned to the States, where he met the Intrepid when she made
it back to San Francisco for repairs.

Buck was awarded the Distinguished Flying Cross for his valiant
action in the Battle of Leyte Gulf, along with 2 Air Medals for the numerous missions he flew against the enemy.

S kipping ahead to another kind of action in Air Group 18's splendid history:

"On 8 Nov., we turned toward Ulithi and, after running through another typhoon, reached that haven on the ninth. There are still no boats, there is no liberty. Discontent mounts. Our air crewmen are in working parties with the rest of ship's company, laboring night and day to bring aboard tons of ammunition and supplies. Heat is terrific.

"In desperation, a group of pilots spearheaded another assault on the beach and made it. They swilled beer all day and returned to the ship in a LCI, with Tom O'Conner and Rudy Van Dyke standing in the bow like Vikings, screaming insults at all the battleships they passed: 'What fleet do you belong to?' 'Are those guns real?' etc.

Several pilots from another air group, in the same boat, let it be known that their group had sunk the entire Jap fleet. They passed several remarks about the 'Queen of the Dry Docks.' and her 'green' air group. Duke Delaney quietly worked himself around beside one of these gentlemen and when he opened his mouth again, he hit him and knocked him 10 feet to the deck. Duke jumped on him and looking around said, 'Anyone else from his group here?'

"There apparently wasn't.

"Air Group 18 and the Intrepid have come a long way together since they first met. The air group will listen to no slurs on the name of their ship and hopes that Intrepid ship's company no longer considers Air Group 18 green."

The Intrepid's radarmen, along with the entire crew, had the utmost respect and admiration for A.G. 18's pilots, radiomen and gunners. They were all brave, valiant warriors, true heros who flirted with death, putting their asses on the line everytime they took off from the Intrepid's flight deck to battle the enemy.

Admiral "Bull" Halsey

1 November 1944.

Aboard Admiral Halsey's Flagship Off the Philippines

Correspondent Philip G. Reed, describing the United States Third Fleet victory against the Japanese quoted, Adm. William F. Halsey as saying: "The American Navy now rules the Western Pacific from the North Pole as far south as you want to go."

Excerpts:: from Reed's report:

"Stocky, four-starred commander of the Third Fleet was weary with fatigue but firmly buoyant over the accomplishments of his 'Phantom Force' that the Japanese radio claimed was destroyed off Formosa a bare 10 days ago. Reports of the action that he continued to receive as we talked caused him to comment happily. 'The Japanese may get away with two, maybe three or more units, but nothing we can't take in stride, nothing that will bother us.'

"Never has there been anything like (this battle) in naval history or warfare, for the number, power and variety of units in this action, and for distances involved, it stands alone. According to Halsey himself, it ranks with the Battle of Jutland.

"All branches of the United States Naval service – airplanes, surface ships, submarines – teamed up to achieve the victory, but the major share of credit must go to the carrier pilots under Vice Adm. Marc A. Mitscher.

"The enemy, apparently following the battle blueprint designed to interrupt the Leyte landings, aimed those three spearheads at the central Philippines section.

"It may have looked good on drawing boards, but it didn't work in battle. Neither Halsey or Kincaid, Seventh Fleet commander, waited for the Japanese plan to develop as written.

"Battleships and light escorting units waded into the southern force before they had a chance to get through Surigao Strait, the night of Oct. 24.

"The following morning, the 25th, planes opened their terrible assault on the central Japanese forces squirming their way through the narrow island passages between Cebu, Panay and Mindoro. Separate carrier groups personally directed by Mitscher deployed in flanking barrier northward off eastern Luzon. Its planes and ships' guns met and routed a full-throated air attack from Japanese carrier planes that had been staged from enemy flattops northward, reinforced by twin- engined land-based bombers. At least 150 Japanese planes were destroyed. None penetrated as far south as Leyte.

"Almost bare-decked Japanese carriers flowed on, apparently to rendezvous off East Luzon, where they expected to meet their planes coming out after refueling, spending the day at Luzon. Instead they met deadly swarms of American carrier planes speeding into dawn skies.

"Combined torpedo, dive-bomber attacks caught the Japanese by complete surprise. Their shattered forces poked their way through San Bernardino Strait. The morning of the 25th, they found clouds of planes from our carriers waiting for them.

"American hard-hitting warships were off eastern Luzon. Japanese units and carrier groups were trading punches in Leyte Gulf, 300 miles southward. We pounded on through the afternoon and night.

"General alarm startled us at 1 a.m.: far-away tracers arched through the darkness. Our cruisers and destroyers had been deployed around a crippled escort carrier off San Bernardino, as surrounding ships poured salvos into trapped Jap vessels.

"Suddenly a volcano of shower sparks hurled high against the horizon cloud bank. Great bunches of flame leaped high into the clouds and the smoke was inky black even in the darkness.

"A destroyer identified a vessel in the glare (before its death burst) as a cruiser of the Atago class. Ships of our force were hungrily in search of victims, but the sea was unbroken. The main body of the Japanese fleet was leaving their crippled to be killed."

Admiral "Bull" Halsey

A dmiral (Bull) Halsey was a smart, tough minded man of action who probably rubbed some fellow officers the wrong way, but he was universally admired, respected and even loved by enlisted men. He had an anchor tattooed on his shoulder and didn't, except for rare exceptions, trust anyone who didn't smoke, drink and cuss. Halsey was one of the only senior officers who ever stood up to pompous General MacArthur, disagreeing about a strategic tactic during a meeting with Admiral Nimitz.

He was heard to say this about MacArthur:"He's a self-advertising son-of-a-bitch."

At Ulithi, while Halsey was inspecting Intrepid's damage from two kamikaze hits, my friend, Marine corporal Tony Zollo, was on duty outside the wardroom entrance during a coffee break. Tony overheard Halsey say: 'There are no great men, only ordinary men capable of rising to great challenges. The crew of the Intrepid are such men.'

When leaving the wardroom, Halsey stopped, put his hand on Tony's shoulder and asked,"Who's your tailor?"

Tony replied,"I am,. sir, and I alter all the Marine's uniforms."

Tony took pride in his uniform, especially his summer tans. His shirt was tailored with two seams in the back, to make it formfitting.

Halsey was driven by his wrathful passion for wiping out the Japs. He

**Cpl. Tony Zollo,
Intrepid Marine.**

worked closely with Adm. Chester Nimitz in planning and executing a strategy designed to expedite victory. The Army had Patton in Europe; we had Bull Halsey in the Pacific.

After the war, when questioned about certain pithy statements he made, he said,"I stand by all that was said (about the Japanese). After that one successful sneak attack, panicky eyes here saw the monkey men as supermen. I saw them as nothing of the sort and I wanted my forces to know how I felt. I stand by the opinion given then, that the Japanese are bastards, and I stand by this one, too."

Admiral Halsey's Third Feet Flagship, the U.S.S. New Jersey, was like the admiral, tough and formidable. It was some 867 feet long and was armed with nine 16" guns, twenty 5" guns, fifty 20-millimeter guns and a crew 0f 2,700.

Unlike the carriers, with their wooden flight decks, the New Jersey was protected by thick 16-and 19-inch armor plate. During a kamikaze raid, one struck the Missouri, sister ship of the New Jersey, forward of the gun turrets. Our concerned fighter direction officer, Lt. Cmdr. Mitchell, queried the Missouri via radio,

"Black Bear...this is Lucky. How's it going?"

The prompt reply:"We're O.K. Lucky. Just piped, sweepers, man your brooms."

Battlewagons like the Missouri and New Jersey could take it as well as dish it out and, like the fast carriers, they too were fast. During the Battle of Leyte Gulf, when the Intrepid headed south as the battle-line carrier for the striking force of surface ships, it maintained a speed of 31 knots, which is about 36 miles per hour.

Legend has it that Halsey preferred Duggins Dew of Kirkentilloch, the mythical Scotch whiskey consumed by Horatio Hornblower.

Legend also has it that this was his favorite toast:

"I've drunk to your health in company.

I've drunk to your health alone.

I've drunk to your health so many times,

I've damn near ruined my own."

Supporting the Philippines Invasion

On Oct. 30, Vice Adm. Marc A. Mitscher was relieved of command of T.F. 38, replaced by Vice Adm. John S. McCain. Like Mitscher, McCain was a respected, skillful carrier tactician.

T.F. 38's three Groups continued the daily strikes against targets on Luzon and the nearby waters.

Highlights from T.F. 38's action activity: Planes from the task force's carriers destroyed some 400 enemy planes while losing 25.

On Nov. 6, the aircraft carrier Lexington was badly damaged by kamikazes.

On Nov. 11, planes from eight carriers attacked a convoy sinking four destroyers, one mine sweeper and five troop transports with nearly 10,000 men on board.

On the 14th, carrier planes attacked shipping near Manila. One cruiser and four destroyers were sunk.

On the 18th, one cruiser and three other vessels were sunk in Manila Bay.

On Nov. 25. seven carriers from T.G. 38.2 and T.G. 38.3 attack and sink two cruisers. Four U. S. carriers, including the Intrepid, were hit by kamikazes during the days action.

It was the worst damage suffered by our carriers, in one day, during any WW II battle.

WHEN THE LAST STRIKE CAME BACK TO LAND JUST BEFORE SUNSET, A HEAVY STORM CAME OVER SHIP AND SOME COULD NOT LAND - 18 HAD TO MAKE WATER LANDINGS - ALL BUT 2 PERSONNEL WERE PICKED UP NEXT DAY.

Oct. 30 - SEARCH FOR SURVIVORS. 2 JAP PLANES SHOT DOWN.

Oct 31. - FUELING

NOV-1ST. STAND BY

NOV-2ND - NOV-25TH - VARIOUS STRIKES IN THE PHILLIPINES - ON THE 25TH ATTACKED BY LARGE GROUP OF JAP PLANES

168

The Worst Day

A shrill order blared from the speaker: "Now hear this! General quarters! General quarters! All hands, man your battle stations!" Hear it we did, and I was at my battle station, in C.I.C., for long periods of time and didn't have time to keep up my diary notes in early November. These intense days are covered by one terse diary notation: "Various strikes in the Philippines–On the 25th attacked by large group of Jap planes."

The next page continues: "2 kamikazes crashed into us with bombs. We burned for a few hours and finally got fire under control and out. Many men killed and wounded–out of my division 32 Radar men killed." (A later count set the number at 26. The six other men killed were from another division.) These radarmen were my good buddies, we were close, standing watches, sharing life, and now death.

The following accounts of "The Worst Day" are from crew members, made during a memorial service held years later, on board the Intrepid, Nov. 25, 1994:

Tony Zollo, Corporal, U.S. Marine Corps

"I was a young marine aboard the Intrepid. My G.Q. post was at a .20-millimeter in gun tub No. 3 on the starboard side of the ship's island.

2 KAMAKAZIES CRASHED INTO US WITH BOMBS. WE BURNED FOR A FEW HOURS AND FINALLY GOT FIRE UNDER CONTROL AND OUT. MANY MEN KILLED & WOUNDED - OUT OF MY DIVISION 32 RADAR MEN KILLED SHOVED OFF FOR ULITHI, ENIWETOK, PEARL HARBOUR & FINALLY ARRIVED IN STATES DEC 20 - STARTED ON 21 DAY LEAVE - GOT HOME CHRISTMAS DAY. LEFT STATES ON FEB 20TH FOR PEARL HARBOR MAR. 3 LEFT PEARL FOR ULITHI. MAR 13 - ARRIVED ULITHI MAR 14. LEFT ULITHI

The Worst Day

"During the early morning hours of Nov. 25, 1944, the U.S.S. Intrepid was steaming off the east coast of central Luzon in the Philippines.

"The Intrepid was the flagship of Task Group 38.2, composed of the fleet carriers Intrepid and Hancock; the light carriers Independence and Cabot; the battleships Iowa and New Jersey; light cruisers Biloxi, Miami and Vincennes; and 17 Fletcher Class destroyers.

"The Intrepid carried the flag of Adm. Gerald Bogan. The New Jersey, was Adm. William F. (Bull) Halsey's Third Fleet flagship.

"T.G. 38.2, one of four groups that made up the famous Fast Carrier Task Force 38, was under command of Vice Adm. John S. McCain.

"Only one other of the four Groups, T.G. 38.3, was part of Task Force 38 at this time; the force was operating at half strength.

"Exactly one month before, the Intrepid and the other ships participated in history's largest naval battle, the Battle of Leyte Gulf, which destroyed the Japanese Navy as an effective fighting force.

"The Japanese high command had become desperate and resorted to suicide attacks against American warships, especially the carriers.

"Nov. 25, 1944, was that day in history when the U.S. carriers received their heaviest one-day damage. Four carriers were hit by kamikazes and bombs."

Ray Stone, Radarman 2/C

"At 0405, on Nov. 25, 1944, I was on duty in C.I.C. We picked up a bogey on radar, 49 miles out. Cmdr. Jim Winston, Admiral Bogan's staff fighter direction officer, whom it seems was always on duty, had gone to his cabin for a quick nap, after advising me to come wake him if I thought he was needed. I don't know why, but he always asked me, not one of our officers, to make the decision about if and when he was needed in C.I.C.

"His cabin had a small anteroom with a round table and a bottle of Scotch on it. After shaking him out of his slumber, he told me, 'Pour yourself a shot, throw it down, and make sure I'm on my feet before you leave.

"The bogey turned out to be a snooper, which closed in on the task group to within eight miles, turning away when it came under A.A. fire by the destroyers in the outer ring. It was tracked on radar until it dissapeared from the screen some 60 miles out.

"At 0640, the Intrepid launched its first strike of the day: 12 fighters, 9 dive bombers and 7 torpedo planes. Targets: three heavy cruisers, survivors of the Battle of Leyte Gulf, and an air base on Luzon.

"At 0723, G.Q. sounded as another snooper was detected 80 miles out. The plane turned away when chased by C.A.P. fighters and disappeared from the radar screen. G.Q. secured at 0755.

"At 0905, G.Q. sounded again when more bogeys were picked up, heading for the task group. The Hancock's C.A.P. fighters intercepted them, breaking up the attack. G.Q. secured at 0926. I was relieved on the S.M. radar, got some coffe and had a smoke.

"At 0930, the Intrepid landed planes from the first strike and launched the second strike of 10 fighters, 9 dive bombers and 8 torpedo planes. Twelve additional fighters were launched to take over C.A.P. duty over the ships and four additional fighters and two dive bombers were launched for antisnooper patrol duty."

Hank Scrocca, Quartermaster 2/C

"I was at my battle station on the navigation bridge, with Capt. Bolger, our commanding officer. Being high up in the island structure, I was able to see approaching enemy planes first-hand – an experience that I'll never forget.

"At 1215, a formation of unidentified planes was approaching at a distance of only 19 miles. G.Q. was sounded for the fifth time today. C.A.P. from the Hancock shot down two of the Jap planes.

" At 1223, the Intrepid ceased zig-zagging and steadied on a base course of southwest, when the task group turned into the wind.

"At 1227, the Intrepid started launching her third strike of the day: 12 fighters, 10 dive-bombers and 8 torpedo planes.

"C.I.C. informed Capt. Bolger that there were at least three Val dive bombers over the formation. They had either come in under the radar or had been mistaken for friendlies. The strike launch ceased, and at 1232 the antiaircraft guns opened fire. One Val was shot down about 3,000 yards off the starboard beam, and the C.A.P. splashed another.

"At 1233, a burning Jap plane disintegrated over the carrier Hancock with parts and the plane's main body crashing into the flight deck, causing a fire. Fortunately, its bomb fell into the sea, exploding alongside without causing serious damage.

"At 1239, the remainder of planes in the third strike resumed launching, with the last plane off by 1244.

"At 1243, C.I.C. reported a low-flying plane, 14 miles astern. Task group's ships on the Intrepid's starboard quarter started firing at 1247 as Admiral Bogan ordered the group to make an emergency turn.

'At 1250, Admiral Bogan ordered another sharp turn as ships astern of the Intrepid opened fire on two approaching Jap planes.

"The air space over T.G. 38.2 was filled with planes returning from earlier strikes, and the air around our ship momentarily appeared free of enemy planes.

"At 1252, the Intrepid's after-fire-control radar picked up two Zeros, eight miles out, approximate altitude 8,000 feet. At this time, several of our planes were in the landing pattern, about to land and were obstructing our A.A. fire.

"The two Zeros dropped to an altitude of 100 feet, jerking violently from side to side as they passed over a hail of A.A. fire from our screening ships.

"The Intrepid's gunners hit one Zero, exploding it 1,500 yards astern. A 'hold fire' order was issued as an Avenger and a Hellcat crossed the line of fire. At the same time, another Zero was blasted by our starboard A.A. batteries.

"The Hellcat attempted to intercept the other incoming Zero, but it first swept low to the water, then began to climb as the guns opened up on him.

"One thousand yards astern, the Zero, now afire from A.A. hits, went into a power stall, did a wing-over at about 500 feet and plunged into Intrepid's flight deck, between elevators 2 and 3. Its 500-pound bomb penetrated the flight deck, buckling it and sending up a large cloud of smoke, fire and debris.

"On the gallery deck, in after-ready room No. 4, 32 men were killed instantly as the bomb exploded. (Twenty-six of the men were radarmen on standby duty waiting to relieve in C.I.C.). The explosion's force also vented downward, spewing shrapnel and flames onto the hangar deck.

"On the flag bridge, Admiral Bogan ordered the task group into a hard turn, causing the Intrepid to heel to portside and the water and flaming gas to spill over the portside, away from the island and critical systems on the starboard side.

"Fires on the Hangar Deck were fed by exploding planes that were gassed and armed with ammunition. The ship's fire marshal, Lt. Donald Dimarzo, and his men in Repair 1, were confident they could get the conflagration under control."

Cmdr. Lewis Schwabe, Intrepid's gunnery officer

"My battle station was above the navigation bridge, on the forward air defense platform, where I directed the Intrepid's antiaircraft guns. While fires from the kamikaze burned on the flight and hangar decks, my attention was drawn to starboard and an enemy plane directly over the battleship New Jersey. I directed our starboard gun batteries to open fire and, after taking a number of hits, the aircraft went into a tight spin and crashed into the water.

"Then, my attention was drawn to two more Zeros closing from astern on the Intrepid's port quarter.

"Both were coming in fast and low, partially obscured by smoke from the Intrepid's fires, resulting in minimizing effectiveness of the few antiaircraft guns we could bring to bear on the planes. The intense smoke from the flight deck neutralized our after 5-inch, twin-mount guns.

"Despite handicaps, one Japanese fighter was ripped apart and crashed into the water. The second Zero led a charmed life. As Intrepid made a broad starboard turn, the portside 40's and 20's had their fields of fire blocked. The incoming plane took violent evasive action and somehow avoided the hundreds of .40 and 20mm. tracers all around him.

"He climbed, went into a power stall, was riddled by our A.A. and set afire. But it was too late.

"The kamikaze pilot dove into our flight deck, tearing his plane apart around him. On the way down, in what was only a second or two, he released his 500-pound bomb and opened fire with his machine guns.

"The bomb crashed into and through the flight deck, leaving a round hole. The plane followed close behind and slammed into the flight deck. A portion of the plane and the pilot's body did not penetrate the deck, but slid forward along the flight deck.

"At the same time, the 500-pound bomb passed through the gallery deck and into the hangar. It hit the armored hangar deck, causing a depression next to the No. 3 aircraft elevator. The bomb bounced up and hit the deck again; its trajectory caused it to skid forward, where it exploded. This occurred at 1259, just 5 minutes after the first kamikaze and bomb explosion.

"The devastation in the hangar was frightful. The bomb had exploded amidst Fire Marshall Lieutenant Dimarzo and the men of Repair 1 as they were fighting fires from the first hit."

Lt. Lowell Keggy, U.S. Marine Corps

"I was with Lew Schwabe on the forward defense platform, in charge of the antiaircraft guns on the starboard bow quadrant.

"The explosion of the second kamikaze's bomb in the hangar caused the worst damage. Huge pillars of fire and smoke billowed out of our ship. I could hear the planes inside the hangar exploding as the flames reached their gas tanks and ammunition.

"Those of us in the gunnery department knew the ship was in great peril. Our guns were our prime means of defense, yet there were massive fires below them, dangerously close to their ammunition supplies.

"The huge pillar of smoke reached hundreds of feet into the sky. Only about 200 feet of the forward portion of the Intrepid was visible by the ships around us. It looked like we were a doomed ship. Most of our guns were blinded by the column of black smoke.

"Our defense was now up to the ships next to us., ships like the battleships New Jersey and Iowa.

"Twenty-two planes were destroyed inside the hangar; bulkheads were riddled with holes from explosions and shrapnel. The overhead burned out; elevator pits flooded; smoke began entering the engineering spaces. The forward engine room was so full of smoke that it was on the verge of being abandoned.

"Many men were trapped by the fires and smoke, especially in the gallery deck.

"It took 15 minutes to get the flight-deck fires under control, but the interior fires took hours to subdue.

"From my position on top of the island, I could see that the Cabot had also been hit and was burning. We then got word from the other task group that the Essex had also been hit by a kamikaze.

"Four of our carriers had been damaged in the space of half an hour. It was the toughest day in naval aviation history and Intrepid had been the worst hit."

Jack (Botts) Alexander, Radarman 2/c

"Nov. 25, 1944, was the worst day in the history of the U.S.S. Intrepid. Two kamikaze planes hit our ship and caused extensive damage plus the loss of many lives and wounding of many others. Our division V-3 Radar, was the hardest hit. We lost forever 26 courageous, young men.

"I was a radar-plotter for Admiral Bogan in the island structure, flag compartment, tracking the location and distance of enemy planes. When the initial reports were received, concerning damages and casualties, the news was not good.

"My initial reaction at the time: I was shocked, frightened and very scared.

"We received word that volunteers, trained in performing C.P.R., were needed. Those qualified were requested to report to the flight deck immediately. I told Admiral Bogan I could help and he gave me permission to leave my battle station and provide assistance to those in need.

Flames shoot skyward after first kamikaze crashed into Intrepid's flight deck.

175

Doctors, corpsmen and volunteers treating the wounded on the flight deck.

"It was a terrible, horrible scene to see, 40 or more unconscious men lying on the flight deck.

"The doctors in charge assigned two volunteers to each victim. The injured were bleeding from the mouth, indicating a possible concussion. My C.P.R. teammate and I were assigned to work on, as it turned out, one of my buddies, a fellow radarman.

"Our team, and the other volunteers, performed C.P.R. for several hours. Sadly, each of these men died, leaving us with a terrible, sad feeling when the doctors pronounced them all dead.

"While performing this treatment, one lost all sense of fear, even though the ship was on fire in many areas and there was still the possibility of another attack by enemy planes

"Negative thoughts raced through my mind. I was enraged, mad and upset because these shipmates of mine were dead. I felt a tremendous loss and hatred toward the kamikaze pilots who caused this terrible tragedy."

The word pictures painted by these men, survivors of this day's terrible horrors, is a tribute to all who died performing their duties – to their ship, their shipmates and their country. Those survivors who are alive today still shudder at thoughts of that day's horror.

Back to C.I.C. from 1035 on:.

The next two-plus hours were most intense, as radar screens filled with bogeys and interceptions. It seemed that every gun on the ship was blasting away at attacking planes.

Commander Winston seemed calm as he made rapid-fire decisions, assigning raids to be handled by our and other carriers' C.I.C.'s.

Fortunately, my good buddy Smitty, who had been the petty officer in charge of the standby radarmen, in after ready room No. 4, had asked Commander Mitchell just the day before for permission to change his G.Q. station back to C.I.C., saying: "Sir, I'm a damn good radar operator. I belong in C.I.C., not back with the relief radar team."

Mitchell agreed, and Smitty was back on G.Q. duty in C.I.C.

In the thick of the action, Mitchell returned from a trip to the head with the wide-eyed pilots' ready room steward's mate, whom he found in the passageway, all alone, down on his knees praying.

Mitchell told us: "Get him a cup of coffee. Talk to him. Let him stay here until it's over."

At the same time Red Jones and CJ King, who had been back standing by in the after ready room, followed him through the door and asked, "Stoney, do you know how long this shit is going to go on?"

Before I could answer, Jake Fegley, who was hooked up with headphones to the lookouts, shouted, "Hit the deck, hit the deck!"

Whenever Hit the Deck Jake yelled, you heard the sound of the 20's blasting away and knew a plane was diving on the ship.

Earlier, a brand-new 90-day-wonder, an ensign, admonished Jake for his hit-the-deck warning, saying, "John Paul Jones would be ashamed of us for ducking."

And according to Jake, after the first hit by a kamikaze, Jake said to the officer, who had ducked under a plot table, "John Paul Jones would be ashamed of all of us, sir!"

The ensign got pissed and said, "Fegley, one more word out of you and your ass is on report."

Jake shut up, just smiled, but once again he shouted, "Hit the deck!" as another kamikaze was diving on the Intrepid.

Hitting the deck, I ended up nose-to-nose with Commander. Mitchell, to whom I suggested: "Sir, I want an instant transfer. Now! I want a transfer to shore duty, some place nice and quiet, like Frisco."

His droll reply:"No way, Stoney. As long as I'm here, you're stuck right here with me, and that's for at least the duration, plus six."

"Thank you for your kind words, sir. I don't know what I was thinking. A transfer to shore duty. What an inappropriate bird-brained idea."

(When scared, we tried to make light of the situation, and relieve the pressure with either humorous or asinine banter.)

Getting up from the deck, I returned to the S.M., a two-man, air-search radar, with Doc seated next to me. Raids were closing in from all directions. As they came within range, every gun on the Intrepid began blasting away at them. Even when hit and afire, the kamikaze continued in its death dive until it crashed onto the the flight deck with its bomb exploding between the flight and hangar decks, just aft of C.I.C.

The ear-splitting explosion that rocked us was followed by thick smoke and heat from the hangar-deck fires.

I didn't know it at the time, but my pals, my good buddys, all the radarmen on standby duty in after ready room No. 4, were killed instantly by the force of the concussion.

The men from Repair 1 were fighting the hangar-deck fire, trying to contain and extinguish it, when, some five minutes later, the second kamikaze plunged into the ship. Its bomb bounced on the hangar deck, skittering forward, before it exploded, killing all the men from Repair 1, who were battling the sea of flames ignited by the first kamikaze.

The time between hits is a blurred memory, but Smitty, Doc and I were still at our radar sets when the second kamikaze smashed into the Intrepid. I don't think we volunteered, but we stayed when everyone abandoned C.I.C., which was now thick with smoke and hot as hell.

Leaky Evans and Merle Hossler were manning back-up radar in the after con, up in the island structure, but the phone lines connecting them to C.I.C. and other areas were blown. So Leaky and Merle had no idea what was happening elsewhere on the ship.

Years later, Leaky told me: "Merle and I were cut off; didn't know what to do. He kept fiddling with, and replacing, the headphones. Nothing worked. It was about two hours before we opened the door and saw what was going on. It was scary as hell!"

We could barely see one another through the smoke when the starboard passageway door opened and in stepped Stoner, my adopted country cousin.

"Hey, guys, anything I can do to help?"

"Country cous', what in the hell are you doing here?"

"Came back. Thought you guys might need some help."

"Grab the headphones. Man the main plot board."

We all tried, but we couldn't do much good; breathing was almost impossible. We'd get down on the deck where the smoke was thinner, take in some foul air and pop up trying to see a pip on the radar screen.

Choking violently, eyes burning from stinging tears, blinded, we finally give up. Crawling to the starboard passageway door and into the midst of a gasping, pushing, tightly packed cluster of confused men, trying to find and get up the ladder, away from the hangar deck's raging inferno, I thought: "Oh God, we're trapped. Is this the way I'm going to go?"

Someone hit me full force in the chest, knocking me on my ass, right onto a step of the ladder we were groping for, the ladder leading up to the flight deck and air.

I yelled: "I've got the ladder. Got it, here!"

Someone shouted: "Pipe down! Hold hands! Everyone, hold hands! Stop shoving. We'll all get out!"

We did, stumbling up through black smoke onto the flight deck, which was covered with bodies strewn around the island area.

I started to breathe easier, but still couldn't see very much. I took my knife, cut off part of my shirt and dabbed my eyes. It helped some.

A corpsman who was treating a badly burned sailor asked: "Anyone got morphine? There's some in your first-aid kit."

I gave him my kit and began picking my way through the bodies.

Our two chaplains were bent over, giving comfort to the wounded and Last Rites to the dying.

Dazed, while moving away from this area, I grabbed onto a passing fire hose, being pulled in the direction of the flames shooting up through huge holes in the flight deck. Looking down, I noticed one of my treasured non-regulation penny loafers was missing.

A guy pulling the hose asked: "Hey., did you hear that? Sounded like something about reporting to your abandon ship station? Did you hear it? Did you?"

I said: "No, I wasn't listening. Did you say, we are to report to my abandon- ship station?"

The Worst Day

Looking around, I saw most men on the flight deck were looking up at the captain's bridge, shaking their heads in emphatic "no's" indicating they were not giving up. They were staying with their ship, saying they would rather fight the fires and save their ship.

For sure, I didn't want to go over the side, but did remember our abandon-ship station was starboard, forward on the flight deck. There, in the midst of about a dozen other radarmen, was Polack, pencil in hand, checking names in his watchbook list. We shook hands and kept patting one another on the back, happy that we were alive, when I asked, "Polack, I don't remember, did we ever have any abandon ship drills?"

"No drills. We were just told where, not how. God, it must be 100 feet down to the water."

"Polack, you see any lines hanging down, or will we have to jump?"

"Stoney, I'm not a good swimmer. If we go over the side, I'll only be able to swim about five yards away from the ship, then it will be 5,000 feet straight down."

Thank God we didn't have to abandon ship and become shark bait. Sharks were my worst fear.

Later, while looking for my lost shoe, I remembered the radar set, up in the flag bridge cabin. Climbing up, I opened the door, stumbling right into the arms of Admiral Bogan himself. He steadied me while looking me over. My face was covered with soot, my shirt cut in half and I only had one shoe, but at least there was no blood.

"Had a rough day, son?"

"Yes, sir, but I'm O.K. I'm here to man the radar, sir."

My buddy Botts Alexander had been on radar duty in the flag cabin, until he had responded to the call, for all hands who knew how to perform C.P.R. He was down on the flight deck trying to help save lives.

Winston Goodloe, Aviation Machinest Mate 3/c

"Because Intrepid's crew was so well trained and worked as a team, we all, together, were able to save our ship. By November 1944, we were all battle-tested veterans. This ship was home to each of us.

"After the fires were out and the holes in the flight deck temporarily plated over and our casualties cared for, only then did we stop to rest.

"Over 150 of our crew were dead, missing or wounded; 69 died this terrible day. Those of us who rescued our trapped shipmates, treated our wounded or recovered our dead can never forget how close we came."

Winston's heroism and devotion to duty earned him the Bronze Star with the following citation:

———————

In the name of The President of the United States, the
Commander Second Carrier Task Force, United States Pacific Fleet,
presents the BRONZE STAR MEDAL to
WINSTON SPERRY GOODLOE, AVIATION MACHINIST
MATE THIRD CLASS, UNITED STATES NAVAL RESERVE
for service as set forth in the following

CITATION

"For distinguishing himself by heroic and meritorious achievement while serving on an aircraft carrier during the action on 25 November 1944. He heroically and with utter disregard for his own personal safety manned the first hose from the Flight to the Hangar Deck. He then went to the Gallery Deck to assist in rescuing trapped personnel, again fearlessly disregarding his own personal safety, repeatedly returning to compartments filled with asphyxiating intense heat and smoke to evacuate trapped and wounded personnel, taking risks beyond the call of duty. His heroism, devotion to duty, fearlessness and meritorious achievement were at all times in keeping with the highest traditions of the United States Naval service."

(signed) J.S. McCain
Vice Admiral, U.S. Navy

———————

Lou Valenti, Signalman 3/c

Lou's view of action from the signal bridge in the island was both enviable and scary. Seeing what was coming at you had to be more frightening than not seeing. He saw, and this is his account:

"It wasn't much of a day, no presage of things to come. Just a promise of a very hot Nov. 25, 1944, in Task Force 38. We of the signal gang had just read that some P-38's had skip-bombed an enemy destroyer in the E.T.O., and we were cracking wise about whether the Japanese had done that, too!

"At this time, Rear Adm. Gerry Bogan, commander Task Group 38.2, flew his flag from the Intrepid. He and his officers were occupying flag plot, which was directly forward of the signal bridge. The admiral's gang also included extra signalmen, who were added to the Intrepid's gang to help with the extra work that his being aboard would necessitate. However, during previous G.Q.'s, it was found that the signal area had become too crowded and that only the section on watch, and the admiral's gang, should report to the bridge. All men who were off duty were spread around and told to report to various 40 mm. mounts around the ship.

**18 year old
Louis Valenti**

"Each quad had two signalmen assigned to it, one from the starboard and one from the port watch. Odell Cooke and I were assigned to gun mount 13, aft, and starboard of the after elevator. Since I was on watch, Odell reported to mount 13. As we went about our duties G.Q. sounded and we donned our helmets: and some men put on flash gear and flash cream, which had the consistency and color of liquid putty; anybody who smeared on the cream took on a ghastly, scared look.

"In no time, all guns began firing and here and there a Jap plane was seen and was taken under fire. Most were shot down. As the battle wore on, I found myself feeling very alone on the starboard side of the bridge, crouched down so that only my helmet, eyes and nose were above the splinter shield, and I was holding onto the top of the shield with my fingers. I must have looked like *Kilroy was here*.

"It's odd what one will do in a time of panic. I turned away from the suicide bomber and ran forward until I got to the door to flag plot and I opened it and entered the inner sanctum, something I would never do under normal circumstances.

"The admiral and his staff turned to look at me as I burst through the door and I pointed aft and said, "Suicide plane," as if I were really bearing a message instead of looking for a place of protection. Since flag plot was buttoned up very tightly and the men inside could not see out, they looked upon me as the bearer of important news. This lasted for a short time until the admiral's chief of staff, a captain, came bursting in from the port bridge and said, "Suicide plane!," and I wondered if he was looking for a place of protection, too.

"We all went out the port side of the flag bridge; I found a parachute that had been torn from one of the dead Japs, hanging from the port running light and knew it would be a great souvenir. I was trying to cram it inside of my chambray shirt when the chief of staff said, "Give me that, boy," and I did. Who's gonna argue with a four-striper?

"The carrier Hancock was on our starboard beam. A little forward and between us was the Iowa with no air bursts blooming around it. Suddenly a plane did a wing-over and started to tumble toward the ocean. As it crashed into the sea, Buchanan, one of Bogan's signalmen, tapped me on the shoulder and pointed aft. As I looked in wonder and fear, I saw the plane was already over the fantail, its wings level and on fire, as it was about to hit the flight deck.

"By then the fires were raging on the hangar deck, and we also learned that the sky-search radar antenna was jammed. Bogan's gunnery officer formed a crew of lookouts around the forward splinter shield and we spent the rest of the afternoon serving as the eyes of the ship.

"As the fire burned below, the inside of the island could only be entered at your peril. This was because the island became a giant chimney, sucking up the caustic smoke from below.

"After the first plane hit us, the reaction of the repair parties and the men in the immediate area must have been instantaneous, because the second bomb killed many of the men in the immediate area who were fighting the first fire.

"We can only assume that Odell Cooke was helping fight the fire. After the fires were extinguished and G.Q. was over, Odell did not answer at roll call. Some of our signalmen were ordered to search among the dead to see if they could find Odell, and to do it fast because the casualties were already being sewn into their body bags. The search was futile. Odell either jumped to avoid the fire and smoke or he was blown overboard."

Edward Coyne, Seaman 1/c
Another Plankowner with a vivid memory of this horrible day was Ed Coyne, a young sailor who enlisted in the Navy at 17 and came directly to the Intrepid from boot camp at the Great Lakes Naval Training Center. He was assigned to V2G Division and his job was to make sure the planes were fully gassed before takeoff.

The Worst Day

Ed's battle station, during G.Q. was on the flight deck, where he manned headphones.

"Little did we know what was coming when I chowed down at breakfast with one of my good buddies, Ray Rucinski, boatswain's mate 2/c. We were at our battle stations, on the flight deck, when the first kamikaze hit.

17-year-old Edward Coyne

"Ray requested permission and was allowed to go down to the hangar deck to help fight the fires. In less than five minutes, a second kamikaze crashed into the midst of the men fighting the fire. Rucinski, and two other brave men from my division, were killed instantly.

"Hours later, when the fires were extinguished, we were able to crawl into the sacks in our hangar-deck compartment. Shortly after we had stretched out, the ship's organ, which was located nearby, started to play: "Where will we all be a hundred years from now?" A scary, but true ending to a horrible day."

(Occasionally, during the darkness of night, the sound of shrill notes from the organ reverberated throughout the hangar deck. No one was ever found at the keyboard.

Kilroy appeared in a simple line drawing, like this, everywhere in the world that American servicemen touched. Some joker even managed to have a Kilroy sign on the beach, greeting the marines, as the first wave landed on Guadalcanal.

Jack Norton

W hile checking off names in his ever present watch-book list, Polack asked: "Hey! Any of you guys seen Norton?"

Someone answered: "He was O.K. when we left C.I.C., but I haven't seen him since then."

Norton, it seems, was going about his duty in his typical grab the bull by the horns manner.

Jack Norton Radarman 2/c

"I believe I was still a bit dazed by the time the fires were under control, but one thought kept running through my mind. Where are the portable S.N. radar sets stored? Fortunately, I ran into Ensign Ewing and we went and got one. It was an unwieldy, 3-foot, box-like square with an antenna on top, set on a spindly tripod base. Finally we maneuvered it a bit forward of the island structure on the flight deck and ran a power cable to it.

"It took a while before I remembered how to operate the S.N. All I could scan was the 180° forward. Ewing was called away before we set up a headphone connection, leaving me alone with no way of reporting on whatever I picked up.

"It was getting dark and I kept expecting someone to come and help. Apparently, no one knew I was there and I was afraid to leave my post. So I stayed there through the night. I don't believe I ever felt so alone as I did there on the flight deck. I could barely make out the shadowy figures on the bridge. It was the downright eeriest night I ever spent.

"In the morning, when I finally found that the S.N. radar wasn't needed and that nearly half of my good buddies had been killed when the first kamikaze hit ready room No. 4, I was overwhelmed. I have never been able to get over the grief and anger I felt that day."

I didn't run into Smitty and Doc until later, not having seen either of them since we left C.I.C. hours before. As close as we were, sharing wine, women and song, our innermost private feelings were usually kept private. It wasn't until years later that Smitty told me: "I never prayed to God before, but I did that day. I prayed, God, let me get through this horrible day. I'll be a good boy. I'll take care of my mother and father."

When the hangar-deck fires were finally extinguished, I made my way through the charred wreckage, heading back to my sleeping compartment, aft on the starboard side. Past the flooded No. 3 elevator pit there were bodies lined up in rows.

A corpsman asked: "You're a radarman, aren't you? Maybe you can help with ID's? Most of these men are from ready room No. 4."

The stench of fire and charred flesh was overpowering and became more potent as I looked over my dead pals. Two of them were locked in a fright-induced rigor-mortis hug.

The corpsman asked, "How are we going to bury them?"

A fountain of tears flooded my eyes. "Break their arms," I said as I turned and walked away. The floodgates of sorrow finally burst into a sea of tears. I stood alone amidst the rubble, sobbing.

Dog tired, I went down the ladder to our sleeping compartment. It was grimly silent. Those stretched out in bunks were staring at the overhead. We spoke to one another in hushed tones.

I had something to do before I could hit the sack.

Nearly all the radarmen killed had been quartered in an after berthing compartment. Here, the bunks were mostly empty.

I went back there to find three officer-training washouts who had recently come aboard as radarmen. They were bitter about being enlisted men, not officers. I understood the bitterness but didn't appreciate their attitude, particularly when they vented their anger and superiority on someone like Stoner.

Stoner was a rube, yes. A farm boy from Lima, Ohio, yes. And the butt of many jokes and pranks before he became my adopted cousin. Cruel humor was habitual entertainment for some men.

Stoner was sent for left-handed wrenches and sky hooks. Sent to look out for the mail buoy, spurred on eagerly by hope of getting a letter from "Forty Acres," our name for his girl back home.

On this horrible day, it was Stoner who came back to C.I.C., through the smoke and fire, to see if he could help. Just him, no one else.

Our three officer washouts had been assigned to standby stretcher duty, or they too would have been killed in ready room 4 along with the other radarmen.

Someone had told me about their performance this day: one fainted, one pooped in his pants, the other puked.

I don't hold any of this against them; it could happen to anyone. But I wanted to make sure they knew how valiant Stoner acted under battle pressure. I didn't mention that I knew about their performances, I just saluted Stoner and implied they should treat him with well-deserved dignity from here on. Or else.

Back in my compartment, I crawled into the sack fully-clothed, exhausted and bone-tired. I tried to pray, but it was difficult with ghastly distractions flashing through my mind, short-circuiting thoughts. Finally, I did thank God that I was alive and whole, as I have every day since then.

Of the 69 men killed, 26 were radarmen who were mostly teenage warriors, yet all heroes who gave their lives for God and Country. (My diary indicates 32, however; six of the men were from another division.)

Compton would never "grow the gal-darn-dest, biggest cabbages and carrots you ever did see, up thar in Alaska."

Casteel would never get to entertain people as an actor.

Nitro would never play first violin with the San Francisco Philharmonic.

Schultz wouldn't dance at any more wild three-day Polish wedding receptions in Chicago.

Yoeder wouldn't get to change diapers on his newborn baby.

Robinson wouldn't have to explain why he got "The Bluebirds of Happiness" tattooed across his chest.

Krouch would never know how his young sons matured and how they, and their children, would visit his ship many years later.

All their talents and aspirations were buried with them, deep in the middle of the Pacific Ocean.

One of my least-favorite shipboard duties was emptying lockers and packing the belongings of dead sailors for shipment home. You had to carefully monitor the contents of certain guys' lockers for things they wouldn't want their wives or mothers to see.

One locker had 12 bottles of Vitalis Hair Tonic stashed in back. Curious, I sprinkled some on my hands and was greeted by the unmistakably pleasant, smokey aroma of Scotch whiskey.

This prime booty was salvaged and rerouted to our "Something to Celebrate" locker. Later, I learned how his wife always shipped the tonic, surrounded and protected by unshelled peanuts.

The Worst Day

Photographer, Ed Ulatowski

I had already packed ship's photographer, Ed Ulatowski's locker contents a couple of days before he and the pilot, Ensign Weaver were rescued from their life raft and I knew exactly what to go for, his collection of nudes. Now most of us, in this pre-Playboy era had rarely, if ever, seen any pics of naked women. To me, his collection was, at best, pitiful: photos of the scroungiest bunch of nonbeauties, with either lemon-size or sagging breasts and matching flaccid faces. Not knowing who at home would receive this heap of crap, I offered the pics to anyone who wanted them. They were snapped up and his sea bag was transferred to a destroyer later that same day

After a couple of days in sick bay he learned that his girlie pictures were gone. Ulatowski blew his top at me for giving his photos away and at everyone else who he thought had, and wouldn't return, his prized girlie photos. His rage was amplified, because he had been returned directly to the Intrepid and therefore would not get the standard survivor's stateside leave of 20-to-30 days. However, he calmed down after a couple of days and, while not quite forgiving me, Ed said that he sort of understood.

Cleaning up the hangar deck was a grimy, grisly task, with plane parts and twisted metal covered with slime and soot. Frank Fodor, from Emaus, Pa., who usually manned the now-disabled No. 3 elevator that moved planes between the hangar and flight deck, was helping the cleanup detail and, while sifting through the rubble, he retrieved an oversized blue helmet, like the one worn by his division officer. To his horror, his division officer's head was in it.

Frank never really recovered from this terrible shock. At war's end, he joined the religious, becoming Brother Vincent at the Graymoor Fathers hospice on the Hudson River. He helped tend to and rehabilitate the derelicts, addicts and alcoholics that the good Fathers rounded up from New York's Bowery.

Crewmen covering the body of the kamikaze pilot who crashed on the flight deck.

During the ship's cleanup, an odd message was repeated over the P.A. speakers several times during the day:"Will the man who has the testicles please bring them to sick bay."

Apparently one of the mountain men had promised his sweetie that he would bring home a pair of Jap's balls as a trophy. He got his chance to keep the promise when the kamikaze pilot's body flew forward on the flight deck, when his plane crashed into it.

Later, I heard scuttlebutt that he had his trophy preserved in a jar of torpedo juice.

Ulithi & One-Eyed Willie

The next day, while the Intrepid, and T.G. 38.2 continued on course back to Ulithi, funeral services for our fallen shipmates were held at 1400.

I can't describe the depth of sadness we felt standing there next to rows of our fallen comrades in canvas body bags. The chaplains eulogized them with proper prayers and praise. The sound of taps filled your eyes with tears. The booming rifle salute made you shudder. But when they tilted the boards to let the bodies slip, one by one, into the sea, you ached from the empathy that enveloped you.

At an Irish wake, there's a joke or two, an attempt to relieve tension. There's was nothing to help you here; burying 69 shipmates is a numbing experience of both body and mind.

You couldn't dwell on your sorrow. You had to learn to look back – but not stare. Thank God, working as a radarman kept you focused on your job, even when not under enemy attack. I remember thinking how fortunate we were to always have challenges that were interesting and involving.

Certain radar sets became your favorites, your pets. Mine was the S.M., our most advanced radar. It could outperform other radars and as you became more experienced and more proficient operating it, you became a team. You and the machine. You knew it, and it seemed to know you. All radar sets had temperaments, which needed constant fine-tuning, calibrating and almost daily fixing.

Ensign Ewing was the bright material officer who kept our radar up and running. He practically lived in C.I.C., always ready to fix a sick set. He passed time drinking coffee and doing New York Times crossword puzzles. Ewing was good officer, and good at his job, too.

On Nov. 28, 1944, the Intrepid arrived at Ulithi Atoll and dropped the hook. This vast lagoon, surrounded by coral reefs, was a near-perfect anchorage and it became one of the fleet's main forward bases. We anchored amidst what looked to be at least a thousand ships, ships of every description: carriers, battlewagons, cruisers, destroyers, destroyer escorts, supply ships, transports, oilers and even floating dry-docks. More ships than I had ever seen in one place.

Ulithi was relatively safe from enemy attack. The Jap island bases had either been invaded, secured or rendered isolated and useless by devastating bombardment. Enemy submarines reportedly lurked near-by, hoping to intercept radio intelligence. We were told to be on the lookout for a lone spy plane, "One-Eyed Willie," a stripped-down twin engine Betty that came in low under radar detection, climbed and streaked over the ships on a photo reconnaissance run.

The Intrepid was assigned to radar watch with fighter direction control of the C.A.P. this day, and we were operating with only a half-watch section; eight radar operators and one fighter-direction officer.

I relieved Mother Stefanich's watch section at 0800 and found we had an Ensign, who had just reported aboard. He was very nervous and I, acting as the watch's leading petty officer, assured him nothing unusual would happen today and that he would have an opportunity to get acquainted with us and C.I.C.'s operations.

I then contacted the C.A.P. which had 3 groups of 4 fighter planes and passed on the flight orders to the orbiting planes, stacking them at 5-10 and 15-thousand-foot altitudes, rotating them every 10 minutes to conserve oxygen. This was the first time I ever gave direct orders to the pilots and I was feeling rather smug, signing off with a hearty "Over and out." As I heard the last words leave my lips, I panicked, realizing my transmission went out in plain English, not in the daily code. I was in hot water for sure. What if a Jap submarine was monitoring? Worse, what if someone on Halsey's flagship on the New Jersey heard?

Soon, I had something else to worry about. We had a bogey on the radar screen, coming in fast from the east, heading right at Ulithi.

The new ensign seemed uncertain and confused. "What should I do?" he asked. With time a factor, I jumped into the fighter director's chair and advised him: "Sir, get on that squawk box to the bridge. Report that we have what appears to be a single bogey, closing fast."

As G.Q. was sounding, I checked plots on the board and gave the fighter pilots a vector to intercept, trying to bring them in on the enemy plane's tail. C.I.C. quickly filled with officers and radarmen reporting to and manning their battle stations. Seeing Commander Mitchell approaching, I slipped out of his fighter director's chair, fortunately just as the pilot jubilantly reported, "Tally Ho!"

While taking his seat, Mitchell looked at me, demanding, "Stoney, what in the hell is going on here and what are you doing?"

Before I could answer, the fighter pilot's voice came blasting out of the speaker: "Splash...one Betty! Splash...one Betty!"

C.I.C. burst into a resounding cheer. "One-Eyed Willie" was ancestor-bound. After the ship secured from G.Q., I explained to Commander Mitchell how I happened to be in charge of things during the interception. I didn't bother to mention how I fouled up with the earlier instructions to the pilots by failing to put them in code.

Helping splash Willie gave me a special, more personal feeling of combat contact with the enemy. Possibly because this bogey had a name, instead of the usual Raid "A" or "B" next to X's plotted on the board. I was quite happy, even though I didn't even receive a basic "well done" for my part in it.

I thought of the pilot, how elated he must have been, watching Willie go down in smoke, adding another notch on his guns, along with another rising-sun meatball stenciled under his cockpit window.

Later that morning, Captain Bolger returned to the Intrepid, bringing Admirals Halsey and McCain with him. After they inspected the battle damage, it was decided that the ship would return stateside for repairs. Hearing Halsey was on board, I more or less went into hiding. I was afraid Halsey would ask to see that dumb son of a bitch who sent the uncoded radio message earlier that morning.

Some of the crew got to go ashore on Mog Mog Island for a recreation party. Each man was given two cans of beer from the ship's cooler. It wasn't enough beer for a real party, and once on Mog Mog, all you could do is drink it before it got too warm and then roam the coral reef looking for exotic shells. That was the recreation.

At noon, Admiral Bogan departed, shifting his flag to the U.S.S. Lexington, another Essex Class sister ship of the Intrepid. I'm not sure, but this was either the third or fourth time Admiral Bogan and his staff had been blown off an aircraft carrier and had to move the flag to another ship.

Commander Winston asked if I would consider joining him as part of the admiral's staff? Even with offers of rapid promotion and as much as I admired and respected Winston, I declined, saying: "Sir, you've been blown off three or more carriers now and you haven't been stateside for years. As much as I enjoy working with you and would like to continue, I think I'll opt for staying with my ship and getting back stateside for repairs and home on leave."

His reply was simple, as he shook my hand: "I don't blame you one damn bit. Smooth sailing, sailor."

Before leaving the ship, he took time to write a quick, simple note and had it posted in C.I.C. "To: V-3R division's enlisted men: You are among the finest radarmen that I've served with. Thanks, and happy hunting. Jim Winston."

He was concise, to the point, just as he was when he issued orders, assigning and directing interceptions. If he was ever flustered, it never showed.

We all admired him for his skills and character. If the commander knew that we hadn't had any decent food because of battle conditions, he would order a couple of plates of bacon and eggs, homefries and toast delivered to him in C.I.C. Then, when the food arrived, he'd say he wasn't hungry and invite us to dig in.

After he left the ship, I sometimes wondered about my decision not to go with him. Winston was a cut above the very best, exactly what I thought a leader should be – smart, tough and fair.

On a Familiar Course

The Intrepid left Ulithi, stopped at Eniwetok, took on many wounded troops and headed for Pearl Harbor, escorted by two destroyer-escorts. Among the wounded passengers was a Jap pilot who was bound for interrogation at Pearl.

We docked at Pearl and, in less than two hours, we radarmen were off the ship and on our way to see a resident Navy shrink. Upon arrival, we were informed that we were to spend the night and see the doctor in the morning. That was fine; it gave us time to party in the PX.

Copious amounts of beer were consumed, along with canned sardines and crackers, before we were told to report for a radar proficiency test. We protested loudly, until an officer arrived and herded us into a room and told us we could resume partying after the test.

The test was three or four pages of questions with multiple-choice answers. It didn't take long to check off the answers, since we didn't bother to read the questions. Back to partying, merrily we went, until the PX was closed down.

Someone discovered there was a prisoner-of-war camp on the base and suggested we pay a visit. That sounded like a great idea and a small group of us staggered over to the stockade. The chain-link fence must have been 30 feet high, with guard towers on the corners. There were about 50 prisoners, squatting on their haunches and ignoring the insults and challenges we hurled at them. One of our huge radarmen, Sundeem, stripped off his shirt to display his muscles while daring them to produce a champion to fight him. They remained passive, not even looking in our direction. We then headed back to the barracks, played poker and hit the sack.

I was shaken out of a deep slumber before reveille by Commander

Mitchell, who was more than upset:"John the Baptist (he called me that after I grew my beard), last night I was searched for and found, while enjoying myself, only to be told I was sailing with the dumbest radarmen in this entire fleet. What in hell did you men do here?"

I explained: "Sir, we too were enjoying ourselves, drinking beer, when they sprung that darn surprise test on us – interrupting our partying. Our drinking. You know."

"Partying? Everybody hit the deck, get in the showers. Get dressed. You're going to take that test again in 10 minutes. Move it."

Mitchell kept close watch on us while we took the test. It was not difficult, and most of us scored in the high 90's. Satisfied, he left mumbling something about the dumbest in the fleet and telling us:"No more beer until after you've seen the psychiatrist. Now, that's an order!"

I think the psychiatrist should have been tested; we all thought he was seriously in need of help. We never did find out what he thought of us or if he drew any conclusions about what working in a dark room, staring at a radar scope for hours at a time, did to us..

I don't think being a radarman had any adverse effects. It certainly didn't make me sterile, as early rumors prophesized. And the eye exercises that we were taught must have actually helped me, since today I still don't need glasses to read a telephone book.

Pilots in their ready room, relaxing between strikes against enemy targets.

Stateside for Repairs

Heartfelt "Happy hunting" and other farewell good wishes were bid to the pilots from Air Group-18 as they left the ship for duty on the Hancock. About 800 officers and enlisted men boarded as passengers for the trip to San Francisco. We off-loaded some radar equipment at Pearl, but we still maintained normal watch sections in C.I.C. during the voyage.

I've searched my mind over and over but I still can't come up with Dingy's proper name. Dingy was a radarman from Georgia's mountains who had an eccentric, Robin Hood-type personality. Dingy loved to steal from those who had stolen.

If Dingy liked you, he couldn't do enough for you; if not, you had to be wary. He happened to like me and Doc and showed it by stealing pies that mess cooks had already stolen and hidden. He would pull pies, still warm, from under his shirt and present them with a broad grin and a knowing wink. Dingy loved outhustling the hustlers.

He once showed me his secret cache, which included the rifle of one of our shipboard marines. The marine had been rude, insulting Dingy, and was paid back by having his weapon stolen. I never could figure how Dingy ever managed to steal this marine's rifle from the gun rack in the marine sleeping compartment.

Wilkins also was rude and insulted Dingy. One night after a watch, as Doc and I returned to our compartment, we found Dingy pointing a Jap rifle at Wilkins head, reciting a litany of Wilkin's transgressions as the reasons why he was going to kill him. He punctuated his remarks by ejecting a bullet from the rifle's chamber as he loaded in another from the clip.

Wilkins, with sweat cascading down his face was frozen in fear.

Dingy's eyes were locked in on his target as Doc asked, "Hey Dingy, what the hell's this all about?"

"Gonna kill this low-life bastard, that's all. And I'm telling him all the reasons why he deserves to die."

I chimed in. "Can't say he doesn't deserve it, but..."

Doc interrupted, "Not worth it. You kill him, you will be caged for a while before they put you in front of a firing squad. Think about that. Caged!"

Dingy just stared at Wilkins as he ejected another shell from the rifle. I picked up from Doc's lead and said: "You won't ever run the hills again. And never make love to your gal anymore."

We were hitting him with things we knew about him. During G.Q. Dingy was assigned to the mess hall to make sandwiches. He wouldn't, he couldn't, stay down below decks. Even when the ship was under attack, with all our guns firing away, Dingy was up on the flight deck running nonstop, hell-bent from one end of the deck to the other.

Dingy was sent to see a shrink while the ship was in Pearl Harbor, and he told us: "This dumb doctor asked me dumb questions. He wanted to know, if I preferred to go out with boys or girls?"

"I told him: That's dumb Doc. It's all according to where I wanta go and what I wanta do. You know what I mean!"

"Next, he tells me I'd be safer below decks in the mess hall than I am up there running around on the flight deck. He said, "Don't you know, that's where all the strafing hits, where the bombs explode?"

"I asked him, Tell me, Doctor, just tell me where those torpedoes hit?"

We also knew that when home on leave, Dingy and his girlfriend spent much time running in the hills, with stops to make love. And while making love, she always sang *"Take It Easy"* to him.

Doc kept applying the *being caged, running free and "Take It Easy"* themed therapy on him, until Dingy finally lowered the rifle.

It took more convincing before he gave it up. He did, though, after being assured that no one present saw anything or would say anything about anything. Wilkins readily agreed to "anything" that would get the gun away from his head. As far as we know, Wilkins never did report the incident or bring charges. Shortly thereafter, however, Dingy and about a dozen other radarmen were transferred off the ship.

Doc and I missed Dingy, his pies and his mischievous antics.

Excerpts from *"Intrepid"*

Another radarman, Royal E. Smith, used "the pen is mightier than the sword" maxim to express his contempt for Wilkins with a satirical newsletter, "Newsy News," that he produced for limited distribution. (One typewritten copy was passed around.)

It was a tongue-in-cheek romp, all in good fun, except for the verbal poison darts he hurled at Wilkins.

"Under cover of darkness, the dishonorable Wilkins and his unscrupulous crew decided to raid Mare Island..."

The ship's official publication, *Intrepid,* had a staff of officers and men who wrote, edited and printed the articles, along with some fillers supplied by Camp Newspaper Service.

A short C.N.S. example:

NEW YORK (CNS)–This sign hangs in an East Side tailor's shop that specializes in uniforms for WACS and WAVES:

"We fill out government forms."

The back page of our publication, *Intrepid,* had a mailing label for sending it back home.

The following pages show more excerpts from *Intrepid's* contents:

Masthead of Intrepid's publication proclaiming THEN! (First Intrepid) NOW! (1944) FOREVER! (At this time we did not know the ship would survive and, years later, become a permanent Air/Space Museum in New York City.

-From an early article:

Just after we left the states last time, the rumor was confirmed that our original Air Group, AG No. 8, would not take part in our first operation; they were being relieved.

This knowledge was received with some dismay by all hands; the ship's company and our first Air Group had come to regard themselves as a unit.

We had the greatest confidence in the skill and general excellence of our "Air Group," hence it was a double hardship to lose them, for not only were they confidence-inspiring, but also they were old friends and, in complete contrast, nothing was known about the group coming aboard.

The situation made an excellent spawning ground for scuttlebutt. Since not even the number of the group was certain, you could hear anything you wanted about them. It was an old group, a new group, they had little or no experience. One thing was certain, however, they were certain to be superior and hypercritical of a new ship.

When the new group came aboard just outside Pearl after the relieved group flew off, the first of our doubts was dispelled. Down to the last unfamiliar (to us) Dauntless, they landed in a business-like way right in the slot. Shortly thereafter they were part of the ship. We found that they were a seasoned group in every sense of the word (having seen action in the Central Pacific). The illustrious "Butch" O'Hare had been their skipper, and when he was lost in a heroic action against the Jap night torpedo bombers, his place was taken by equally able Lt. Commander Phillips. Their record was excellent and, like true veterans, they were anything but haughty and uncooperative. It became apparent Intrepid was lucky in its new air group.

Excerpts from *"Intrepid"*

If any doubts remained, the abbreviated shakedown period certainly removed them. This group went through take-offs, maneuvers and landings with deadly precision and machine-like accuracy that was thrilling to watch. Here were a bunch of men to be proud of, men who knew their business to the last detail.

Our first offensive action justified the faith in the ship and the air group. Acting with calm efficiency, they did the bulk of the damage to the area assigned to our task group, shooting down numerous planes in the air, destroying many on the ground, blowing up dumps, installations and wrecking numerous gun positions. In addition, Lt. Commander Harrison (the VF skipper) spotted for one of our battleships, enabling it to sink a cargo ship,

On this first action, Lt. (jg) Vraciu, already credited with two planes, earned numbers 3, 4 and 5, and entered the elect society of Aces. The exploits of the group as a whole cleared the air of enemy aircraft and enabled our battlewagons to move in with their devastating bombardment, without which the actual landings would have been immeasurably more difficult.

The next operation was no less spectacular and demonstrated the courage of the group even more decisively. The previous objective had been a known quantity; there had been numerous long-range bombing attacks and photo reconnaissances and part of the group had made flying strikes there, but this job was clothed in ominous mystery.

With their habitual coolness, our pilots moved in boldly and when the day was over, they had destroyed many planes in the air, more on the ground, sank several ships (with an assist on a cruiser which they stopped dead in the water for our battleships to finish) and damaged others including a cruiser and a destroyer. One of the ships sunk was an ammunition ship which was completely destroyed by Lt. Bridges, a torpedo pilot who was lost with his crew in the ensuing terrific blast. Here also, Lt. (jg) Vraciu accounted for five more planes, although he claimed but four, the other being attested to his wingman, bringing his total to at least nine.

The Air Group had nothing but praise for the ship. They liked how the Captain brought her into the wind with no loss of time. They admired the excellence of the plane-handling crews. They lauded the landing signal officer, the repair parties and all others they came in contact with. The group stated that no other ship operated better in any detail, nor was more cooperative and anxious to assist. Such a statement covered a lot of ground and should be a source of pride to the INTREPID considering the source and the standards of comparison.

And so this Air Group has returned for a well-earned rest and rehabilitation, except for Lt. Vraciu who had himself transferred to another squadron while still in the Pacific. The Intrepid is sorry that its associations with the Air Group is at an end, and wishes them all good fortune when they return later in the year to embellish their brilliant record.

From an *Intrepid,* "Early Aviation" article.

Modern Naval Aviation with its countless carriers, advance bases, clouds of planes and thousands of men, started in WW I with 22 seaplanes (none fit for operational use), 38 naval aviators and 163 enlisted men.

Naturally, ordinary operations and training were hazardous, but at that time aviation was still feeling its way. After all, what would you expect of wire-bound, canvas-covered crates? The mere act of taking off and landing in one of those flying machines was worth a D.F.C.

The bombing of enemy Naval Bases was accomplished by Naval aviators, using Army land planes. Enemy sub bases at Zeeburg, Bruges and Ostend were frequently blasted.

We owe much to these intrepid aviators of the last war. They actuated the idea of the Naval Air Force, prov-

Intrepid's Air Plot Officer, Lt. Cmdr. Mattheissen, is Naval Aviator # 757. He served overseas in Paris, Rome and Bolsano during WW I..

ing it a powerful part of the fleet. Among early Naval aviators who are still with us are Naval Aviator #3-Vice Admiral, H.J. Towers, #8-Rear Admiral P.N. Bellinger, #24-Rear Admiral A.C. Reed, and #33-Vice Admiral M.A. Mitscher.

Other early Naval aviators include such men as Admirals: E.J. King, W.F. Halsey, J.H. Hoover, J.S. McCain, R. K. Turner, and Intrepid's own first Captain, Rear Admiral T. L. Sprague.

Excerpts from *"Intrepid"*

–From: *Intrepid*, April 1945

The Fair-Haired Bastards

When Dr. Margaret Chung of San Francisco became a benefactress to seven down-and-out American aviators in 1932, she little realized that their number would double and triple until it would reach its present total of 755. However, that is the number that Captain G. E. Short wears today on his silver ring that is given by Madame Chung to every member of the famous group.

Intrepid

INTREPID'S 9,000TH LANDING

Some of the most famous names in the Navy today are members of this exclusive group, and it is interesting to know that Commander R. P. Kauffman, our Executive Officer, outranks Admiral Halsey when the "Fair-haired Bastards" get together. Commander Kauffman was one of the first members. His silver ring bears the number 116 and consequently he is Admiral Halsey's superior officer.

Madame Chung has divided her famous organization into three groups. First, are the "Fair-haired Bastards" who must fulfill the following requirements before they can become members. The applicant must be: *"A good guy, who can fly, who's not afraid to die, a courageous man who is loyal, tolerant. A 'square' man who contributes to the progress and glory of aviation, who makes the world a better place because he lives."*

Other officers of the Intrepid who have become "Fair-haired Bastards," besides Commander Kauffman, are Commander Lanman, Commander Ellis and former Commanding Officer, Captain Bolger. Other famous naval personnel who belong to this group are Admiral Halsey, Admiral Mitscher and Admiral Ragsdale.

In her second group, Madame Chung designates a *"Kiwi"* as exceptionally good *'bastard'* material, but one who does not fly." Commander Wallace and Lt. Comdr. Hogan (recently detached) are both members in good standing in this group.

The latest addition to Madame Chung's group is the "Golden Dolphin" who must be a member of a submarine crew which has sunk over 100,000 tons of enemy shipping.

Affectionately known as "mom" to her "beloved sons" Madame Chung is a prominent physician and surgeon in San Francisco and famed as a patron of the arts and opera.

Captain Short receiving Battle Flag from Madame Chung as Commanders Kauffman and Lanman look on.

Dr. Chung, recently presented a new battle flag to Captain Giles E. Short. In making her presentation to Captain Short, Madame Chung said: "Captain Short, I proudly present to you, as skipper of the USS Intrepid, this flag of the United States of America, the flag you and your gallant men defended so successfully and so valiantly. Guard it and cherish it as well as you have fought for it.

"My earnest hope is that we at home, for whom you have fought so heroically, may prove ourselves worthy of your valor.

"To this I pledge my life in humble gratitude. Wherever you may be, my prayers for your safety and my love will wing their way to you. May God bless you and your men of the Intrepid and may the Lord watch over you while we are absent, one from the other."

A Top Carrier Ace: Lt. (jg), Alex Vraciu, shown on Intrep
after shooting down the ninth, of his nineteen plane tot

VICTOR OVER 19 ENEMY PLANES
TO GET $100 FOR EACH

(CHICAGO (AP) --- Lt. Alexander Vraciu Jr., 25, of Ea
go, Ind., who once declined a furlough from the Pacific b
"there are a few things I want to clear up," was en rou
Monday with 19 Japanese planes

From a Chicago newspaper...

CHICAGO (AP)...Lt. Alexander Vraciu Jr., 27, of
Chicago, Ind., who once declined a furlough from
Pacific because "there are a few things I want to clear
was enroute home Monday with 19 Japanese pla
downed and $1,900 in his wallet. (June Issue "
Intrepid.")

He stopped off at the home of his uncle John Ti
Chicago manufacturer, to collect on a little wager. Mr T
had promised Alex $100 for each plane he shot down."
glad he came home now because if he stayed there
longer I'd have to buy the Jap air force," said Mr Tinsu

VRACIU
A SURVIVOR

Top Carrier
Ace Missing

By United Press

EAST CHICAGO, Ind., Jan. 4.—
Lieutenant Alex Vraciu Jr., the
Navy's top carrier-based flying ace,
is missing in action in the South
Pacific, his wife reported today.

Lieutenant Vraciu, who twice was
rescued by destroyers after being
forced down in the South Pacific,
was credited with sinking a Jap
transport and with destruction of
19 enemy planes in combat, 18 on
the ground, and two other "probables."

A telegram from the War Department yesterday said Lieutenant
Vraciu failed to return from a mission. No other details were given.

Lieut. (j.g.) Alexander Vraciu destroyed
six Japanese planes with 300 shots in air
battle west of Guam on June 19, brought
his score to 18, highest for carrier pilots.

Two of the carriers V
flew off were torpedo
he had to ditch into t
sea twice, also parac
ed from his plane tw
times. He was shot d
in December '44 dur
raid on Manila's Clar
Field...he survived, b
out with Filipino
guerrillas for five
weeks until joini
up with American
forces.

Joan Gough Frost
1944 WASP Pilot

19-year old Joan Gough

You could have knocked my socks off when I opened a letter from my high-school pal Joan Gough. Out fell a photo of her in pilot's mufti. Joan had enlisted in the Woman's Airforce Service Pilots and was training at Sweetwater, Texas.

After earning her wings, she joined the other 2,000 women who were flying planes from factories to Army air bases throughout the United States. They flew every type of plane – bombers, fighters and transports – from coast to coast in all types of weather. During WW II, they flew over 30 million miles, with 38 women losing their lives. The WASPs had little recognition for this valuable service and they were considered civilians until 1977 when Congress finally granted them much deserved "military veteran status."

One of Joan's dubious distinctions: she was the first woman pilot to crash land at Kennedy (then Idlewild) Airport in New York. Fortunately, she walked away from the plane, uninjured and was able to attend her WASP Reunion.

Over 280,000 women served in the armed forces during WWII. There were 100,000 WACS (Women's Army Corps Service); 86,000 WAVES, (Women Accepted for Volunteer Emergency Service); and 18, 000 Women Marines (They had no catchy acronym; we simply called them BAM's; Broad-Assed Marines.)

We owe a most significant debt of gratitude to those 57,000 Army and 11,000 Navy nurses who nursed and comforted our wounded.

Katherine Baker
SPAR, Storekeeper 1/c

When my neighbor, Katherine Baker, first tried to enlist in the SPARS, which stood for the Coast Guard motto: "Semper Paratus–Always Ready," she was 5 pounds under the 100-pound minimum weight. Determined to enter the service, she returned home and consumed huge quantities of bananas. On her second try, although still one pound light, she was accepted.

After boot-camp training at the famous Biltmore Hotel in West Palm Beach, Katherine attended store-keeper's school and then reported for duty to the Coast Guard captain of the Port of Baltimore. During her service of two years-three months duration, Katherine rose in rank to store-keeper first class.

Elizabeth Fisher
USO Volunteer WW II

The USO, the servicemen's home-away-from-home, lifted their spirits entertaining them both at home and overseas. I remember how special it was when stars like Mickey Rooney and Bob Hope performed aboard the Intrepid. We really appreciated and looked forward to these great USO shows.

Besides the big-name stars, there were hundreds of USO volunteers, like Elizabeth Fisher, who helped entertain servicemen overseas. She was a Zigfield showgirl and in her free time between shows, she spent hours in hospitals visiting and comforting the wounded.

Years later, while still dedicated to supporting the men and women of the armed services, Elizabeth and her husband, philanthropist Zachary Fisher, led a team that rescued the Intrepid from the scrap heap. The Intrepid Sea, Air & Space Museum is now a major New York Historic Landmark, visited by over one-half million people a year.

"Its new mission is to honor our heros, educate the public, and inspire our youth." A fitting legacy for the Intrepid.

My thanks to members of the Fisher family who continue to provide the strong leadership and guidance that will keep "my ship" afloat and on course during its long voyage into the future.

He Died Instantly

Nitro, one of my good buddies killed in ready room 4, was a native San Franciscan and we felt obliged to pay our respects to his family. None of us were experienced in expressing feelings and extending condolences to the family of a fallen shipmate. We felt awkward just talking about it. How to act? What to say?

Wanting to spare his mom additional heartache, we decided to tell her that Nitro died instantly, one of the 26 radarmen killed in the ready room.

Actually, one of Nitro's legs was blown off when the first kamikaze hit; he was alive and being carried on the shoulders of a rescuer when the second kamikaze hit. The concussion from the explosion buckled the hatch door, trapping them. The would-be rescuer was finally able to squeeze through a narrow opening, but he couldn't pull the unconscious, or already dead, Nitro through it. He had to leave or be cremated by the raging inferno.

After phoning Nitro's mom, Polack, Botts, Jake, Leaky and I went to see her one afternoon. We stood staring at the front door of the house for a while before ringing the bell. When the door opened, his mother reached out and gave each of us a hug. She kept thanking us for coming and, like any good Italian mama, she had prepared enough food to feed a multitude. After she made sure we all had a plate of goodies, she asked the question we were dreading: "Tell me how my son died?"

Polack started. "He died instantly."

I picked up from Polack. "All the radarmen were on standby duty in the ready room. They were killed by concussion from the first bomb explosion."

Botts added, "They didn't suffer ma'am."

He Died Instantly

Tears rolled down her cheeks, ours too, and we were wiping our eyes when once again she thanked us for coming. Each of us got another hug, and a "God Bless" as we were leaving.

Later, while downing a couple of drinks, I couldn't stop thinking of the sadness in Nitro's mom's eyes and how unpleasant it would be for my mom, if she ever got a "how he died" visit."

The dreaded telegram was the way most people were informed of the death of a loved one. "I deeply regret to inform you that your husband, John Doe, was killed in action during a kamikaze attack on the U.S.S. Intrepid. etc.

Heading Back

The closer we were getting to going back into action, the more I started to think as pilots did: in mathematical equations. Simply, the greater the number of missions you flew, the fewer the chances you had of returning from the next one.

So far, the ship had been torpedoed, hit by a single kamikaze, and then hit by two more kamikazes. Concern about my own, and the ship's, invincibility kept seeping into thoughts of the future.

The closer we came to the Japanese home islands, the more intense and fierce their defenses. With their backs against the wall, they would defend like cornered rats. It was going to be bloody, with heavy casualties on both sides, and kamikazes were their last resort and most effective weapon.

The night before we were to sail under the Golden Gate Bridge to head back into action, we pooled our money and got a couple of rooms in a flea-bag hotel and two bags of booze. To buy a bottle of bourbon then, you also had to include a bottle of some crap like Rock 'n Rye or creme de menthe. Ours was a two bottles of bourbon party, and after a couple of real heavy belts, we naturally thought it was time for girls. The game plan was: Botts, Jake and I would hit the local U.S.O. and capture a bevy of beauties. Our hunting party included Hayworth, who was Hollywood-leading-man handsome but not glib with the gab with the ladies. Using him as a lure, we netted four Canadian WACS who were party-ready.

Walking back to the hotel, I began to feel very drunk; my feet had huge springs that made me bounce as I walked. I made it to the door of our hotel room before I went stiff. For the first, and only time, I was paralyzed drunk. I could see, hear, sort of think, but I couldn't move.

Heading Back

They laid me out in the middle of the double bed, where I was surrounded and ignored by the revelers. Above the din, I could hear Jake shouting something about Japs. There was a small hand sink on the wall next to the bed - before Jake ripped it off. I was sprayed and soaked until someone found a shut-off valve on the pipe.

Next, I was shoved over on the bed and Jake was deposited next to me. He apparently decided I was a Jap, grabbing me by the throat and choking me. I tried to but couldn't move, shout or do anything to defend myself. One of the WACS noticed what was happening and Jake was pulled off me. He then passed out, as everyone was leaving us to go dancing back at the U.S.O.

After some sleep, I came to, no longer paralyzed but hungry as heck. Jake was unwakeable, so I set course for some chow and then returned to finish sleeping it off.

Being first to awaken early in the morning, I checked out the other room down the hall. It took plenty of poking, pulling and water to get my shipmates on their feet. I reminded them of the implicit threat in the notice we had received before we left on liberty:

Anyone who misses the Intrepid's scheduled sailing will be considered a deserter and will fall under jurisdiction of the local Naval District - for subsequent trial and punishment.

Rumor had it that punishment would be most severe: many years of hard labor, long days of loading munitions in extreme desert heat.

I knew a couple of guys who were thinking of either jumping ship or faking mental illness to keep from going back into action. They weren't cowards. They were scared as hell by what they had experienced. There is a difference. Maybe they weren't mentally fit for combat anymore, and if you couldn't count on them in battle, you might as well leave them behind.

While waiting for my pals down in the lobby, a Shore Patrol wagon pulled up in front of the hotel and four S.P.s entered. It seems the desk clerk had sent someone to check our rooms, who reported the wreckage. You could tell that these S.P.s were not regulars, probably from the Navy radio school. They were nervous, as the petty officer in charge announced: "We're taking you in to book ya!"

I advised him: "There's no way you guys are going to prevent us from going through that door. You have clubs; we have these ash tray stands. We absolutely must be back on our ship on time. We'll fight like hell to get there. I suggest that you send one of your men up to look at the room. It's a mess. But we left our last three-bucks for the chamber maid who has to clean it up."

Wisely sizing up the situation and his options, he agreed. When the room inspector returned, he also was wise, reporting, "Yeah, it's quite messy, but the maid should be able to handle it."

As we made our hasty exit, past the S.P.s, the room clerk was sounding off with threats and complaints.

There were a few crewmen who deliberately, or accidentally, did miss getting back to the ship on time. As the Intrepid was slowly pulling away from the dock at Alameda, I saw a couple of them running, shouting, supposedly trying to stop the ship and get aboard. I don't know what happened to them, but I do know what happened to my good pal Winston Goodloe. His account follows:

Winston Goodloe,
Aviation Machinist Mate 2/c

"When the ship was in port, I was in charge of the 'starboard-watch' transportation department. In other words, I was on call to chauffeur or be a 'go for' during this watch period.

"As I recall, on Feb. 20, 1945, the officer of the deck ordered me to pick up some spare airplane parts from a distant supply depot. Our battle damage repaired, the ship was moored at the

Winston Goodloe

Alameda Naval Air Station and we were to soon depart for Pearl Harbor. However, neither the O.D. nor I knew just how soon.

"To my surprise, as I was returning, and in about in the middle of the Golden Gate Bridge, I saw the "Big I" below, on the way to Pearl without me.

"What to do now? I decided to report to headquarters for Com. Air. Pac. I explained my plight to an officer, who picked up the phone and arranged for me to be on a P.B.Y. flying boat for a flight to Pearl. I was there waiting when the Intrepid arrived, days later.

"And now, for the rest of the story:...

"About a month later, I received a letter from my mother telling me that the Navy had declared me a deserter and that my photograph was hanging in all the local post offices. (Don't you just love the Navy.)

"The O.D. who dispatched me didn't have either the brains or guts to say that he had sent me ashore to pick up special airplane parts. And God knows how long it took the Navy to correct their mistake.

"Poor Mom, with four sons on the front lines. One, 20 years of age, died after being wounded for the second time, during the battle of the Bulge. The oldest, 25, was missing in action behind German lines. A third, after two years of island hopping in the Pacific with the Army Corps of Engineers was sent back to the States, to be hospitalized with a bad case of jungle rot.

"Now, Mom also had to endure the humiliation of my false desertion charge. Eventually, Mom and Dad were able to smile again – after they received a letter of explanation from my division officer, Lt. Charles Devens, the man I admired most during my two and one half years service on the flight deck of the U.S.S. Intrepid. May God forever bless and keep him.

"P.S. A month after my "Wanted" picture was plastered on post-office bulletin boards, the citation that accompanied the Bronze Star Medal that I had been awarded finally appeared in The Washington Post, one of my hometown newspapers."

1943 pencil sketch of the Intrepid by Winston Goodloe. Winston presented the drawing to Capt. Thamas Sprague before the captain left the ship.

Back in Action

As the Intrepid passed under the Golden Gate Bridge with the crew lined up at quarters on the flight deck, there was a gaggle of girls out on the bridge waving with scarves, brassieres and even panties. It was a pleasant surprise, visually delightful and everyone, even Capt. G.E. Short, who had replaced Captain Bolger five days previously, got a good chuckle out of this unique and colorful sendoff.

The passage to Pearl Harbor and on to Ulithi was routine, with the usual gunnery and air-operation drills and practices. In C.I.C. we worked on mock interceptions.

After arriving at Ulithi, Intrepid was assigned to Task Group 58.4 and proceeded north with the Fifth Fleet, under command of Admirals Spruance and Mitscher. The prime targets the first day were Kyushu's airfields. Response to our raids was intense and fanatical.

The ship's gunners saved the Intrepid from another direct kamikaze hit by blasting a diving twin-engined Betty's tail off, forcing it to crash off the starboard bow. As the plane exploded, it showered our hangar deck with debris and flaming gasoline. Damage-control parties quickly extinguished the flames, preventing extensive damage. Intrepid was at G.Q. continuously, defending against kamikazes.

MAR 18 - MADE ATTACK ON KYUSHU
UNDER ATTACK CONTINUOUSLY ALL
DAY - 1 BETTY SHOT DOWN BY SHIP.
GUNS - EXPLODED ON STBD. SIDE,
PARTIALLY HIT HANGAR DECK & STARTED
FIRE - NOT MUCH DAMAGE OR CASUALTYS
MAR 19 - CONTINUED ATTACKS ON KYUSHU
& THEY CONTINUED ATTACKING US.
MAR 20. FUELED CANS & STILL ATTACKED
BY JAP PLANES.
MAR 21 - COVERING RETREAT OF ONE
DAMAGED SHIP WERE STILL UNDER
ATTACK - GROUP OF 24 BETTYS & 4 ZEROS
INTERCEPTED 4 BETTYS & 4 ZEROS SHOT
DOWN BY OUR C.A.P. REST EITHER SHOT
DOWN OR DRIVEN OFF BEFORE

Back in Action

That night, radar screens were full of bogeys, and our night fighters were kept busy intercepting multiple raids. Tired and tense, I still savored my stints on the S.M. radar, working closely with the night fighter direction officer, while he vectored a F-4-U (my favorite fighter plane) onto the tail of an attacking Jap.

A kamikaze crashes close to the Intrepid's starboard bow – off Japan's Kyushu Ialand.

Reading and deciphering pips on the "R" scope, which allowed you to zoom in on a five-mile area, was intriguing. You had a sense of the hunted and the hunter as you watched the gap between pips quickly closing on the scope. Hearing a pilot's resounding "Tally ho!" – followed by, "Splash one bogey!" was a beautiful, exhilerating, soul-satisfying sound.

Task Group 58.4' had a powerful one-two punch. First from the carrier planes from the Yorktown, Enterprise, Intrepid, Independence and Langley. Next, from the combined and awesome firepower of two battleships, the Wisconsin and Missouri, plus cruiser support from the Guam, Alaska, St. Louis and San Diego, plus fifteen destroyers: the McCord, Remey, Trathen, Norman Scott, Hazlewood, Mertz, Heerman, Monssen, Haggard, Melvin, Franks, McDermut, Hailey, McGowan and McNair.

There were three other groups in T.G. 58, each with ships of similar composition and force, stretching over 50 miles of ocean while pounding the airfields, shipping, naval bases and other military targets on Kyushu.

These heavy attacks on Kyushu continued the next day, March 19, and the Japs kept up intense air attacks on us.

At G.Q. that morning, a little after 0700, we received word that the Franklin, our sister Essex Class carrier, was hit and burning badly. I slipped out of C.I.C. and climbed a ladder to the flight deck, trying to see the Franklin some 20 miles away. A towering column of fire and smoke marked it, like a Viking funeral pyre.

Hearing the numerous, repeated explosions from the fully-armed, about-to-be-launched planes, was sickening. And, you could virtually feel and smell the fire. "God help them," I prayed.

214

Returning to C.I.C., I had to shake out of a deep lethargy and focus on my duty. It wasn't easy. Two of my favorite officers were on the Franklin: Lt. Cmdr. MacGregor Kilpatrick, in command of Air Group 5's fighter squadron and Cmdr. Jim Winston, on board with Admiral Bogan, who was scheduled to replace Admiral Davison.

Preliminary reports had the Franklin in serious trouble, with the strong possibility of having to abandon ship. I hoped and prayed they would survive, knowing, but not knowing, how they could.

Commander. Winston didn't. He, along with all radarmen and officers in C.I.C. was killed. Had I accepted his offer to join him on Admiral Bogan's staff, I wouldn't be here. I would have been one of the Franklin's 832 dead crewmen buried in the seas off the coast of Kyushu.

As the saga of the Franklin unfolded, it was a story of one of the most heroic crews ever to man and stick with a ship. It's vividly told in a great book, "The Franklin Comes Home," by A.A. Hoehling.

Three hundred of the wounded were transferred to the cruiser Santa Fe which stayed alongside helping to fight fires and rescue crew men. Many of the men who were blown off, or jumped into the water, were picked up by destroyers.

Captain Leslie Gehres and 704 officers and enlisted men who stayed on the Franklin managed to sail to Ulithi, Pearl and finally to the Brooklyn Navy Yard in New York.

From the book, I learned details of what happened to MacGregor Kilpatrick, correcting misinformation given me by a Franklin crew member, months later. He told me MacGregor was shot down while taking off in pursuit of the bomber that dropped the two 500-pounders on the Franklin. For years, I believed MacGregor was dead.

One day, sometime in the early 1960's, I was the promotion art director at This Week Magazine, and was on a photo shoot at a studio near my favorite watering hole. While waiting for delivery of a missing prop, I ducked out for a quick martini at the Mont d'Or. While seated at the small bar, I scanned the dining area to see if any of my buddies were having lunch. Like radar on a target, I locked onto a man sitting with two others. All I could see of his face were two blue eyes, sparkling like jewels, crowned by snowy white hair. Stunned, I thought, I know those eyes, but...

"No way. It can't be MacGregor. He's dead."

I had to run back to the photo studio, so I asked Martin the barman to find out the name of the man in the middle, saying, "He looks like someone I once knew, who is dead."

Leaving, I told Martin, "I'll be back, in an hour or so, for a late lunch."

When I returned, Martin told me, "The gentleman's name is MacGregor Kilpatrick."

I was stunned – happily so. To think after all these years ... he's alive, alive, not dead. I celebrated with a few more martinis. Finally when I made contact with MacGregor, years later, he told me his version of what happened in the Mont d'Or that day.

"I was having lunch with my brother and Billy Graham – the boxer, not the preacher. This character comes in, sits at the bar and downs six or more martinis. He kept staring at me; then he jumps up, points at me and runs out the door, shouting, "He's dead, I know he's dead.""

When I corrected him with my version, he replied, "Maybe that's the way it was, but my version made a much better story, and I sure told it my way, many times."

Via faxes and letters, I tried to convince MacGregor to attend the Intrepid's 50th anniversary reunion. He declined, saying he didn't like (and never attended) reunions. I'm sorry that he died a couple of years later before we could get together and I could tell him how much we admired and respected him. The man was the epitome of an officer and a gentleman.

The day the Franklin was hit, Mac's life was saved by a fluke, by doing something he hadn't done before. He accidentally rode down from the flight deck on the munitions elevator, just seconds before the bombs hit and exploded.

Mac sensed that the Franklin was going down and he figured, "If I was going swimming, I might as well have some cash." Somehow he made it to his cabin on the forecastle deck and back. He then organized and worked with crewmen throwing five-inch shells and sizzling bombs over the side to keep them from exploding.

When the cruiser Santa Fe was alongside taking off wounded, Mac wanted to stay and help save the Franklin, but Captain Gehres told him: "You are an aviator, not a firefighter. Take your pilots and get moving."

And an aviator he was, having served with honor on three of WW II's finest aircraft carriers: the Enterprise, Intrepid and Franklin.

Okinawa—Where You Catch The Fast Express to Tokyo

Map from May 1945 issue of *Intrepid*.

Each day off Kyushu was a horrendous replay of the previous one. On the third day, while the Intrepid was refueling a couple of tin cans that had come alongside, the attacks continued. And on March 21, while helping cover the withdrawal of a damaged ship, a raid consisting of 24 Bettys and 4 Zekes was intercepted by our C.A.P. Fourteen of the Bettys and 4 Zekes were downed by our fighter planes. The rest were either shot down or driven off by planes from other carriers.

The next day the Intrepid pulled back to be refueled and, for the next two days, pre-invasion strikes against Okinawa were launched.

After capture, Okinawa's airfields would shorten the range to Japan's industrial cities to 800 miles. Nagasaki, Yawata and Shimonoseki, plus the Naval bases of Sasebo and Kure, would then also become land-based bomber targets.

Nakagusuku Bay would provide our ships with one of the finest anchorages in the Pacific. One drawback: Okinawa lies in the path of typhoons that menace air and sea operations from July thru October.

Another day of refueling was followed by two more days of heavy air strikes against prime Okinawa targets, as our battleships, cruisers and destroyers bombarded the beaches.

Destroyers were deployed on picket lines, positioned between the fleet and the Japanese Home Islands, supposedly in place for early warning detection and defense. More likely, destroyers were stationed there to lure kamikazes into attacking them first, before they reached the fleet.

SHIPS PLANES.
MAR. 22 - FUELED BY TANKERS
MAR 23&24 - STRIKES ON OKINAWA
MAR. 25 - FUELED BY TANKERS
MAR 26-27 - HEAVY STRIKES ON OKINAWA - BATTLESHIPS, CRUISERS & CANS SHELLED BEACHES.
MAR. 28 - FUELED AGAIN.
MAR 29 - MADE STRIKE ON KYUSHU LOOKING FOR JAP FLEET WHICH WAS SPOTTED BY PATROL PLANES - WE DID NOT FIND THEM.
MAR. 30-31 - MORE STRIKES ON OKINAWA
APRIL 1 EASTER SUNDAY - COVERED & SUPPORTED INVASION OF OKINAWA. OPERATIONS WENT

On Mar. 29, patrol planes reported spotting the Jap fleet. Strikes were redirected to search the seas off Kyushu. Not finding the Japanese ships once again, Okinawa became the primary target, with the objective of nullifying the enemy's airfields and clearing the beaches for landings.

The invasion started on Easter Sunday, April 1, with landings on Okinawa's beaches by an army-marine amphibious force. Early resistance was light but stiffened when the defenders countered from predetermined fortifications.

WELL FOR ARMY & MARINES.
APRIL 3&4. WERE SUPPOSED TO FUEL ON 3RD BUT COULDNT DUE TO TYPHOON. WEATHER CALMED ON 4TH-FUELED THEN APRIL 5- MADE RAIDS ON REST OF ISLANDS IN SAKISHIMA GROUP. APRIL 6- FUELED - PART OF JAP FLEET SIGHTED SOUTH OF KYUSHU. OTHER T.G. UNDER ATTACK SHOT DOWN 60 PLANES. WE HEAD NORTH AFTER JAP FLEET- 1BB -2CL&8DD SIGHTED APRIL-7- SENT PLANES AFTER JAP SHIPS-RESULTS GOOD 1BB - THE YAMATO, 2CL, 3DD-SUNK 2DD ONFIRE - 3DD DAMAGED PLANES FROM OUR SHIP

While launching early morning and midday support strikes, a cautious eye was kept on a slow-moving typhoon that was heading our way. High winds and rough seas prevented fueling on April 3 until late afternoon, when the Intrepid was able to take on some fuel and aviation gas. The next day, the Intrepid took on more fuel and launched strikes against Sakishima Gunto.

The following day, the strikes against Sakishima Gunto continued in direct support of our troops on the beaches. One hundred forty-one sorties were flown this day and they met intense and accurate A.A. fire. Three of our planes were shot down; one crew was rescued.

On April 6, Japanese warships were sighted south of Kyushu: one battleship, two cruisers and eight destroyers were reported in the group. As we proceeded north to engage them, we learned that one of our task groups had been under heavy attack, during which it shot down 60 planes.

April 7 was a lucky day for the U.S. Navy – first because the Japanese ships were finally in range; second, it was kick ass, big time.

The Intrepid's planes were among the first to attack, sending torpedoes and scoring bomb hits on the super battleship Yamato, the pride of the Japanese Imperial Navy.

When caught, the Yamato was steaming toward Okinawa in the

East China Sea and, like the kamikazes, with only enough fuel for a one-way trip. Yamato's objective: annihilate the invasion fleet's ships with her huge 18-inch guns.

In little over two hours, after wave after wave of the torpedo, bomber and fighter planes' punishing attacks, the Yamato rolled over and sank. Two cruisers and three destroyers also went down. Two destroyers were left burning, and the other three were damaged.

Planes from the Intrepid were credited with helping sink the Yamato, one cruiser and two destroyers.

> CREDITED WITH SINKING OF THE YAMOTO, 1 CRUISER & 2 DESTROYERS.
> APRIL 8 & 9TH SUPPORTING THE GROUND TROOPS ON OKINAWA - ONE OF OUR CANS SANK SUB NOT FAR FROM US.
> APRIL 10 - TOOK FUEL & AMMO
> APRIL 11TH, 12TH, 13TH, 14TH MADE STRIKES ON REST OF SAKISHIMA GROUP, PRINCIPALLY AMAMI. WAS AT G.Q. MOST OF DAYS & NIGHTS. LONGST STREKH BEING 7 HRS. SOME OF OUR SHIPS SUNK & DAMAGED. MANY JAP PLANES SHOT DOWN - RUGGED DAYS -

Of the hundreds of planes that attacked and sank these Imperial Navy ships, only 10 were lost.

On April 9, three of our task group's destroyers responded to a submarine contact, dropped depth charges and sank a sub near us.

For the next couple of days, the Intrepid's planes provided support strikes against targets on Okinawa, and the ship replenished fuel and ammo supplies.

The next four days, while planes from T.G. 58 hammered away at Okinawa's airfields and military targets, we were almost constantly at G.Q. Our C.A.P. was busy, day and night, splashing bogies. Our night fighters nailed one close to the formation and it was a visible flaming streak as it plunged into the sea.

Kamikazes scored hits on the Missouri and the Enterprise and several of our radar picket ships. The destroyers on picket duty had especially hazardous duty; they did their share of shooting down attacking kamikazes, but with so many attacking at once, it was impossible to stop all of them.

And, on April 14, my 20th birthday, the battleship New York was hit by a kamikaze. This was followed by a relatively calm day of fueling and taking on ammo.

April 16 was full of fierce action on board and in the air. One division, consisting of four of our fighter planes, knocked down 18 Japs during a dogfight. One pilot splashed seven, another six, another three, and the last pilot got two. Our Air Group's grand total for the day: 43 downed by its fighter planes.

Kamikazes were attacking us from all directions. The ship's gunners were active and accurate, downing four as they were attempting suicide crashes on the ship.

Coming in from the stern, one kamikaze, though hit by our AA fire and aflame, managed to get through the barrage and crash into our flight deck, with its bomb exploding on the hangar deck.

The attack on the Intrepid continued while we were fighting the hangar deck fires. During this time there were a couple more near misses with our gunners blasting two diving planes out of the sky.

Ten shipmates were killed and others wounded. This time, the kamikaze hit far enough aft of ready room No. 4, and none of our radarmen, on standby duty there, were killed or injured.

Again, my fears surfaced – as they usually did after the action subsided – when I began to think about how lucky I was. If the flight deck had a target painted on it, the meatball, in the center, would be right over C.I.C. The wooden flight deck and thin steel ceiling above us wouldn't stop much. One day, I thought, one of these bastards is going to hit the bull's eye and that will be it.

I don't remember how many times Jake yelled, "Hit the deck!" that day as kamikazes were diving on us – probably more than a dozen. We had a small chuckle when we talked about it later. If a kamikaze hit any closer to us, diving and laying prostrate on the deck wouldn't protect you any more than if you remained seated at your radar. But by now it was a self-preservation, reflexive action. Dropping down at least gave you something to do when you were scared.

APRIL 15" FUELED & TOOK AMMO
APRIL 16TH MANY JAP PLANES IN AIR. AT ONE TIME 1 DIVISION (4) OF OUR PLANES SHOT DOWN 18 PLANES GETTING 7-6, 3 & 2 PLANES PER MAN RESPECTIVELY. ENTIRE SCORE FOR OUR SHIPS PLANES FOR DAY ABOUT 43 PLUS 4 KNOCKED DOWN BY SHIPS GUNS WHEN WE WERE UNDER ATTACK. WE TOOK A SUICIDER THROUGH FLIGHT DECK CAUSING DAMAGE - TEN KILLED & OTHERS WOUNDED. HEADED FOR ULITHI APRIL 19TH ARRIVED ULITHI AND REPAIR SHIP CAME ALONG SIDE, PATCHED HOLE IN FLIGHT DECK

& HANGAR DECK - COULD NOT
FIX #3 ELEVATOR - THANK GOD.
MAY 4 - STARTED FOR PEARL

FROM MAR 18 TO APRIL 16 WHEN
WE GOT HIT WERE THE RUGGEDEST
DAYS I EVER PUT IN. NOT MUCH
SLEEP OR CHOW AS WE WERE
UNDER ATTACK & AT G.Q
MOST OF THE TIME. NIGHT FIGHTERS
DID VERY WELL IN BREAKING UP
NIGHT ATTACKS & SHOOTING DOWN
PLANES. THE JAP SUICIDERS
WERE THICKER THAN USUAL & TG 58
+ THE OLDER SHIPS IN INVASION
SHIP KNOCKED DOWN MANY PLANES

BOX SCORE FOR OPERATION.
AIR GRP 10 (OUR PLANES)
97 JAP PLANES SHOT DOWN IN AIR
6 DAMAGED
81 DESTROYED ON GROUND
104 DAMAGED "   "
6 SHOT DOWN BY SHIPS
GUNS +3 ASSISTS.
1 BB (YAMATO)
1 CL
1 DD   } SUNK
+ MANY LIGHT (CRAFT)
1 x BB CV
1 CVE
1 CL   } SHIPS DAMAGED
3 DD
VARIOUS SMALL

Once again, we had to abandon C.I.C. because of thick smoke and fire. This time we had no problem making it up the ladder to the flight deck, fresh air and safety.

It was again time for me to thank God that it wasn't my time. I was now 2 days into my 20th year and I had serious doubts about ever reaching my 21st birthday.

Damage-control parties moved in quickly to extinguish the fires, but they were hampered by parked planes catching fire and exploding. The No. 3 elevator was damaged and inoperable.

The Intrepid was ordered to proceed to Ulithi, with three destroyers providing screen and antisubmarine coverage. While under way and after the ceremony of burying the dead at sea, a fourth destroyer joined the group.

Proceeding at 23 knots, the Intrepid entered Ulithi's anchorage and dropped the hook shortly after noon on April 19. A repair ship came alongside to evaluate the the damage and estimate how long repairs would take.

Repair estimate: the Intrepid could be repaired to 80 percent capacity by May 5. No. 3 elevator would have to remain inoperable.

On April 30, No. 2 elevator was discovered to be out of alignment, but operable. The Intrepid was then ordered stateside for complete repairs.

Back in Action

It was a couple of days after we were hit off Okinawa, when the Chaplin, Lt. Timothy Herlihy, sent for me and told me of my Dad's death. He said that he had received a letter from my cousin, Frank Moore, asking the chaplin to tell me at an appropriate time. Even though I had been expecting the worst all along, it was hard to accept. I sat there, staring blankly at Father Herlihy, his words of condolence were not registering. My thoughts were racing. Poor Dad. How were Mom and Dolly going to make it? When Dad became so sick that he couldn't get out of bed, he lost the diner and everything he had invested in it. There was no nest-egg. Mom hadn't worked at a real job since she was a telephone operator, before she married.

I probably only had a little over one hundred bucks on the books. Not much to help there. What will they do? What can I do?

I left the Chaplin's office, went aft on the hangar deck, climbed the ladder to the cat walk under the flight deck. Sitting there alone and confused, staring at the ship's wake while tears ran down my cheeks. My mind was shooting blanks as I attempted to search for solutions. It must have been hours later when I concluded there wasn't anything I could do from here, some 10 thousand miles away.

I arrived in C.I.C. late for standing my 2000 to 2400 watch. Word about Dad's death had reached them; they knew why I was late and suggested I skip the watch. I declined. I wanted to be near my buddies and have my mind distracted from sorrow. It helped.

On May 4, the ship got underway on an easterly course and on May 8, the Intrepid crossed the 180th Meridian. The next night, I was standing a dog-watch in C.I.C when a radio operator buddy told me that the war in Europe was over. The Germans had surrendered and VE day was here. The first thoughts that flashed through my mind were of my brother and all my friends fighting "over there" in Europe.

They were safe. They had survived their war and would soon be home.

To us, the war in Europe was almost like something being fought on another planet. We were too involved in our own day-to-day action to pay that much attention to fighting in Europe. However, it did hit home when a pal received word that his paratrooper brother was killed at Bastogne. We all grieved with him, reverently sharing in his sorrow and then promptly reverting to our immediate concern, the war in the Pacific.

"Yippie!" someone shouted when I shared the end of war news. "Now they will be able send more troops and ships and stuff to help us. Our war will end sooner."

I asked for permission from the senior watch officer to go below to my compartment and see if anything was in our "something to celebrate booze-stash-locker." I returned with the only bottle left, a pint of Rock 'n Rye. This overly sweet hooch was passed around, each man taking a sip, to toast and celebrate *that* war's end.

It was the middle of the night when we first heard the news; I thought for sure we were among the few on the ship who got the word about VE day. But word had spread throughout the ship as fast as greased scuttlebutt. At 0400, on the way back to my sleeping compartment, I had to step over several passed-out celebrants on the hangar deck. They not only got the word, but also the torpedo juice for a proper celebration of this historic event.

223

A Grandstand Seat

The Baltimore Sun, Monday July 30, 1945
Combat Career of Carrier Intrepid
A Firsthand Account From a Grandstand Seat
by Philip S. Heisler

Washington, July 29, 1945–As a grandstand seat for the violent battle action in the Pacific, few spots could surpass the U.S.S Intrepid – most frequently hit aircraft carrier in the United States Navy. Struck by a Japanese torpedo and crashed by a total of five Japanese suicide planes in just 15 months of combat operations, the big fast carrier Intrepid is once again back in action in the Pacific after her fourth trip to the repair yards for battle damage.

The Navy today permitted the story to be told for the first time. Paradoxically, it was that the Intrepid was in so much action and damaged so often that made her one of the least known of the Navy's major warships.

The Jap torpedo got the Intrepid on her second trip into action. It was during the first daring attack on the Japanese naval base at Truk that a lone enemy plane wormed its way through the protective air screen and dropped a torpedo into the Intrepid's stern. Explosion ripped out the ship's steering mechanism and hopelessly jammed the rudder and she was floundering, unmaneuverable in the open sea.

While medical crews cared for scores of wounded, Rear Adm. Thomas L. Sprague, then the skipper of the Intrepid, used his engines to steer the stricken ship, erected a sail rigged on the forecastle and spotted the planes forward to trap the wind, and shift all possible weight aft to put her low in the water.

THIS TIME IT WAS A DUD. Crewmen told me they thought the Intrepid had all the bad luck by the time I boarded the carrier late in the summer of 1944. I believed them several weeks later, when the Japs made a determined counterattack against the Third Fleet off Formosa. Under cover of darkness, four Jap torpedo planes made a run on the Intrepid and again a torpedo crashed into her side – this time into the very midsection of the ship. The whole ship shuddered from the force of the impact, but there was no explosion. The torpedo was a dud.

We had heard reports that the Japs were beginning to use suicide dive tactics against some of our ships early in October 1944. We heard radio Tokyo propagandize the Jap kamikaze corps and everyone began talking about the weird suicide planes. The same month, the Intrepid was hit by one of the very first kamikaze attacks.

The Intrepid's planes were circling the flattop slowly, waiting for their chance to land after attacking airfields on Luzon, when six Jap planes appeared high overhead. Every gun on the ship opened fire on the tiny black dots, and our own circling planes were given a wave-off as the Jap planes went into their dives. Two of the Jap planes were knocked out of the sky several thousands feet above the water. Two others burst into flames a split second later. The fifth one missed the ship and crashed into the sea, but the last one hit its mark. The Jap plane, a Judy, plummeted into the edge of the flight deck slithered into a gun gallery on the side of the ship. Ten gunners in the gallery, firing their 20 millimeter guns right up to the second the plane struck, were killed and many others injured. Flames from the Jap gasoline tank swept the deck. Firefighters were standing by and, before the flames could reach the planes parked on the the forward part of the deck, they were brought under control and the Intrepid resumed landing planes.

The Intrepid got it again, one month later, when, operating off the coast of Luzon in preparation for MacArthur's invasion there, two Jap planes laden with bombs crashed into her flight deck almost simultaneously. The Intrepid had just finished launching her own planes for a strike against Manila when the Japs pulled a surprise daylight raid. An estimated 100 enemy planes were in the attacking force, but more than 75 were shot down by the fleet's air cover before they reached the ships. From the flag bridge of the Intrepid, I saw eight Jap Zekes high astern. For a few breathless moments they seemed to hesitate, circling slowly before they plunged into their dives. At first only the long range five-inch guns pounded away at the diving planes. Angry black puffs of smoke burst all around them. As the diving black dots got bigger, the chatter of the 40-millimeter and 20-millimeter joined in the furor, filling the sky with streaks of fire and smoke.

Two of the black dots turned red as the antiaircraft fire poured into them. A wing was knocked off a third and it went into a a crazy spin into the sea. All the guns of the fleet were now pounding away but one did not seem to notice the noise. It seemed an incredibly long time since the planes started streaking downward toward us. Two more burst into flames and crashed. Three more were still coming and by now I could hear the scream of their motors and the wind tearing at their wings.

The firing did not let up for a second. Then there was a terrific crash as one Zeke tore into the Intrepid's flight deck. The shock of the blast knocked men to the deck, and burning fragments of deck, planes and men showered down. The bomb carried by the Jap plane ripped through the flight deck, exploding in the pilot's ready room, fortunately empty at the time. Thirty-two men in an adjourning compartment were killed; flames covered the hangar deck below, destroying planes parked there, exploding fuel and ammunition and wounding scores of the ship's crew. Thick black smoke poured from the gaping holes in the deck, but still the guns kept firing as the second suicide plane crashed into the burning ship. Scores more were killed and wounded, and fresh fires started.

The attack was ended now, but the ship was burning furiously. Some men jumped overboard. Others were blown overboard by the explosions. Dead and wounded were trapped in the smoke below. Capt. Joseph F. Bolger, then commanding officer of the Intrepid, arranged for other fleet units to stand by to pick up survivors if, as it then appeared, abandoning the ship became necessary. I blew up my life belt. For two hours and 38 minutes, the flames ravaged the ship. Men and officers alike fought the flames without regard for position or rank.

Maryland men in the midst of it:

Lieut.. Cmdr. John Rames, Baltimore, the ship's air-intelligence officer, helped direct the firefighters on the flight deck, which was soaked with gasoline. Lieut. Cmdr. Joseph Purdy, of Pikesville, Md, organized a rescue party to try to save some of the men trapped by smoke below decks. Lieut.. Harry Cooper, of Eastern Shore, Md., was alone in the ready room where one of the bombs exploded and miraculously fumbled his way out of the inferno despite severe burns. Second Lieut. Harry C. G. Henneberger was standing only 50 feet from the spot where the plane hit, the Marine officer was knocked down by the blast but escaped injury.

Meanwhile, the Intrepid's planes had completed their attack on Jap shipping at Manila and were on their way back to the ship. Smoke and flames still poured from two big holes in the flight deck and landing any planes there would have been impossible.

Some of the planes landed on sister carriers, but there was not enough room on the other carriers to take care of all of Intrepid's planes. Cmdr. George Ghesquire, then the skipper of the Intrepid's dive-bomber squadron and now an instructor at the Naval Academy at Annapolis, gathered together the remaining Intrepid planes in the air and led them to a safe landing at a newly-won landing field on Leyte.

As night approached and the fires were finally under control, exhausted men simply fell to the decks, too tired to move. Rescue squads were still carrying the dead to the captain's cabin, which had been transformed into a temporary morgue, and taking the wounded to the crowded ship's hospital.

One call for volunteers to give blood transfusions to the wounded brought more than 100 exhausted men and officers to the hospital. Although scores of heroes were made that day, no one talked of bravery when it was ended. Everyone, including the bravest, claimed only the honor of having been scared the most.

Repairs were made on the Intrepid in near record time, and for a while her luck improved. She came back to the fleet to hit Japan, Iwo Jima, Formosa and Okinawa. However, on March 16, while participating in a strike on the Japanese homeland, the Intrepid got her fourth battle wound. The Japs had seriously damaged the U.S.S. Franklin and were then making a serious effort to sink her. Again, a kamikaze dive on the Intrepid. Shells from the Intrepid's antiaircraft guns tore into the suicide plane when just several hundred feet above the ship. The Jap plane crashed in to the water so close to the Intrepid that its burning fragments showered the ship, starting fires.

One month later, while attacking Japan again, the Intrepid was hit by her fifth suicide plane in six months. The plane crashed into the flight deck while its bomb tore through the deck and exploded on the hangar deck below, killing and wounding scores.

By this time, the Intrepid's battlewise crew was expert at handling situations like this. Within 50 minutes, the fire was under control. Prefabricated patches were put over the flight deck hole and the Intrepid landed her own planes.

It was now official. The Intrepid had been hit more often than any other

A Grandstand Seat

aircraft carrier in the fleet. But the Intrepid could dish it out as well as take it. Despite all the damage suffered during those 15 months, her planes sunk 110 enemy ships and damaged 179 others. They sank a Jap aircraft carrier and helped sink the Jap super battleship, Yamato. Her planes and guns together destroyed 650 Japanese planes.

A MESSAGE FROM THE BOSS. It was when the flames were highest and it looked like we might have to abandon the wrecked carrier after she had taken the double suicide hit that I decided to give up my grandstand seat on the Intrepid for a safer bleacher seat on some island.

That night, when things had finally calmed down, I mentioned to the Intrepid's communications officer that I had just about enough of the war at sea and was thinking of going on an amphibious operation for a rest.

"That reminds me" the officer said. "We got a message for you on the radio. It came about an hour after we got hit." The message was from Baltimore and signed by my boss (whom I immediately suspected of being clairvoyant) It read: "Suggest you remain with the fleet a while longer."

Intrepid's Aerology gang. (standing) L to R: Robert Parsons, Donald Cruse, William Morris, Lewis Black, Richard Inglima, John Lewis, (below) Peter Iannuzzo, William Tarbox and Robert McShane.

R obert McShane was our favorite aerographer's mate. He owned two great nightclubs in San Francisco, the Dawn Club and the Professional Club.

The Dawn Club was always filled with sailors and a bevy of single girls who loved to dance. Next door, the private membership Professional Club was a civilian oasis away from sailors. However, Bob allowed a couple of his shipmates at a time to enter the adjacent Professional Club through a secret door in his Dawn office. It was a welcome change to be sitting at the bar, having a conversation with some civilians, knowing you were not about to become embroiled in a brawl over some broad.

The Dawn Club was another scene entirely. When alone, I usually occupied a place at the bar in front of a mirror so I could protect myself against a sneak attack by a drunken serviceman.

When a fight broke out, I retreated with drink in hand into the phone booth. Sitting in the dark, with my foot holding the door closed, I phoned the radarman on guard duty in Intrepid's C.I.C. Giving it my best, gravel-voiced imitation of fight announcer Clem McCarthy, I described the action as the S.P.s broke up fights and herded nearly all the sailors out, leaving mostly noncombatant members of the gentler sex. Then, I

The Dawn Club

The Dawn Club was one of our favorite watering holes. Assembled from L to R, Steve Vogrin, Mrs. Johnson, Red Jones, Mrs. Fontenot, Peewee Wildes, Roy Harbour, Ray Stone, B.J. Fontenot, George Vogrin, John Stefanich and Johnson.

would make my grand emergence from my sanctuary. You had to make your move fast; within 10 minutes the evacuated sailors would return, minus those who were hauled off to the brig. And the cycle would start all over again.

McShane invited the officers and enlisted men in our V-3 Division to a private party at the Professional Club on a Sunday afternoon when the club was usually closed. I kept bragging that my date was going to be one of the star strippers from the local burlesque show.

That Sunday morning, I was pondering my foot in my big mouth while sipping coffee in a Market Street cafeteria. The outlook was bleak until I noticed a very attractive tall girl, seated on the other side of the counter. She responded favorably to the note I sent: "Help! I need to speak with you. Important!"

Fortunately, she not only had compassion for my plight but also a great sense of humor. She told me her secret fantasy was to be an exotic dancer, but she was really just a shy, small-town Iowa farmgirl and could never strip down to pasties and a G-string.

We walked over to the small park near Union Square and practiced her bumps, grinds and burly queen walk, with lots of port and starboard hip action. She was great, and Miss Iowa Farm Girl liked her new name, Flame.

Our grand entrance to the party fooled everyone. Flame was as tall as I was, built and extra-animated as we crossed the dance floor to our table. We were immediately surrounded by a horde of my buddies, boasting how they had seen her perform and how she was the best, the star of the show.

We laughed, we danced and we drank. Before a drink was half consumed, the waiter brought another, and another. Poor Flame was a better imitation stripper than whiskey sipper. When she became ill, and at her urging, I put her in a taxi and sent her home.

The party raged on for hours, and it is one of the few times when the officers and enlisted men were equal - all were equally ossified.

Later, when I 'fessed up to my buddies about Flame being a good old farmgirl, but they didn't believe me.

Elsie Lehr, Chief Aerologist Don Cruse, Janeth White and Dick Inglima at the Dawn Club.

Goodbye, My Fair Lady

Word filtered down that, in the senior medical officer's opinion, "The Intrepid's original crew had seen enough battle action for now; they should be assigned to other duty."

That sounded awfully good to me. I was still gung-ho about kicking Jap ass, but felt my foot needed some rest. And though the fiercest fighting was just ahead before this war would be over, I had mixed emotions about being in on the kill and being killed.

That I would even consider leaving my ship, and leaving my buddies, made me feel like a deserter. But even when enticed by an offer to jump a rate to chief petty officer, my response was a prompt negative.

In less than a month, after the ship arrived back in the States, I was emptying my locker, packing my sea bag. I felt as I did when emptying one of my fallen buddy's lockers. Empty.

The Intrepid had been my home for nearly two years, two of the most intense years of my young life. My ship and I were close; we had shared the gamut of emotions from joy to sorrow and everything in-between. It's difficult to articulate love of a supposedly inanimate object, though a ship is not really inanimate. It has almost human life, spirit and soul. It does if you think it – and feel it. I did and still do.

What gave the Intrepid its life were the men who shared in romancing this formidable Fighting Lady. Plain and simple, we just loved our ship and thought she was the best in the whole damn U.S. Navy.

Polack made chief and was staying on board along with a couple of other radarmen from the original crew. The rest of us departed on June 16, 1945, transferred to the receiving ship at Treasure Island. I now started looking forward, not back; an optimist about whatever the Navy had coming my way.

The highlight of my brief stay at Treasure Island was the Navy's attempt to con me into volunteering for its wonderful world of underwater demolition. The petty officer who made the pitch was hooted out of the room by a tough group of battle-hardened Third Fleet sailors.

A couple of days later, I was homeward bound, on 20-day delayed orders, before reporting to the Third Naval District in Brooklyn for further assignment.

The overflow from the Brooklyn receiving ship facility was quartered in a high-rise apartment building where you could grab a bunk and hang out until assigned. The only rule: be there every morning at 0700 for muster, to listen for your name when the officer read the day's duty roster.

It was under 20 miles from home so I usually elected to leave a bar, when it closed at 3 a.m., drive my Plymouth to the building, park in the courtyard and sleep until the bugle call awakened me. Then, if not assigned, I would drive home and get some more sleep.

After a couple of weeks of this routine, my name finally was called and I was assigned to the newest carrier, CV 42, the Franklin D. Roosevelt. I had predicted it would be my next ship, from somewhere in the middle of the Pacific Ocean, when I saw a picture of Mrs. Roosevelt launching it with a bottle of Champagne at the Brooklyn Navy Yard.

New orders instructed me to report and join the F.D.R.'s crew at Newport Naval Base in Rhode Island, by 2400 on a Saturday night. I thought Hell, I've got a hot date to go dancing at the Commodore Hotel, right next to Grand Central Terminal. I'll keep the date, catch a later train and arrive at 0600 in the morning. No one will miss me and if any yeoman gets difficult while checking me in, I'll either cajole or threaten him.

On the train, I was preparing my little explanation for a Marine guard, only to find civilian guards at the gate. I was locked up immediately and put in a small shack until processed as a prisoner at large, awaiting trial, by captain's mast.

Newport Naval Base was what we called a chicken-shit base. It was run like a military school for misfits. If three men were walking to the chow hall, they had to march in step and salute everything in sight.

The prisoner's stockade was more like an enemy P.O.W. camp

Goodbye, My Fair Lady

than an American Navy brig. As you walked by the high cyclone fences, you saw prisoners with shaved heads and big P's painted on the backs of their shirts, usually doing push-ups and calisthenics, night and day.

As a prisoner at large, I spent a couple of hours each day on the back of a truck picking up laundry. One day, I ran into a hometown pal, Jimmy Cummings, a marine assigned to the Newport War College. His evaluation of my situation was bleak, totally negative. The commodore who presided over the captain's mast at Newport, was an old, ornery, hard-of-hearing bastard who sentenced everyone to 30 days piss and punk. (bread and water). I started to prepare three excuses, thinking I would use the one I thought would work best once I saw the commodore in action.

One excuse concerned the death of my dog Rags; she got hit by a car some years previous, but I knew I could relive and tell the story in a sincere, sorrowful way. The next tale was about Mom's old alarm clock; it was unreliable, but she wouldn't part with it because it had been a gift from my deceased Dad. The third, was about having a date with the sister of one of my fellow radarmen, a shipmate killed during the Battle of the Philippines when two kamikazes crashed into the Intrepid's flight deck.

The third excuse was looming as my first choice when I arrived for the mast. At this time, commodore was an almost extinct rank in the U.S. Navy, and this old buzzard was too short to be an officer or even an apprentice seaman; he must have been a political appointment.

He was standing on a milk crate behind the podium, and I don't think he heard much of what was mostly mumbled testimony as sailors were brought before him. He just kept slamming down his gavel as he gave them 30 days, P. and P. Ah ha, I thought, I'll speak very loudly and at least he'll hear me.

And loud as I could, I started giving him some story, a combination of the dead dog, alarm clock and Battle of the Philippines. Hearing myself shouting and realizing my folly I began to giggle, then laugh uncontrollably. I had blown it. Was dead in the water. The more I laughed, the more vehemently he slammed down his gavel, and the more I lost it. Finally, he shouted: "This man is an idiot. He's mad, a crazy fool! Get him out of my sight."

A boatswan's mate escorted me to the door and said, "Go!"

I asked, "What does this mean?"

He said. "Don't ask, just go. You're the first to ever escape him. Go!"

Go I did, grateful to avoid severe punishment for what I considered just a minor transgression. After all, this was a damn land base, not a fighting ship, and to me, reporting six hours late was no big deal.

The war in the Pacific seemed to be going well without me. By June 28, MacArthur announced that operations on Luzon were over except for mopping up die-hard Japs who wouldn't surrender. Then on July 5 MacArthur announced that the Philippines had been completely liberated.

About this time, invasion plans were presented to President Truman scheduling the invasion of Japan, to start with landings on southern Kyushu on Nov. 1, 1945 and followed by landings at Honshu, near Tokyo, on March 1, 1946.

Admirals Halsey and McCain were directing attacks all over the Japanese Home Islands. Fifteen U.S. carriers were joined by British carriers, and on July 10, Tokyo was attacked by 1,022 planes, while our battleships, cruisers and destroyers were shelling land targets northeast and southeast of Tokyo.

The war's finale was building.

The End in Sight

One week after the first successful atomic weapon test in New Mexico, President Truman decided to use the bomb if the Japanese continued to delay in coming to terms. His decision was based on the fact that a quick Japanese surrender would save many lives, on both sides, if the Allies didn't have to invade Japan's Home Islands.

After delivering an atom bomb to the Marianas air base, the cruiser Indianapolis was sunk by torpedos from a Jap submarine. Because of a communications snafu, it was not known to be missing until three days after it was due to report in the Philippines. Therefore, many of the Indianapolis' 316 survivors were not rescued from shark-infested waters until several days later.

Aug. 6, 1945 – The first atom bomb is dropped on Hiroshima.

Aug. 8, 1945 – The second atom bomb is dropped on Nagasaki.

Aug. 15, 1945 –V-J Day,(Victory over Japan Day). Emperor Hirohito's surrender broadcast stuns the Japanese people.

I was in Boston, at the Fargo Building, attending C.I.C. School with a group of the Roosevelt's radarmen when V-J Day was proclaimed. I was so excited, I put on my dress blues and ran out onto the street to a cacophony of cheers, laughter, honking horns and pealing church bells. The sound was almost as wondrous as the faces. Everyone was smiling, laughing, hugging, kissing and dancing. The strain of the war years erased from their faces.

I boarded a bread truck, rode into the heart of the city and joined the wild horde of celebrants; each and every one wanting to buy you a drink. I had a drink with as many as I could, until I couldn't hold another drop of whiskey or dance another step, which was some time close to dawn.

The next morning, the real meaning hit me. The war was over! I was alive – I had survived without a scratch. Soon, I wouldn't have to stand in long lines for anything. I'd be discharged and, if possible, I'd go to art school. If not, I'd get a job, maybe with the F.B.I., as a G-man.

I still had my Navy job, helping train about 20 of the Roosevelt's radarmen for duty in C.I.C. An ex-presidential yacht, The Pilgrim, was being used as a radar training vessel for scanning and tracking exercises outside Boston Harbor. I happened to be in the mess hall, talking to the cook, when a bugler sounded chow call. As first notes sounded over the P.A. speakers, hundreds of huge cockroaches responded, covering the bulkheads near the tables. The cook took this repulsive spectacle in stride, saying: "Some of these roaches have been in the Navy longer than me. For a couple of hitches at least. Didn't you see the hash marks on their wings?"

What I saw was startling. I had never seen even one cockroach on the Intrepid, and these roaches were big enough to carry off a whole slice of bread, along with your appetite.

On Sept. 1, I took my F.D.R. radar crew to Brigantine Island, off Atlantic City, for more C.I.C. schooling. Now the Brigantine Hotel was not like the elegant Cavalier, where I first attended radar school. This hotel was formerly a retreat for Father Divine, a black evangelist, and his followers, before the Navy took it over. It was sparse, but functional. After three weeks of daily classes, and a couple of liberties in Atlantic City, we were back in Newport, joining the rest of the Roosevelt's precommissioning crew.

I was marking time, knowing I would soon be discharged. The Navy had begun releasing sailors, using a point system – so many points for time in service, so many points for months of combat duty and points for having dependents.

Having Mom as a dependent put me in a higher bracket than other sailors my age. When combined with points for sea duty, and battles, I knew my discharge would come shortly after the Roosevelt was put in commission.

I spent my first night on board the F.D.R., and the next day, Oct. 27, 1945, the Roosevelt was commissioned and officially turned over to the Navy by the Brooklyn Navy Yard shipbuilder.

In the short time I was on the Roosevelt, I never had the time to get

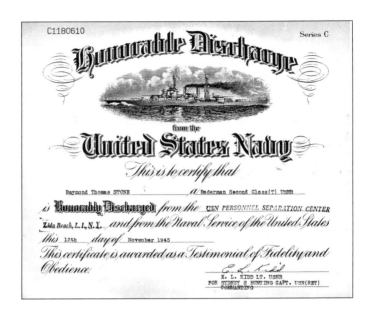

to know her or develop any deep feelings like those I had for the Intrepid.

It wasn't just that the war was over. You had been intimately involved, sharing a passion. The love of your first ship is deepest, truest and longest-lasting. That's the way it was then and that's the way it still is, with me and "My Ship."

I still love the Intrepid. I still choke up and sometimes can't hold back the smiles or the tears, when I speak of her.

WAS IN BOSTON WHEN
JAPS SURRENDERED
SEPT 1- WENT TO BRIGANTINE
N. J. FOR CIC SCHOOL.
SEPT 21, WENT BACK TO
NEWPORT
THEN BACK TO BROOKLYN
PUT F.D.R IN COMMISSION
OCT 27, GOT TRANSFER-
ED NOV8. TO LIDO FOR
SEPARATION & GOT
DISCHARGED NOV 12, 1945
AMEN

The End

16 AUGUST 1945.

--INTREPID PRESS--
-1-

WASHINGTON:
PRESIDENT TRUMAN ANNOUNCED AT 7 O'CLOCK TONIGHT JAPANESE ACCEPTANCE OF SURRENDER TERMS PROCLAIMED AT THE POTSDAM CONFERENCE. THE TERMS WILL BE ACCEPTED BY GENERAL MACARTHUR WHEN ARRANGEMENTS CAN BE COMPLETED.

PRESIDENT TRUMAN READ THE FORMAL MESSAGE, RELAYED FROM EMPEROR HIROHITO THROUGH THE SWISS GOVERNMENT, IN WHICH THE JAPANESE RULER PLEDGED THE SURRENDER ON THE TERMS LAID DOWN BY THE BIG THREE AT POTSDAM.

PRESIDENT TRUMAN MADE THIS STATEMENT: "I HAVE RECEIVED, THIS AFTERNOON, A MESSAGE FROM THE JAPANESE GOVERNMENT IN REPLY TO THE MESSAGE FORWARDED TO THAT GOVERNMENT BY THE SECRETARY OF STATE ON AUGUST 11TH. I DEEM THIS REPLY A FULL ACCEPTANCE OF THE POTSDAM DECLARATION WHICH SPECIFIES THE UNCONDITIONAL SURRENDER OF JAPAN. IN THIS REPLY THERE IS NO QUALIFICATIONS.

ARRANGEMENTS ARE NOW BEING MADE FOR THE FORMAL SIGNING OF SURRENDER TERMS AT THE EARLIEST POSSIBLE MOMENT. GENERAL MACARTHUR HAS BEEN APPOINTED THE SUPREME ALLIED COMMANDER TO RECEIVE THE JAPANESE SURRENDER. GREAT BRITAIN, RUSSIA AND CHINA WILL BE REPRE- SENTED BY HIGH RANKING OFFICIALS. MEANTIME THE ALLIED ARMED FORCES HAVE BEEN ORDERED TO SUSPEND OFFENSIVE ACTION.

THE PROCLAMATION OF VJ DAY MUST WAIT UPON THE FORMAL SIGNING OF THE SURRENDER TERMS BY JAPAN."

SIMULTANEOUSLY MR. TRUMAN ANNOUNCED STEPS TO SLASH INDUCTIONS FROM EIGHTY THOUSAND TO FIFTY-THOUSAND A MONTH. ONLY MEN UNDER 26 WILL BE DRAFTED.

PARIS:
A MONTH AFTER ANY JAPANESE SURRENDER IS SIGNED A COMPLETE REVERSAL IN THE PRESENT EUROPEAN TROOP DEPLOYMENT PROCEDURE WILL TAKE PLACE "THAT WILL BRING THE HIGH POINT MAN INTO HIS OWN", A U.S. SPOKESMAN SAID TUESDAY. ORDERS WERE EXPECTED TO GRANT PRIORITY TO HIGH POINT MEN ON HOMEWARD BOUND SHIPS. AT PRESENT THE LOW SCORE MEN HAVE BEEN GIVEN TOP BILLING AS THEY WERE RUSHED TO THE PACIFIC EITHER DIRECTLY OR BY WAY OF THE UNITED STATES.

WASHINGTON:
STATE DEPARTMENT PRESS SECRETARY MCDERMOTT, SAID SECRETARY OF STATE BYRNES, AT 4:20 EWT WENT TO THE PENTAGON AND WAS CONNECTED ON A WAR DEPARTMENT HOOKUP WITH HIGH OFFICIALS AT LONDON, MOSCOW AND CHUNGKING. HE READ THE MESSAGE RECEIVED FROM OUR MINISTER AT BERNE, LELAND HARRISON, BY PHONE, TELLING THEM THAT HE REGARDED JAPANESE PROPOSAL AS COMPLETE ACCEPTANCE OF POTSDAM DECLARATION. THIS WAS THE ONLY NOTICE THAT THE OTHER GOVERNMENTS HAD OF JAPANESE SURRENDER. THEY AGREED TO ACCEPT IT.

NEW YORK:
MADAME CHIANG KAI SHEK COMMENTING ON SURRENDER OF JAPAN SAID:

"FOR ALL WORLD TODAY IS DAY OF REJOICING AND YET IT IS DAY FOR SERIOUS AND SOBER THINKING, FOR IT CAN BECOME ONE OF MOST SIGNIFICANT DAYS IN ALL HISTORY. WE MUST LEARN THAT OMISSION TO PREVENT WAR IS JUST AS CULPABLE AND DISASTEROUS IN THE END AS COMMISSION TO FOSTER WAR IN THE BEGINNING."

(THIS COPY MUST NOT LEAVE THE SHIP)

Intrepid Reborn

Intrepid's former crew members such as Ray Stone performed heroic deeds to save their ship during World War II, and her later crews loyally served our nation during the Cold War, Space Race, and Vietnam. Whether it was participating in NATO exercises in the 1950's, rescuing Mercury and Gemini astronauts in the early 1960's, serving three tours of duty off Vietnam in the mid to late 1960's, or engaging in anti-submarine patrols in the early 1970's, the Intrepid and her crew will go down in history as one of the twenty-four great Essex class carriers that helped protect the United States well beyond World War II, throughout the dangerous post war decades that threatened the world with annihilation.

When Intrepid was decommissioned in 1974 she, as many of her sister ships, was threatened again–only this time with total destruction, as Essex class carriers were replaced by newer, larger Forrestal, Kitty Hawk, and now Nimitz class carriers, almost twice as large as Intrepid. In the later 1970's and 80's, however, a very few of these venerable Essex class ships were saved by enthusiasts and philanthropists from an ignoble end in the scrapyard. With Intrepid, commercial real estate developer Zachary Fisher stepped in to rescue the ship, bringing her to New York's Pier 86 on the Hudson River where she opened as a museum in 1982.

Today, after a two-year closure for restoration, the Intrepid Sea, Air & Space Museum features a new Pier 86 on 46th Street and 12th Avenue, that holds a British Airways Concord, the early Cold War nuclear-missile submarine Growler, and the restored Intrepid, the centerpiece of the museum complex. The 2008 reopening of the museum showcased newly restored areas of the ship, particularly the historic forecastle, with the spectacular anchor room and junior officers quarters, and third deck with a general mess restored to its unique 1969-70 appearance, complete with chief's and enlisted berthing. Beyond that the museum holds one of the best collections in the United States of Cold War aircraft. Many of them, were restored for the reopening and are exhibited on the flight deck.

Intrepid Reborn

The Intrepid Sea, Air & Space Museum at 46th Street and the Hudson River.

Finally, staff and exhibit designers created a striking new exhibition experience on the hangar deck that explains the history of Intrepid within the larger context of the development of functioning aircraft carriers as well as the history of Intrepid in relation to events of the twentieth century. The new exhibition includes a memorial wall which is also a fitting tribute to crewmen who died while in service on board. Beyond this new museum display lies the Exploreum, an area with seventeen distinctive interactives where kids and families can learn about principles of sea travel, spaceflight, aviation and life aboard ship. The entire new exhibition serves as a very tangible remainder to visitors that the museum's mission is to honor our heroes, educate the public and inspire our youth. Thus the ship was reborn in 1982 to serve society in an educational and inspirational way. Intrepid's 2007-08 renaissance reaffirms that mission for the museum's twenty-fifth anniversary, with a new conviction and dynamic new atmosphere, appropriate to a National Historic Landmark, a major New York City museum experience and a famed part of both American and world history.

The Most Inspiring Adventure In America
Susan Marinoff
Executive Director
The Intrepid Sea, Air & Space Museum

Acknowledgements:

My thanks to my friends: Abbott (Kit) Combes for his editorial assistance and nitpicking, to Lynne Meena for more nitpicking, to Bea Lund and Michael Bruneau for fine-tuning and to Charles Murphy for his crafty imprimatur.

PHOTOS: Most photos were shot by Intrepid's photographers and can be found in The National Archives. Others are from the author's, or his shipmates' private collections as well as family members of former crewmen.
Photo reproduction quality varies due to condition of the photo or if scanned from photo copies. Thanks to Larry Kenney, a man known professionally for his talent imitating celebrity voices, rather than his computer skill retouching pictures. And to Amy Wintering Smith, my patient computer Guru.

REFERENCES: The author's personal, unauthorized diary.*
* During WWII, keeping a diary was forbidden; ostensibly, to prevent the enemy from acquiring classified or secret information.
"U.S.S. Intrepid CV-11 – Day by Day," by Anthony Zollo Sr.
"The U.S. NAVY," by Nathan Miller
"JANE's American Fighting Ships of the 20th Century," Captain John Moore, R.N.
"The World Almanac Book of WORLD WAR II," edited by Brigadier Peter Young
"Island Fighting," by Rafael Steinberg and the Editors of Time-Life Books
Excerpts about the Enterprise, Joel Sheppard, whose father flew off the Enterprise with MacGregor Kilpatrick
"The Franklin Comes Home," by A.A. Hoehling
"Share of Honor," by Ralph Graves
Music: Ed Shanaphy, The Music Group
Various online sources about the U.S. Navy

Book design, typography, graphics & typos by the author

AUTHOR'S BIO

In April, 1943, 17-year-old Ray Stone enlisted in the Navy, and after boot camp at Sampson, N.Y, he attended radar school at Virginia Beach. Ray then joined the precommissioning crew of the U.S.S. Intrepid, an Essex class aircraft carrier being completed at the Newport News Shipbuilding Company in Virginia.

A *Plankowner*, one of the 3,000 men in the Intrepid's original crew, Stone served as a radarman in the ship's Combat Information Center.

C.I.C., the carrier's brain center, was responsibile for airplanes, from the time they took off until they landed back safely on the flight deck. C.I.C's prime radar responsibility was detecting enemy planes and directing our fighter pilots to intercept and destroy them.

Stone survived one torpedo and five kamikaze hits on the Intrepid without a scratch, while 26 of his fellow radarmen were killed during the kamikaze attacks off the Philippines.

He left the Intrepid in June 1945 and was assigned to another carrier, the *Franklin D. Roosevelt,* and was part of the Roosevelt's commissioning crew. Stone was honorably discharged from the Navy on November 12, 1945.

After a couple of years of studies at *The Art Students League* in New York, under the G.I. Bill, he worked as a magazine promotion art director and then as a script and promotion writer at the Newspaper Advertising Bureau. Later he became an advertising-agency creative director, a partner, and finally, president of SSK&F Advertising.

While at the N.A.B., Ray was co-author of a bicentennial book, "*The Spirit of Seventy Six, 1776 - 1976.*"

Ray's new book, "*My Ship!*" *The U.S.S. Intrepid*," is a memoir of his service on the U.S.S. Intrepid in WW II while it participated in seven major battles. Other works in progress include: a cookbook, "*Beyond a Six Pack & Boiled Potatoes*" and a children's book, "*Joe the Crow.*"

Stone lives and works out of his home studio in South Salem, N.Y.

GLOSSARY

AA fire–Anti-aircraft fire. Also AA guns like the Intrepids:20. MM (20 Millimeter), 40. MM(40 Millimeter), and 5 Inch cannons.

Aircraft U.S. Navy–F6F, TBF, SB2/c, F4U (see page 73)

Aircraft Japanese–Betty, Francis, Judy, Zero (see page 131)

Airedale–A crewmember who handles planes, spotting (moving) them about the hangar or flight deck for launchings and landings.

Battle Station–The place you race to and perform your specific duty when General Quarters is sounded.

Battlewagon–Navy jargon for a (BB) Battleship.

Boatswain's Mate–More commonly called a Bosun's Mate, a petty officer with a pipe (whistle) who "pipes" the ship's routine, as directed by the officer of the deck. (a shrill who-hoee-ee followed by:"Now hear this!")

Bogey–Any unidentified aircraft. (also called a bandit by fighter pilots).

C.A.P.–Combat Air Patrol. The fighter planes assigned to orbit above ships and defend against enemy air attacks.

Captain's Gig–A small boat used to transport the Captain ashore, or to another ship. (Not a *gig* appearance by the Capt. at a night club.)

Catwalk–usually a narrow outer passage deck

C.I.C.–Combat Information Center. Where information gathered from the surface and air-search radar is plotted, evaluated and interceptions are assigned to planes by the fighter direction officers.

Fart-sack–The bunk and bedding mattress you sleep in, and on.

Flattop–Navy jargon for a (CV) Aircraft Carrier

Gedunk Stand–Where sailors buy creature comfort items: ice cream, cigarettes, shaving lotion and pogey bait (candy).

ODE TO A BOATSWAIN'S MATE

I think there's nothing quite so great
Or lovely as a Boatswain's mate
A Boatswain's mate with hairy chest,
who gives the new recruits no rest.
Upon whose forearm is tattooed
A dancing woman in the nude.
For the Boatswain's mate is always right;
He shouts at us in line all day
To square our hats, throw butts away.
Any boot can make a dozen rates.
But only God makes Boatswain's mates!

GLOSSARY

General Quarters–The ships highest-alert condition when ready for or involved in action. Also the vocal command, followed by a bugle call, followed by a loud claxon gong which propels the crew into hauling-ass, as fast as possible, to get to their battle station.

Golden Dragon–A sailor who has been duly inducted into the silent mysteries of the Far East after crossing the 180th meridian and the equator simultaneously

Horsecock sandwich–Sweaty slices of salami on dry white bread. Served as a battle ration when the galley is secured during battle.

Intrepid–Resolute, fearless, courageous, gutsy, nervy, ballsy, spirited, dashing, daring, adventurous, brave, valiant, audacious, heroic, gallant, resolute, indomitable and quite invincible.

Knots–A measure of a ship's speed, based on a nautical mile: 6,080 feet. (20 knots=aprox. 23mph)

and knots–as a bowline, formed by interlacing rope.

Lucky–A code name used by the Intrepid when communicating with ships and planes.

Mail-buoy–A fictitious floating post office that love-sick, letter-hungry sailors were told existed when assigned to mail-buoy lookout duty. (The poor chumps were also sent to find left-handed wrenches and sky hooks.)

N.O.B.–Naval Operating Base, such as the Norfolk Base in Virginia.

O.G.U.–The Out Going Unit at a Naval Base.

Pip (or blip)–An electronic signal that appears as a dot or upward peak on a radar screen, indicating direction and distance to a target.

Plankowner–A ship's original crewmember, who owns a deck plank, in name only. and is not allowed to take it with him

Port/Starboard–Port has the same number of letters as left– the side of a ship when facing forward; starboard is to the right side. (Port is also a semi-sweet red wine preferred by ancient mermaids.)

Polliwog–A lowly, slimy crewmember, whose ship has crossed the equator and has yet to be initiated as a shellback..

Radar Scopes–Three types: A., P.P.I. and R.Scopes that display pips (or blips) that indicate a target's relative direction and distance.

Radio/Gunner–An air crewman responsible for operating a plane's radio and machine guns

Shellback–A sailor, who has crossed the equator and is no longer a lowly polliwog, after initiation into the Ancient Order of the Deep.

GLOSSARY

Shore Patrol–A police force. Usually petty officers, assigned to maintain order among sailors on liberty. (A duty, not relished except by boatswain's mates; to be avoided whenever possible).

Scuttlebutt–A ship's drinking-water fountain. Also, Navy jargon for gossip, rumor and, occasionally, the real dope.

Swabby–A seamen who pilots a mop and swabs the decks.

Tin Can–Navy jargon for a (DD) Destroyer

T.F./Task Force–The total armada of battleships, aircraft carriers, cruisers and destroyers that make up an attack force of Navy vessels. T.F.s usually comprise two or three T.G.s–Task Groups of ships.

Torpedo juice–100° alcohol used to propel torpedoes and when mixed with grapefriut juice, 100° guaranteed to propel sailors into orbit.

Torpecker–Navy jargon for a torpedo or a torpedo plane.

Vector–A specific direction within any of the 360° of the compass.